COMPUTER
BOOK SERIES
FROM IDG

CorelDRAW! 5 For Dummies

Cheat Sheet

W9-AGY-060

Command Shortcut Keys

To	Press
Access Full-Screen Preview mode (Esc to return)	F9
Align selected objects	Ctrl+A
Align text to baseline	Alt+F10
Break apart selected object	Ctrl+K
Bring one backward	Ctrl+PgDn
Bring one forward	Ctrl+PgUp
Bring to back	Shift+PgDn
Bring to front	Shift+PgUp
Combine multiple objects into one object	Ctrl+L
Convert shape or text to curves	Ctrl+Q
Copy	Ctrl+C
Create new document	Ctrl+N
Cut	Ctrl+X
Duplicate an object	Ctrl+D
Exit Corel	Alt+F4
Group selected objects	Ctrl+G
Open document	Ctrl+O
Paste	Ctrl+V
Print	Ctrl+P
Redo an undone operation	Alt+Enter
Repeat an operation	Ctrl+R
Save document	Ctrl+S
Toggle between Wireframe and Color mode	Shift+F9
Toggle grid snap	Ctrl+Y
Undo	Ctrl+Z or Alt+Backspace
Ungroup selected object	Ctrl+U

Dialog Box Shortcuts

Dialog Box	Shortcut Key
Close dialog box	Alt+F4
Edit Text Fonts dialog box	Ctrl+T
Fountain Fill dialog box	F11
Outline Color dialog box	Shift+F12
Outline Pen dialog box	F12
Preferences dialog box	Ctrl+J
Uniform Fill dialog box	Shift+F11

Text Movement Shortcuts

To Move	Press
Beginning of current line	Home
Beginning of current paragraph	Ctrl+↑
Beginning of current text block	Ctrl+Home
End of current line	End
End of current paragraph	Ctrl+↓
End of current text block	Ctrl+End
One page backward	PgUp
One page forward	PgDn
One word to left	Ctrl+←
One word to right	Ctrl+→

. . . For Dummies: #1 Computer Book Series for Beginners

 ™

References for the Rest of Us

COMPUTER BOOK SERIES FROM IDG

Are you intimidated and confused by computers? Do you find that traditional manuals are overloaded with technical details you'll never use? Do your friends and family always call you to fix simple problems on their PCs? Then the *... For Dummies™* computer book series from IDG is for you.

... For Dummies books are written for those frustrated computer users who know they aren't really dumb but find that PC hardware, software, and indeed the unique vocabulary of computing make them feel helpless. *... For Dummies* books use a lighthearted approach, a down-to-earth style, and even cartoons and humorous icons to diffuse computer novices' fears and build their confidence. Lighthearted but not lightweight, these books are a perfect survival guide for anyone forced to use a computer.

> *"I like my copy so much I told friends; now they bought copies."*
>
> **Irene C., Orwell, Ohio**

> *"Quick, concise, nontechnical, and humorous."*
>
> **Jay A., Elburn, Illinois**

> *"Thanks, I needed this book. Now I can sleep at night."*
>
> **Robin F., British Columbia, Canada**

Already, hundreds of thousands of satisfied readers agree. They have made *... For Dummies* books the #1 introductory level computer book series and have written asking for more. So, if you're looking for the most fun and easy way to learn about computers, look to *... For Dummies* books to give you a helping hand.

CorelDRAW! 5
FOR
DUMMIES

CorelDRAW! 5 FOR DUMMIES

by Deke McClelland

IDG
BOOKS

IDG Books Worldwide, Inc.
An International Data Group Company

Foster City, CA ♦ Chicago, IL ♦ Indianapolis, IN ♦ Braintree, MA ♦ Dallas, TX

CorelDRAW!® 5 For Dummies®

Published by
IDG Books Worldwide, Inc.
An International Data Group Company
919 E. Hillsdale Blvd.
Suite 400
Foster City, CA 94404

Library of Congress Catalog Card No.: 94-75903

ISBN: 1-56884-157-4

Printed in the United States of America

10 9 8 7 6 5 4 3

1D/RX/QU/ZV

Distributed in the United States by IDG Books Worldwide, Inc.

Distributed by Macmillan Canada for Canada; by Computer and Technical Books for the Caribbean Basin; by Contemporanea de Ediciones for Venezuela; by Distribuidora Cuspide for Argentina; by CITEC for Brazil; by Ediciones ZETA S.C.R. Ltda. for Peru; by Editorial Limusa SA for Mexico; by Transworld Publishers Limited in the United Kingdom and Europe; by Al-Maiman Publishers & Distributors for Saudi Arabia; by Simron Pty. Ltd. for South Africa; by IDG Communications (HK) Ltd. for Hong Kong; by Toppan Company Ltd. for Japan; by Addison Wesley Publishing Company for Korea; by Longman Singapore Publishers Ltd. for Singapore, Malaysia, Thailand, and Indonesia; by Unalis Corporation for Taiwan; by WS Computer Publishing Company, Inc. for the Philippines; by WoodsLane Pty. Ltd. for Australia; by WoodsLane Enterprises Ltd. for New Zealand.

For general information on IDG Books in the U.S., including information on discounts and premiums, contact IDG Books at 800-434-3422 or 415-655-3000.

For information on where to purchase IDG Books outside the U.S., contact IDG Books International at 415-655-3021 or fax 415-655-3295.

For information on translations, contact Marc Jeffrey Mikulich, Director, Foreign & Subsidiary Rights, at IDG Books Worldwide, 415-655-3018 or fax 415-655-3295.

For sales inquiries and special prices for bulk quantities, write to the address above or call IDG Books Worldwide at 415-655-3000.

For information on using IDG Books in the classroom, or ordering examination copies, contact Jim Kelly at 800-434-2086.

For authorization to photocopy items for corporate, personal, or educational use, please contact Copyright Clearance Center, 222 Rosewood Drive, Danvers, MA 01923, or fax 508-750-4470.

is a registered trademark under exclusive license to IDG Books Worldwide, Inc., from International Data Group, Inc.

About the Author

Deke McClelland

A contributing editor to *Macworld* magazine, Deke McClelland also writes for *PC World* and *Publish*. He has authored nearly 30 books on desktop publishing and the Macintosh computer. He started out as artistic director at the first service bureau in the U.S.

Deke's awards include the Ben Franklin Award for the Best Computer Book, 1989; Computer Press Association, Best Product-Specific Book, 1990; and Computer Press Association, Best Software Product Review, 1992.

Deke is also the author of the best-selling *Macworld Photoshop 2.5 Bible*.

Dedication

(To be sung to the tune of "Harrigan")

E-L-I-Z-A-B
E-T-H spells Elizabeth!
When she walks by, the people blow her kisses;
They say to me, "You have a lovely missus."

You know the rest. Thanks for loving me.

Acknowledgments

Special thanks to Leigh Davis, Pam Mourouzis, and Julie King for giving me excellent guidance and editing of this book.

Thanks also to Mike Partington and Steve O'Halloran for their substantial input.

(The publisher would like to give special thanks to Patrick J. McGovern, without whom this book would not have been possible.)

Credits

Executive Vice President, Strategic Product Planning and Research
David Solomon

Senior Vice President and Publisher
Milissa L. Koloski

Editorial Director
Diane Graves Steele

Acquisitions Editor
Megg Bonar

Brand Manager
Judith A. Taylor

Editorial Managers
Tracy L. Barr
Sandra Blackthorn
Kristin A. Cocks

Editorial Assistants
Stacey Holden Prince
Kevin Spencer

Acquisitions Assistant
Suki Gear

Production Director
Beth Jenkins

Supervisor of Project Coordination
Cindy L. Phipps

Pre-Press Coordinator
Steve Peake

Associate Pre-Press Coordinator
Tony Augsburger

Project Editor
Julie King

Editor
Pamela Mourouzis

Technical Reviewer
Michael Partington, *Partington Design, Fourth Place Winner in Corel Art Show 3*

Production Staff
Valery Bourke
Linda Boyer
Mary Breidenbach
Chris Collins
Dominique DeFelice
Dwight Ramsey
Gina Scott

Proofreader
Chuck Hutchinson

Indexer
Sherry Massey

Book Design
University Graphics

Cover Design
Kavish + Kavish

Contents at a Glance

Cartoons at a Glance

By Rich Tennant

page 1

page 80

page 245

page 7

page 179

page 222

page 378

page 339

page 341

page 65

Table of Contents

Introduction

*I*f you've ever seen or worked with CorelDraw, you know that it's one of the most ample, expansive, immense, sprawling, capacious, and comprehensive graphics programs in the known universe. CorelDraw is an all-in-one artist's studio that allows you to create precise illustrations, draw free-form artwork, edit digital photographs, represent data in charts, assemble simple presentations, and even construct animated sequences.

All these features combined with the program's reasonable price may explain CorelDraw's phenomenal popularity. By some accounts, it's the most popular piece of graphics software for the personal computer.

Why a Book . . . For Dummies?

But all this power comes at a price. At last count, the CorelDraw package comprises 12 programs. The central program is CorelDraw, which lets you design professional-quality pages and artwork, but there's also Corel Photo-Paint, CorelVentura, CorelChart, CorelShow, CorelMove, and a bunch of others. If Corel could figure out how to market its KitchenSink and SwissPocketKnife programs, they would be in there as well.

Needless to say, there's no way to sit down cold with 12 programs and figure them out overnight. How can you tell which of these programs are worth your time and which you should ignore? I can tell you from years of personal experience that a few Corel programs are very interesting, some are somewhat interesting, and the rest are pretty darn forgettable.

So rather than pack your brain full of a bunch of utter nonsense about a bunch of programs you'll never touch, I cover just those aspects of those programs that I think you'll find exciting, entertaining, and ultimately useful. Being a generous guy by nature, I leave the boring stuff for another book.

About This Book

I've tried to write this book so that you can approach it from several perspectives, depending on how you learn:

- ✔ If you're a reader — it's been my experience that only hard-core readers put up with introductions — I hope that you'll find my writing lively enough to keep you from falling asleep or collapsing into an information-age coma.

- ✔ If you just want to find out how a command works and then toss the book back into a dusty corner, you'll find that IDG Books creates an ample, expansive, immense, sprawling, capacious, and comprehensive index, on par with CorelDraw itself.

- ✔ If you already know your way around CorelDraw, flip through the book, check out a few of the tips here and there, and see how much stuff there is to glean.

- ✔ If you hate to read anything without pictures, just read Rich Tennant's cartoons. I fall into this learning group (good news, huh?). Folks like you and me won't learn anything about CorelDraw, but by golly, we'll get in a few yucks.

- ✔ If you want to get a quick idea of what this book is like, read the five chapters in Part V. Each chapter contains a series of short sections that not only prepare you for the high-falutin' caliber of information in this book but also mesmerize you with my enchanting style and wit. Well, perhaps mesmerize is the wrong word. How about clomp you over the head?

   ✔ If you don't much like the idea of reading a computer book but you're so
   confused that you don't even know what questions to ask, start at Chapter 1
   and see where it takes you. I promise not to leave you wallowing in the dust.

This book has been read and reread by folks who don't know the first thing
about CorelDraw, and to this day, they are only marginally confused. Consider-
ing that they all led happy and productive lives before they read *CorelDRAW! 5
For Dummies* and that only three of them had to seek therapy afterwards, I think
I've got one heck of a book here.

How to Use This Book

To make sure that you understand what I'm talking about, this book uses
several conventions to indicate what you're supposed to type, which menus
you're supposed to use, and which keys you're supposed to press.

If I describe a message or something you see on-screen, it looks like this:

```
Insert Disk #2 into Drive A:
```

Menu commands are listed like this:

   Arrange⇨Group

This statement means that you open the Arrange menu (with the mouse *or* the
keyboard — whichever you prefer) and then choose the Group command.

This books uses two different kinds of key combinations.

This is a *menu shortcut:*

   Alt,A,G

This shortcut means that you should press and release the Alt key, press and
release the A key, and press and release the G key. (Don't type the commas.)
This shortcut accesses the Arrange⇨Group command.

This is a *keyboard shortcut:*

   Ctrl+G

This means that you should press and hold the Ctrl key, then press the G
key, and then release both keys. (By the way, this shortcut accesses the
Arrange⇨Group command, too.)

This book also sticks tools in the margin to let you know which of Corel's
gazillion tools you should use and when.

How This Book Is Organized

I've divided *CorelDRAW! 5 For Dummies* into five digestible parts, each of which contains three to six chapters, which are themselves divided into gobs of discrete sections, which contain these funny little letter-units called words.

Part I: The Stuff Everyone Pretends They Already Know

This part of the book answers all those questions that you have and didn't know you had, and even if you did know, you wouldn't ask anyone because all your friends would have laughed at you and branded you an Industrial Age cretin. It's like a CorelDraw information pill. Swallow it and be smart. Or at least better informed.

Part II: Let the Graphics Begin

Now that you've bared your soul and learned the basics, it's time to start expressing yourself and creating some bona fide computer art. Not an artist? Not to worry. Neither are thousands of other folks who use this program. In fact, CorelDraw is specifically designed to accommodate artists and nonartists alike, enabling you to express the uniquely individual creative impulses that surge through, well, all those places that things tend to surge. That is to say, you're able to get the job done. You can even throw in a few special effects for good measure.

Part III: Getting the Message Out There (Wherever There Is)

Many people feel the special need to share things with other people. Reports, newsletters, and internal memos allow you to show off your personality and mix in a bit of your literary expertise. Bold headlines like "Joe Bob Receives Employee of the Month Award" or "Sales Up in March" tell a little something about who you are and how you live.

CorelDraw knows that it's not enough to draw pretty pictures; you have to be able to back up those pictures with hard-hitting text. In these chapters, you'll discover that CorelDraw is half drawing program and half document-creation software. You can enter and edit text, design logos and special text effects, create multipage documents, and print the whole thing out on 20-pound bond paper.

Part IV: Corel's Other Amazing Programs

As I mentioned earlier, I try to steer you away from Corel's boring and mostly useless programs and concentrate on the good ones. This part covers five good programs: Photo-Paint, Chart, Show, Move, and Ventura. You also learn how to share information between CorelDraw and all the other programs. None of this is required reading; in fact, most folks never venture out of CorelDraw. But if you take the time to read through these chapters, you'll learn about some exciting capabilities that you very likely didn't even know existed. The fact is, you paid for these programs, so you may as well at least give them the once over.

Part V: The Part of Tens

This part of the book is a savory blend of real information and the sort of chatty top-ten lists that prevent people from understanding too awfully much about anything. In these chapters, you'll find lists of special effects, timesaving shortcuts, obscure features, file formats, and advice for everyday living. Prepare to be entertained as you learn. Prepare to laugh and be somber. Prepare to chortle until factoids come out your nose.

Icons Used in This Book

To alert you to special passages of text that you may or may not want to read, the National Bureau of Wacky Graphics has designed the following universal margin icons and thoughtfully interspersed them throughout the book.

Here's an example of something that you may want to avoid. This icon highlights a close encounter of the nerd kind, the variety of information that could land you in intensive care if you were to utter it at the Annual Gathering of Hell's Angels. In other words, read if you must, but don't repeat.

Here's something you didn't know, or if you did know it, you're smarter than you thought. Don't be surprised if a single tip makes you fractions of a percentage point more efficient than you were before. It's been known to happen to people just like you.

This may be something that I've already mentioned. But you may have forgotten it, and I want to drill it into your head. Metaphorically speaking, of course. Or it may be something that I just thought you might like to know — a friendly gesture on my part.

This icon spells danger. Or, at least, something to be watchful for. Try to steer clear of the stuff I describe here.

This icon calls attention to information that, while mildly interesting, is not in the least important to your understanding of CorelDraw. I just throw it in to keep the scandal-mongers happy.

In CorelDraw, as in any other computer program, you'll find yourself performing a few tasks on an almost-daily basis. This icon shows how to accomplish such a task while expending the tiniest amount of mental and physical energy.

This icon indicates features that are new or significantly different in Version 5, the most recent version of CorelDraw. This information serves you users who just upgraded from Versions 3 or 4 and want to be sure that you're getting your money's worth.

Where To First?

Different people read in different ways. You may want to check out the index or table of contents and look up some bit of information that has been perplexing you for the past few days. Or you might just close the book and use it as a reference the next time you face an impasse or some horrible, confusing problem. Then again, you could just keep on reading, perish the thought. Personally, I couldn't put the book down, but you probably have more will-power.

How to Bug Me

If you want to share your insights, comments, or corrections, please write to me at the following address:

Deke McClelland
c/o IDG Books Worldwide, Inc.
155 Bovet Rd., Suite 310
San Mateo, CA 94402

If you're on America Online, drop me a message at DekeMc. You can also reach me via CompuServe at 70640,670. Don't fret if you don't hear from me for a few days, months, or ever. I read every letter and try to implement nearly every idea anyone bothers to send me.

Part I

The Stuff Everyone Pretends They Already Know

The 5th Wave　　　By Rich Tennant

In this part...

Imagine this: You're enrolled in an introductory computing course. The professor asks you to write a simple program. Let's say that the code creates a series of *As* in a column, or something equally pointless. Who cares? It's not important. He, she, it — I'm talking about the professor, here — takes time to carefully explain the language and logic behind the exercise. Because you secretly harbor an unusually immense brain — granted, you only use it on special occasions — you understand thoroughly. No sweat.

But when you sit down in front of a terminal at the computer lab, you realize that you lack a key bit of information. How are you supposed to get to the point where you start entering your code? The computer is on, but it just sits there blinking at you. Anything you enter results in an error. You're so utterly clueless and overwhelmingly frustrated that you don't even know how to ask one of the pompous lab assistants what the heck is going on.

I've been there. I empathize. It sucks. The fact of the matter is, any amount of knowledge is worthless if you don't know the basics. The difficulty, of course, is that lots of folks act like they already know the basics because they don't want to look like, well, dummies. But let's face it, when it comes to computers, remarkably few people know what's going on. And those that do tend to be insufferable.

So here are the basics. The following chapters explain all the easy stuff that you've been pretending to know, little realizing that 90 percent of the people around you don't know it either.

Chapter 1

What's With All These Programs?

orelDraw used to be a single program. Weird, huh? Nowadays, your CorelDraw 5 box includes 12 separate programs, each of which you can use independently or in conjunction with its electronic friends. This chapter introduces these programs and explains their benefits and relative degrees of usefulness, which range from truly stupendous to barely worth yawning over. I also tell you which chapters, if any, contain more information about the programs. "Go, aye, and be ye no longer confused when back here thou mayest get," as I'm fairly certain Shakespeare never said.

You Bought What?

For the record, here are the three ways you can purchase the various bits and pieces of CorelDraw:

    ✔ CorelDraw 5 is the most recent version of this obscenely popular graphics product. It includes all programs discussed in this chapter. It's totally new and state of the art and — need I mention? — hot, hot, hot.

✔ Right before CorelDraw 5 came out, some clever upstart in the marketing department said, "Hey, just a moment here. A lot of users don't have tons of money. Look at Windows Draw. For about $100 by mail order, that sucker sells through the roof!" Of course, the folks in the marketing department didn't want to miss out on all those users. So the upstart rallied, "Why don't we keep CorelDraw 3 and CorelDraw 4 on the market and slash a few hundred bucks off the price of each?" And you know what? The upstart was right. CorelDraw 3 and 4 have reached an eager audience of new users, the kind of folks who know the value of money.

✔ But wait. CorelDraw 3 users are missing out on a program included with CorelDraw 4 and 5, CorelMove, which is your ticket to the veritable hog heaven of computer animation. And CorelDraw 5 has remarkable enhancements to *all* of the programs *and* includes the new CorelVentura (also known as Ventura Publisher). Corel saved this wonderful desktop publishing (DTP) program from the dreaded "shelfware" or "garage-sale-ware" environment — or even worse, the quarter-page ads in the back of computer magazines.

These same people can also tell mythical lore of a GUI (graphical user interface) called GEM for the PC. Yep, the Redmond boys may hide this fact, but there was a Windows-like GUI for the PC before Windows. The most bizarre fact about Corel buying and integrating Ventura Publisher is that CorelDraw started off as a Ventura add-on utility for the GEM version of Ventura Publisher and was called Corel Headline! Any of you who have this prehistoric (from the 1980s), proto-Draw software should hold on to it; it's the Archeoptyrex of the soaring software evolution.

What a Bargain!

CorelDraw's many programs make it a unique value. I mean, where else are you going to find 12 independent pieces of software, several of which hold up quite nicely on their own, for, er, whatever it is you paid? The answer is *nowhere*. You have the right to be consumed with the pride of a savvy shopper.

Lots of computer companies package additional programs with their core product to increase its perceived value. In commercial circles, this technique is called *bundling*. For students of bundling, Corel is about the most aggressive case study around.

CorelDraw

This program started it all. Not only is CorelDraw (or Draw for short) the program for which the package is named, but it's also the most powerful and the most useful of the bunch. Not surprisingly, therefore, it's the one I talk about in the most detail. Chapters 2 through 13 talk at length about this wonderful piece of software.

What can you draw with Draw? Why, you can draw *anything*: free-form graphics of butterflies or unicorns, architectural plans for a bathroom off the linen closet (I wish *I* had one of those), maps of downtown America, technical drawings of car engines before and after reassembly, or anatomical illustrations that show food going down the trachea (and the ensuing coughing fit that follows). The list is endless, or at least close enough to endless that I run the risk of boring you into a coma if I continue.

There's more. You can open and edit *clip art* — you know, those drawings that other people create specifically for you to mess up. You can create wild text effects, such as a logo for Stuckey's. You can even design documents, such as advertisements for Stuckey's, fliers for Stuckey's, and posters for Long John Silver's. (Stuckey's doesn't need posters. We know all about their pecan logs.)

Thar's math in them thar' objects d'art

Math is the driving force behind CorelDraw. I know, it's strange, but it's true. When you draw a wiggly line, for example, Draw takes the coordinates of its beginning and end points and calculates a mathematical description of the curve between the two points. Draw thinks of each line, shape, and character of text as an independent mathematical object, which is why Draw and programs like it are sometimes called *object-oriented* software. When you print your drawing, the program explains all this math to the printer, which in turn draws the objects as smoothly as it can so that they look like you drew them by hand and not with a computer.

If your printed drawings look jagged, you're probably using a cheap printer. You can improve the appearance of your drawings by buying a better printer or by paying to have your drawing printed at a service bureau. Either way, you have to outlay some additional cash. For the whole story about printing, see Chapter 13.

CorelVentura

CorelVentura is the odd man out in the CorelDraw 5 suite of applications: It doesn't make any pictures. Nothing! Nada! Nyet! Other words that mean "no!" If you think of CorelVentura as a word processor on steroids, you've got an inkling as to what this baby can do. Legal writers, document specialists, publishers, and trekkies cooped up in their basements writing scripts for "Star Trek: The Next-Next-Next Generation" drool over CorelVentura.

CorelVentura can help you write your diary. It can help you write that novel that you know will make you a bundle. It can help you write the NAFTA agreement. In short, CorelVentura is a comprehensive document publisher that can sit on a network and integrate multiple word-processor files from multiple sources.

Draw vs. Ventura: Text with Pictures or Pictures with Text?

Those Corellians who have CorelDraw 4 know that it handles huge blocks of text on multiple pages about as elegantly as Ross Perot is subtle. Corel was intending to put DTP functions into Draw that you could find only in programs like Ventura Publisher (guidelines, gutters, form-flow text, kitchen sink, and so on). They were so impressed with Ventura Publisher, however, that they went out and bought it (yes, it doesn't happen just to electric shavers).

Now Corel has two DTP programs — sort of. As far as DTP is concerned, CorelDraw is great for creating four-page flyers, menus, leaflets, baby announcements — any document that has a few pages, lots of images (clip art), and text that needs to be flashy. CorelDraw is the Chevette of DTP. For anything more than that, you should seriously consider CorelVentura, which is DTP's Corvette. The bonus here is that you can drop any picture made in Corel Photo-Paint or CorelDraw into CorelVentura and still edit it (known as *OLE,* or *object linking and embedding*). You get the best of both worlds.

Corel Photo-Paint

The primary purpose of Corel Photo-Paint, discussed in more detail in Chapter 15, is to let you make changes to photographic images. You can change the color scheme of a family photo so that your relatives look like they had the sense not to wear bright orange and avocado green in the seventies. You can apply special effects so that Grandma Edna's face appears to be molded in lead.

You can retouch subtle or bothersome details, such as Junior's unusually immense chin. You can even combine the contents of two different photos so that Uncle Mike and Aunt Rosie are standing shoulder to shoulder, even though the two would just as soon hang out in the same room together as take a flying leap into the Grand Canyon. And if that sounds like an accurate description of your family, you need all the help you can get.

Corel Photo-Paint was originally sold under the name PhotoFinish by ZSoft, the same folks who make PC Paintbrush. Photo-Paint 3.0 and PhotoFinish are nearly identical products. However, to create Photo-Paint 5.0, Corel pretty much rewrote the program from scratch to make it a totally new and better product. Whew, titillating stuff, eh?

Where to find photos on disk

The following list gives a few ways to get photos on disk so that you can edit them in Photo-Paint:

> ✔ You can take a photograph to a service bureau and have it *scanned,* which means to read the photo and convert it to a digital image, sort of like recording music to a CD. Some folks call scanning *digitizing.* This proposition is generally pretty expensive, around $2 to $10 per photo, depending on whether you scan the photo in black and white or in color.

> To locate a service bureau, look in the Yellow Pages under "Desktop Publishing." Some cities have lots of them; San Francisco, Los Angeles, Seattle, Chicago, New York, and all those other coastal towns have as many service bureaus as they have adult bookstores. But out in the heartland, both are a little harder to come by. You may have to search around a bit. If you have friends in the computer graphics biz, ask them for recommendations.

> ✔ If you intend to do a lot of scanning, you may want to purchase your own scanner. Prices range from a few hundred bucks for a cheap, handheld scanner to $1,000 and up for a top-of-the-line, color model.

> ✔ Kodak's Photo CD technology provides the best quality at the most affordable price. For around $100, you can transfer up to 100 photos from slides, negatives, or undeveloped rolls of film to a compact disc, identical in appearance to the kind that plays music. However, to take advantage of Photo CD, you have to invest in a CD-ROM drive, which can cost hundreds of dollars. Be sure to ask for a *multisession* drive so that you can use it to read Photo CDs.

> ✔ You also can buy CDs filled with photographs shot by professional photographers. Called *stock photos,* these images run the gamut from famous landmarks to animals, from textures to people engaged in people-like pursuits. Stock-photo CDs start at $100 each.

✔ You also can buy CDs filled with photographs from Corel Corporation (hey, is this a plug?). Corel has about 200 different Photo CDs, each of a different title (Bridges, People, Cars, Patterns, Butterflies, Orchids, Tigers, and so on) at about $50 each. Interestingly, these images are royalty free; you don't have to pay the photographer diddly for using the images. Use 'em and abuse 'em — you bought 'em. They also double as great screen savers (with music if you forget to take them out of your CD-ROM drive).

✔ If you subscribe to an on-line service such as CompuServe or Prodigy, you can download photos by using your modem. But watch out. Because of their large size, photos take several minutes — sometimes hours — to download. You can waste some major bucks in access charges if you're not careful.

✔ All these solutions are pretty expensive, huh? Well, if you have a few friends who work with computer graphics, they may be willing to loan you a few photos on disk to help you get started. Tell them how much you admire their work and what a daily inspiration they are to you. Eventually, they'll give in. Artists crave compliments.

Painting from scratch

Photo-Paint allows you to do more than just edit photos; you also can paint images from scratch. The difference between drawing in CorelDraw and painting in Photo-Paint is that the painting process is a lot more intuitive. In fact, you don't need my help to paint an image. It's totally easy. You sketch a little here, erase a little there, fill in some details, and keep working until you get it right. Kids love painting on a computer. You'll love it, too. It's the easiest thing you can do with *any* computer program, I swear.

Picture yourself done up in pixels

Alas, even in the Simple-Simon world of computer painting, Technical Stuff rears its nerdy head. Remember how CorelDraw defines lines, shapes, and text by using complex mathematical equations? (If not, and assuming that you care, check out the preceding Technical Stuff icon.) Well, Photo-Paint defines the entire image, whether it's a photograph or something you painted from scratch, by thousands or even millions of tiny colored squares called *pixels*.

Photo-Paint treats the image like a mosaic. When you get close to a mosaic, you can see the individual colored tiles. When you get far away, the tiles blur into a recognizable picture. Pixels function just like those tiles. When you magnify an image in Photo-Paint, you can see the individual pixels. When you restore the image to its regular size, the pixels blur together.

Draw and Photo-Paint Duke It Out

Although both are forms of computer artwork, *drawings* and *images* are different. Drawings created in CorelDraw feature sharp edges, as demonstrated in Figure 1-1. The right side of the figure shows enlarged detail so that you can see what a difference math makes. Even when printed on a really large scale, a drawing retains its detail.

Images created with Photo-Paint feature softer edges. One shade flows continuously into the next. *C'est magnifique, trés* artsie fartsie, *n'est-ce pas?* But like Achilles (you know, that Greek guy with the bad heel), images have a fatal flaw: They look better when printed in small sizes, as shown in Figure 1-2. When they are printed large, you can see the jagged transitions between colors. (If you read the preceding Technical Stuff thing-a-ma-jig, you'll recognize the colored squares you see as pixels.)

Figure 1-1:
No matter how large or small you print your drawing, it's all smooth lines and high contrast.

Figure 1-2:
When printed small, paintings look marvelous. When printed large, they look like a stinky pile of goo.

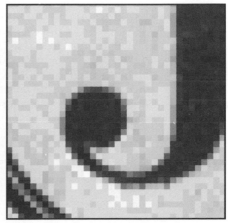

You can't use CorelDraw to edit scanned photos. Because photos are images, you can only edit them in Photo-Paint. Likewise, you can't edit drawings in Photo-Paint; you must make adjustments in CorelDraw.

CorelTrace

CorelTrace is a conversion program. It converts Photo-Paint images to CorelDraw drawings by tracing the outlines of the lines and shapes of the image. Suppose that you put pen to paper and sketched out that bathroom off the linen closet that I discussed earlier. Now you want to convert the plan to a CorelDraw drawing. Here's how the process might work:

1. **Scan the sketch at your local service bureau or wherever you can find a scanner.**

2. **Open the scanned image in Photo-Paint and clean it up a bit.**

   Erase all the dust marks and stuff. Scans always need some tidying here and there. They like to be fussed over. (See Chapter 15 for more details.)

3. **Save your changes to disk.**

   I explain this opening and saving stuff in detail in Chapter 3, so for now, don't worry about it. Just let it wash over you.

4. **Open the image in CorelTrace.**

   Play with the zillion levers and dials that tell CorelTrace how to do its work and convert the image to a drawing.

5. **Open the drawing in CorelDraw.**

   Be prepared to edit the drawing at length to get it to look good.

Converting an image to a drawing is an iffy proposition. It relies on something called artificial intelligence, which is about as reliable as military intelligence. The program tries to emulate your brain but invariably does a pretty poor job. That's why you have to do so much editing to the drawing in CorelDraw.

The fact is, most folks don't need to learn CorelTrace. In a time when magazine articles, TV commercials, and CNN news blips remind you on a daily basis how much new stuff exists that you're totally unaware of, isn't it nice to know that you can get away with *not* knowing something? Although it's very capable, CorelTrace is a special-interest program of limited value to most users. I never use it myself. And if *I* never use it, well, need I say more?

Oh, yes, that's the word "ojoucd" — or is it "qohoot"?

CorelTrace 5 can read, too. If you scan a page of text, Trace can convert the page to a computer text document that you can open and edit in a word processor such as WordPerfect or Microsoft Word. This capability is called *optical character recognition,* also known simply by its initials, *OCR.*

Unfortunately, OCR involves even more artificial intelligence than converting images to drawings. Depending on the quality of the page you want

Trace to read, the program can easily confuse one letter for another. For example, the word *optical* might be read as *optkal, ogucd, ojoucd,* or *qohoot.* Don't get me wrong — CorelTrace is as good as most other OCR programs on the market. But it's highly unlikely that it will read *any* page 100 percent correctly. In some cases, it's easier to enter the text from scratch.

CorelCapture

This program is hardly a program at all. It barely cuts the mustard, as 'twere. What I'm trying to say here is that CorelCapture barely warrants mention. In fact, why don't you go ahead and skip to the next section? You have better things to do than read about CorelCapture.

Oh, all right. Now that I've gone and gotten you all excited about this program, I'll tell you a little bit about what it does. CorelCapture takes pictures of your screen, which are called *screen shots*. This book is chock full of such pictures. They allow me to show you CorelDraw's interface while I describe it to you at the same time.

Pretty cool, huh? The only problem is, you'll probably never need to use this program. What do you need with screen shots? Do you want to wallpaper your room with the insides of CorelDraw? Heck, no. So unless you're documenting a program like I am in this book, CorelCapture is of no use to you.

Just in case you find yourself loving this program in direct violation of my specific instructions, here's a little something you should know: You can use Photo-Paint to edit the pictures you shoot with CorelCapture. In fact, that's exactly what I did to refine many of the figures in this book.

CorelKern

CorelKern is a little gadget-utility that opens Adobe Type 1 fonts and builds and modifies kerning pairs. If you know what kerning pairs are, this application could interest you. If you don't know what kerning is all about, I cover the topic later on in the book. To sum it up, this application is a screwdriver among power tools; 99 percent of Corel users will never touch it.

Corel DataBase Editor

This program is, well, a database editor. In other words, it allows you to build and modify database files. What's it doing in CorelDraw 5? Beats me. Corel picked it up when they purchased the Ventura-ball-o-wax deal. It no doubt has some connectivity to CorelVentura, but nothing to do with CorelDraw at all. Save this application for a rainy decade.

CorelQuery

CorelQuery is the last of the yawners. You can use it to search database files (like the ones you spent all night generating from Corel DataBase Editor) for specific information. For example, you can tell it to "Look for DTP fanatics in Colorado who use CorelDraw." Or "Look for people on this planet who bought CorelDraw to get their hands on CorelQuery." Like Corel DataBase Editor, this one has absolutely no links to CorelDraw.

CorelChart

Have you ever heard of Harvard Graphics? Like CorelDraw, it's an insanely popular piece of graphics software. But instead of letting you create free-form artwork, Harvard Graphics makes serious business charts — you know, bar charts, pic charts, and anything else that shows how well the company is doing, how much market share everyone can expect, or how much money is going down the tubes. The *Graphics* in Harvard Graphics means graphs, not artwork.

CorelChart fulfills the same function. Sure, if it came to blows, Harvard Graphics would stomp CorelChart pretty soundly, but Chart's more than adequate for the occasional charting enthusiast. You enter some data — how many popsicles sold in February, that kind of thing — whack a few buttons, and bingo, you have a serviceable chart that you'll be proud to show associates and clients alike. Read about how great the program is in Chapter 16. Be there or be pie shaped.

CorelMove

Do you like cartoons? The Saturday morning variety? Well, you'd better, because this book is one big cartoon: informative, entertaining, and fun. You can create your own — cartoons, that is, not books (I can do without the competition, thank you very much) — by using CorelMove.

This program lets you animate virtually anything. Suppose that you want to make your company logo hop around on-screen. I don't know why. Maybe you're trying to show how energetic your staff is. Or how nervous everyone gets near payday. Either way, you can make the logo move in any direction at any speed for any length of time. It can zigzag in all directions, gyrate, pitch, tumble, seethe, or do the Watusi. You can even set the scene against a backdrop, like maybe the Uffizi Gallery, to show how your company survives the test of time. Dang, what a bad example. Okay, if not the Uffizi, then Michelangelo's *David* because he's really monumental and huge and . . . wait, no, he got his toe whacked off. If I mention the Pyramids, they'll probably be leveled before this book is published, so why don't I just leave it at some generic long-standing testament to humankind. There behind your gyrating logo. What a movie that would make!

If you're really motivated, you can create movies one frame at a time. To animate a person running, for example, you would draw the left leg down and the right leg up, then both legs fully extended in opposite directions, then the right leg down and the left leg up, then the right foot snagging on a tree branch, then both feet fully above the head, and so on. If this kind of animation seems like too much hard work, Move can automatically fill in the movement between two extremes. To see this program in action, try your luck at Chapter 17.

CorelShow

CorelShow lets you combine elements from other programs, including CorelDraw drawings, Photo-Paint images, Chart charts, and Move animations, into a business presentation. You can print Show files to slides, but face it, slide shows are a thing of the past. Dark rooms. Click click. Blah blah. The perfect recipe for a slumbering audience. CorelShow shines in the creation of on-screen presentations. One slide can dissolve into the next. Animated logos can fly in front of jazzy charts, Uffizi or no Uffizi. You can even create self-running demos that run on other people's computers. The end of Chapter 16 contains a brief look at this program.

CorelMosaic

What with all the stuff you can create with these programs, Corel thought that you might need a librarian to keep track of it all. That's where Mosaic comes in. This program is capable of generating *thumbnail* (that is, tiny) previews of every drawing, image, chart, animation, and presentation stored on a disk. With this approach, you don't have to open each file individually to see what's inside it. You can also use Mosaic to organize files. Just drag the thumbnails to different locations on-screen and you're in business.

Groovy as Mosaic may be, it differs from Corel's other programs in that it doesn't let you *create* anything. It's just a muck-about-and-organize-things tool. That's why I don't discuss it in this book. You can get by without it. Later, when you've mastered everything else, you may want to check it out. But in the meantime, you and I have more important territory to cover. Hi ho!

But Wait! There's More!

That's right, if you act now, you'll also receive thousands of clip-art drawings, hundreds of typefaces, and more animation files and predrawn cartoons than you can shake a Douglas Fir at. No other program comes close to this variety of ready-to-use artwork. It's truly amazing and well worth the price of admission on its own. I feature much of this artwork throughout the book in hopes that you can follow along more easily. I'm just that kind of guy.

With CorelDraw 5, most clip art, fonts, and so on are packaged on CD-ROM, which means that you need a CD-ROM drive to access this stuff. If your computer doesn't have a CD-ROM drive, you may have a friend who has one. Or maybe some other computer in your office is equipped with CD-ROM. Either way, I suggest that you borrow the services of this machine to copy some of your favorite clip-art drawings to disk so that you can use them on your computer. If you don't know how to copy files, ask a friend for help or buy a copy of *DOS For Dummies*.

Feeling Overwhelmed?

I don't blame you. Corel has gone a little nuts in the value department. But the fact is, CorelDraw remains the central and most useful program of the bunch. Frankly, few users would buy a program like Trace or Mosaic if it weren't bundled with Draw.

To wit, most of this book is devoted to Draw. But I bet you ten comes a runnin' to five (actually, I don't gamble, so I'm a little rusty on the vocabulary) that after you learn how to use CorelDraw, you'll find that you can pick up on the other programs with remarkable ease. And, of course, for those ready to venture beyond Draw already, Part IV walks you through Photo-Paint, Chart, Show, Move, and Ventura. Before you know it, you'll be brainy as all get out. No doubt, then, you'll want to take a gander at my next book, *CorelDRAW! For Bionic-Brained Ultra-Dweebs*. I'll probably devote the whole thing to CorelCapture.

Chapter 2
See CorelDraw Run

CorelDraw is one son-of-a-gun program. But you don't have a prayer of mastering it until you and the program get a little better acquainted. You have to learn its nuances, understand some of its gizmos, study its fruity yet palatable bouquet, and make yourself familiar with its inner psyche. In short, you need to read this chapter. Herein lies the answer to that time-honored question, "What makes Draw draw?"

Draw on the March

Entering the world of CorelDraw is a mysterious but surprisingly straight forward process. It goes something like this:

1. **Turn on your computer.**

   Imagine how embarrassed you'd be if you skipped this step.

2. **Wait for your computer to start up.**

   Ho hum, dum dee dum. Be patient; it'll be finished soon. It may be a good time to get some coffee, buy a doughnut, or use the little whatever-sex-you-are's room.

3. **If your computer gives you the DOS prompt, be afraid, be very afraid.**

    Aagh, it's the DOS prompt! (That C> or C:\> thing.) You know it's coming, but you're never quite ready for it. Quick, get rid of it! Type **WIN** and press Return! Come on, shake a leg!

    If your computer enters a shell, be only slightly agitated.

    Some computers bypass the DOS prompt and directly enter some kind of *shell* (that's what the dweebs call them) filled with menus and options. You should find a Windows option somewhere. Select it. If you can't complete this step on your own, call out for help. Hopefully, some kind and knowledgeable soul will rescue you.

    If your computer starts Windows automatically, be immensely relieved.

    Some computers start Windows automatically. All you have to do is sit back and watch.

4. **Now that you're in Windows, activate the CorelDraw program icon.**

    It should be inside a window called Corel, as shown in Figure 2-1. Use your mouse to move the *cursor,* the white arrow on-screen, over to the CorelDraw program icon and then click the left mouse button. Doing so selects the program icon. Now press the Enter key.

Congratulations! CorelDraw is now starting. In mere moments, you'll be able to use the program. In the meantime, let me share with you a few tidbits of information designed to increase your enjoyment of this terrific program.

- There's more than one way to start CorelDraw. Upon locating the program's icon, you can alternatively *double-click* on it — that is, press your left mouse button twice in rapid succession — or click on the icon once and choose File⇨Open from the menu bar at the upper-left corner of your screen.

- Don't panic — I cover all this mouse and menu stuff in detail later in this chapter.

- It's possible that after you start Windows, the Program Manager window (see Figure 2-1) won't appear on-screen. In this event, no ducking or covering is required. Instead, you should see a Program Manager icon lying about somewhere, most likely in the lower-left corner of your screen. Double-click on it to open the Program Manager and see its innards and entrails, among which you should find the CorelDraw program icon. Please wear surgical gloves.

- If the CorelDraw program icon is missing, you should see a Corel group icon somewhere on-screen (again, see Figure 2-1). When you locate it, double-click on it.

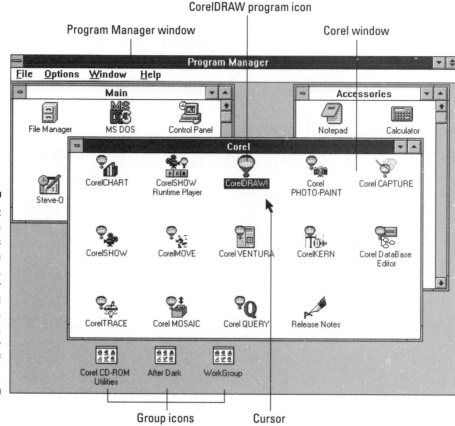

Figure 2-1:
The
Windows
Program
Manager,
your
personal
entrance
ramp to the
hurly-burly
world of
CorelDraw.

✔ If you can't find the Corel group icon, it may be buried under an open window. Try choosing Window⇨Corel in the menu bar. If there is no such command, choose Window⇨More Windows in the menu bar and press the C key one or more times to see whether you can select the Corel option. Once you do, press Enter.

✔ If you still can't locate the Corel group icon, you need to ask yourself a difficult question. Are you sure that someone has installed CorelDraw on your computer? If you aren't sure, ask the person in charge of installing things at your home or office.

✔ Because most folks have already installed CorelDraw, I don't go through the whole process in this chapter. But the appendix at the back of the book tells you everything you need to know.

TIP

✔ Want to bypass all this Windows stuff? Assuming that your system is configured correctly (they seldom are), you can start CorelDraw from the DOS prompt (C:\>, remember?) by typing **WIN CORELDRW**. (If the computer can't locate the CORELDRW file, Windows starts and promptly displays an irritating error message, in which case you have to start CorelDraw the normal way.)

Interface in Your Face

After you start CorelDraw, bang, the whole world changes. What you see on-screen and what Figure 2-2 shows you are CorelDraw's *interface*. The interface allows you to work in and communicate with CorelDraw. All the bits and pieces that you see labeled in Figure 2-2 I bravely cover at great length and personal risk in the following sections.

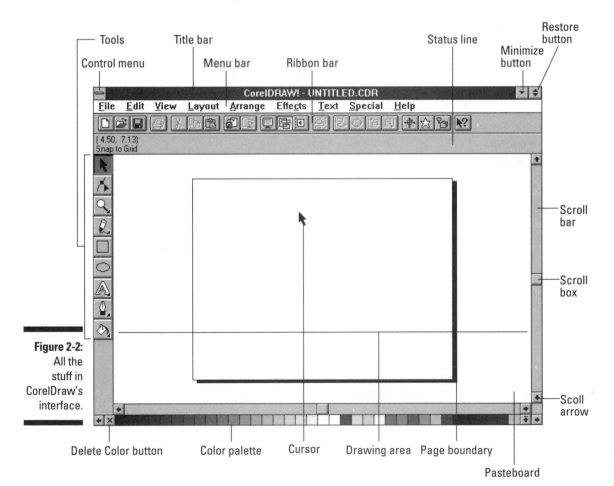

Figure 2-2: All the stuff in CorelDraw's interface.

Title bar

Topping it all off, the *title bar* tells you the title of the program and the name of the document you're working on. In this case, it reads `CorelDRAW! — Untitled` because you haven't assigned a name to your file yet. CorelDraw always creates a new, untitled window when you start the program so that you can start working right away. To the left of the title bar is the *control menu.* To the right of the title bar is the *minimize button.* To the right of that is either the *restore button* (two arrowheads, as in Figure 2-2) or the *maximize button* (a single arrowhead pointing up). These items are common to all Windows programs, but I'll tell you how they work just to while away the time.

✔ When you first start CorelDraw, the interface appears inside a window that hovers in front of the Windows Program Manager and any other programs you may be using. How distracting! To cover up all that background stuff, click on the maximize button. Now the interface fills the screen in floor-to-ceiling cinematic splendor.

✔ To restore the CorelDraw interface to its cramped quarters in a floating window, click on the restore button. This action makes the background stuff accessible again.

✔ You can move the floating Draw window around by *dragging* — that is, pressing and holding the left mouse button while moving the mouse — the title bar.

✔ To change the size of the floating window, position your cursor on one of the window's four corners. Your cursor changes to a diagonal line with arrowheads at either end. Drag the corner as desired.

✔ If you want to get CorelDraw out of your face for a moment and you're really feeling daring, click on the minimize button to hide the CorelDraw window entirely. A CorelDraw icon appears somewhere in the lower-left corner of the screen to show you that Draw is still running but has gone into hiding. Double-click on the icon to bring the interface back into view.

If you don't see the icon in the lower-left corner, it may be hiding under your Program Manager. Do *not* double-click on the CorelDraw icon in the Corel group, which starts another version of CorelDraw. For now, press Ctrl and Esc at the same time to get the Task List box. Double-click on the task: CorelDraw!. (For later, go out and get *Windows For Dummies,* which has some way cool tricks to set up the Program Manager so that this scenario isn't repeated.)

✔ All these options are available as commands from the control menu, but you'd have to be a nut to use them when the title bar and buttons are so much more convenient.

Menu bar

A single *menu bar* appears just below the title bar, as it does in all other Windows applications. Each word in the menu bar — File, Edit, View, and so on — represents a menu. Each menu contains a list of *commands* that you can use to manipulate lines and shapes that you've drawn, change the way text looks, and initiate other mind-bogglingly sophisticated procedures.

Menus are a pretty big topic, so I talk more about them later in this chapter (in the continental "Les Menus sans Soup du Jour" section, to be exact).

Status line

The status line keeps you apprised of what's going on. For example, any time your cursor is in the *drawing area* — the place where you create your drawing, naturally — the status line tells you the exact coordinate location of your cursor. Cool, huh? It also tells you a load of information about selected shapes or anything else you might want to create.

For more information about this splendid feature, check out "Your Four Tools of Control" in Chapter 6.

By default, the status line appears at the bottom of the window. All figures in this book show it on top, just below the ribbon bar. To make your status line move to this position, press Ctrl + J, click on the View tab, and then click on the Place on Top option to select it. Click on OK or press Return to finalize your change.

Ribbon bar

The ribbon bar is a bunch of buttons that you can click on to access certain commands or functions — Group, Align, Copy, Convert to Curves, and so on. It just provides another way of getting the program to work for you. Everything on the ribbon bar can also be invoked with hot keys or via the pull-down menus.

In my not-so-humble opinion, the ribbon bar is a waste of time, for three reasons. One, it's a lot quicker to use keyboard shortcuts (such as Ctrl+A for Align Objects) than it is to hunt, peck, and then press the Align button on the ribbon bar. Two, the ribbon bar reduces the Windows free system resources, which reduces your ability to launch multiple applications. Three, if you ever have to work on a version of CorelDraw that doesn't have a ribbon bar, you'll be scratching your noggin wondering how to do things the old-fashioned way.

If you don't care about these issues, go ahead and leave the ribbon bar turned on. If you want to get rid of it, you can do so via the Preferences dialog box.

Tools

CorelDraw provides nine tools — the same nine tools that the program has offered since street-corner newsboys used to hand out Version 1.0 in 1934 (back when a double feature with newsreel, cartoon, and CorelDraw only cost a nickel). To select a tool, click on its icon. Then use the tool by clicking or dragging inside the drawing area.

To find out more about tools and even give one or two a test run, skip ahead to the "How to Deal with Tools" section. Or better yet, just keep reading. You'll get there soon enough.

Drawing area

Smack dab in the middle of the drawing area is the *page boundary,* which represents the physical size of the printed page. If you position a shape inside the page boundary, it prints. If you position a shape outside the page boundary, it doesn't print. The area outside the page boundary, or the surface on which the page sits, is called the *pasteboard.* Think of the pasteboard as a kind of drawing repository that you can use to store shapes temporarily while you try to figure out what to do with them. It's also a great place to set copies of logos, headlines, ornamental graphics, and other stuff that you use repeatedly throughout a drawing.

Scroll stuff

Scroll bars let you navigate around and display hidden portions of your drawing inside the drawing area. CorelDraw offers two scroll bars, one vertical bar along the right side of the drawing area and one horizontal bar along the bottom. When you click on a *scroll arrow,* you nudge your view of the drawing slightly in that direction. For example, when you click on the right-pointing scroll arrow, an item that was hidden on the right side of the drawing slides into view. Click in the gray area of a scroll bar to scroll the window more dramatically. Drag a *scroll box* to manually specify the distance scrolled.

Navigation is another big topic, one to which I devote a significant amount of energy in the "Getting Around in the Drawing Area" section of Chapter 3.

Color stuff

You can change the colors of the outlines and interiors of shapes in the drawing area by using the color controls at the bottom of the CorelDraw interface. With the left mouse button, click on a color in the *color palette* to change the color assigned to the interior of a selected shape. Click the right mouse button to change the color of a shape's outline. Use the *Delete Color button* (the left button with an X on it) to make an interior or outline transparent.

This topic is another biggie. I cover it in my usual rough-and-tumble style throughout the rolling sagebrush and hilly terrain of Chapter 7.

The Mouse Is Your Willing Slave (and Other Children's Stories)

Have you noticed that when you move the mouse, the cursor moves on-screen? If so, you may be concealing the deductive reasoning powers of Sherlock Holmes. Way to put together that action-reaction stuff. But that's not all the mouse does. It's your primary means of communicating with CorelDraw. Oh sure, the keyboard is great for entering text and performing the occasional shortcut, but the mouse is the primo drawing and editing tool. In other words, it's about time you became familiar with the thing.

The typical mouse features two buttons on top that register clicks and a trackball underneath that registers movement. If your mouse offers three buttons, you'll quickly discover that the center button doesn't work in CorelDraw.

Here's a quick look at some common mouse terminology (not how mice talk, mind you, but how we talk about them, sometimes behind their furry little backs):

 ✔ To *move* your mouse is to move it without pressing any buttons.

 ✔ To *click* is to press and immediately release the left button without moving the mouse. For example, you click on a tool icon to select a tool.

 ✔ To *right-click* is to press and release the right mouse button. I know, it's unfair that the right mouse button is singled out like this, but it's a special-function button that is not used as frequently as its favored cousin to the left.

 ✔ To *double-click* is to press and release the left button twice in rapid succession without moving the mouse. As you saw earlier, you can open a program by double-clicking on its icon. Some programs even accept triple- and quadruple-clicks. CorelDraw does not go to such extremes.

✔ To *press and hold* is to press the button and hold it down for a moment. I refer to this operation very rarely — for example, when an item takes a moment or two to display.

✔ To *drag* is to press the button and hold it as you move the mouse. You release the button to complete the operation. In CorelDraw, for example, you drag with the Pencil tool to draw a free-form line.

✔ To *crush* the mouse is to set it on the floor and stack heavy objects on it. I almost never call on you to perform this technique. In fact, I only recommend crushing to very desperate performance artists, and only then if running the mouse over with a station wagon fails to exhaust your rage.

You can also use the keyboard and mouse in tandem. For example, in Draw, you can draw a perfect square by pressing the Ctrl key while dragging with the Rectangle tool. Or press Shift and click on shapes with the Arrow tool to select multiple shapes. Such actions are so common that you see compound verbs made up from key and mouse combinations, such as *Ctrl+dragging* or *Shift+clicking*. Don't you love the way computer marketers and journalists abuse language? i THinX IT/z Grait.

How to Deal with Tools

You can liken CorelDraw's tools to the pencils, compasses, and French curves that technical artists used back in the bad old days. The difference is that in Draw, tools never wear out, stain, run dry, get lost, or get stepped on. They're always ready to use at a moment's notice.

A quick experiment

To familiarize yourself with the basic purpose of tools as a group, try this brief exercise:

  1. Click on the Pencil tool.

It's the fourth one down — the one that looks like a pencil drawing a wiggly line. Select the tool, and it's ready to use.

2. Express yourself.

I don't want to give away too much stuff about the Pencil tool (I'd spoil the many surprises awaiting you in Chapter 5), but you drag with the tool to create free-form lines. It works just like a pencil. So draw something. Figure 2-3 shows a line I drew, if that's any help.

3. Roam freely.

Recognize no boundaries. Although I stayed inside the page boundaries in Figure 2-3, you don't have to. You can draw anywhere you want inside the drawing area, either within the page boundaries or on the pasteboard.

4. Keep drawing.

Don't stop. When you finish drawing one line, start another one. Draw something really complicated or something really messy. Drawing with a mouse can be a real chore if you're not experienced. So I suggest that you spend some quality time moving your mouse around. I want you two to get acquainted.

Okay, that's enough already. Ixnay with the encilpay.

 5. Arrow tool time. Click on the Arrow tool to select it.

It's the first tool, the one that looks like an arrow. The Arrow tool lets you manipulate the stuff you've drawn.

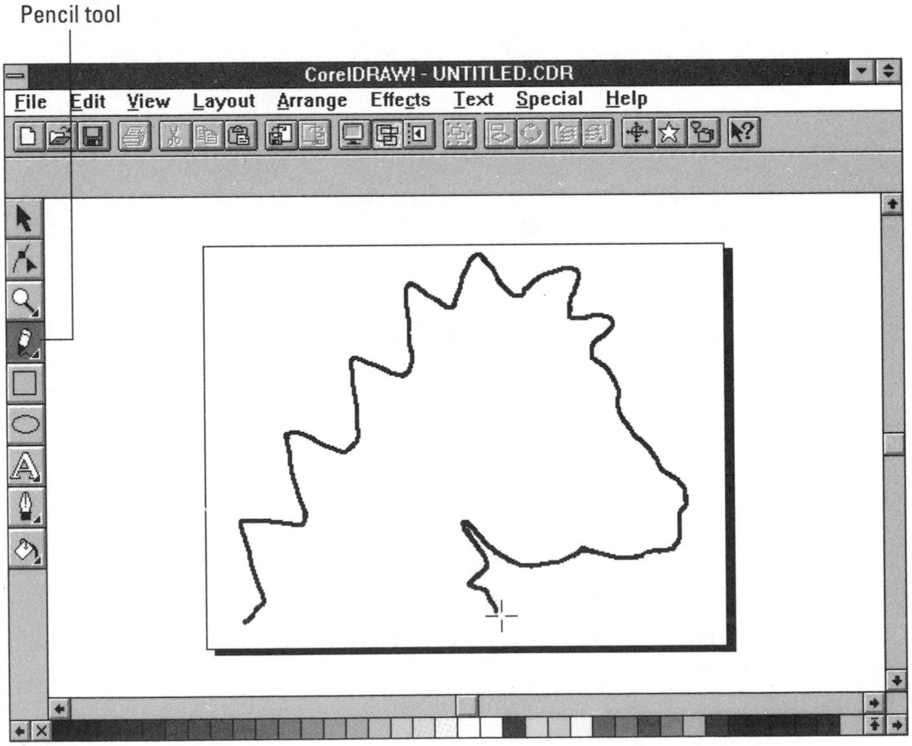

Pencil tool

Figure 2-3:
A spiked thing drawn with the Pencil tool.

6. Select one of them suckers.

> Now click on some entirely random line that you drew in the drawing area. Make sure to align the tip of the arrow with the line before you click. The tip of the arrow is the hot point. I selected my wacky animal's wacky eye, as shown in wacky Figure 2-4.

It's the end of the line, folks. You know those enormous squares that surround the line you just clicked on? They show that the line is selected. Try pressing the Delete key. Oops, the line's gone. You just killed it. Way to go.

See, that was pretty easy, huh? With some time, effort, patience, and other rare commodities, you'll have that whole drawing-with-a-mouse thing down pat.

Tool tricks

You should know a few more things about tools before continuing to the next subject, whatever that may be. First, some tools offer these pop-up McThingies that come up and let you select . . . wait a sec. Let me look this up for you. It's the least I can do, really. You pay $19.95 for a book, you get a little service. And please, no tipping.

Arrow tool

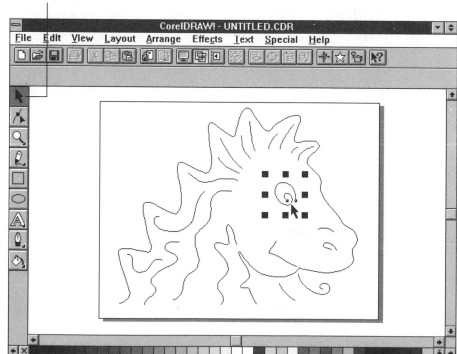

Figure 2-4:
The Arrow tool caught in the act of selecting a line.

The pop-up thingies are called *flyout toolbox menus.* At least, that's what Corel calls them.

When you click on the Zoom tool (third down), Outline tool (second from bottom), or Fill tool (dead last), CorelDraw displays a flyout menu like the one shown in Figure 2-5. Click on an icon inside the menu to select the specific option you want to apply. For example, the Fill tool fills the interior of a selected shape in accordance with the option you select from the flyout menu.

The Pencil and Text tools — the latter looks like an *A* — also offer flyout menus. To access one of these menus, you have to press and hold — rather than simply click — on the Pencil or Text tools (or you can double-click on the tool). The icon you select from the flyout menu then becomes the new occupant of the Pencil or Text tool slot, as demonstrated in Figure 2-6. (The Pencil flyout in CorelDraw 3 and 4 doesn't offer quite so many options.)

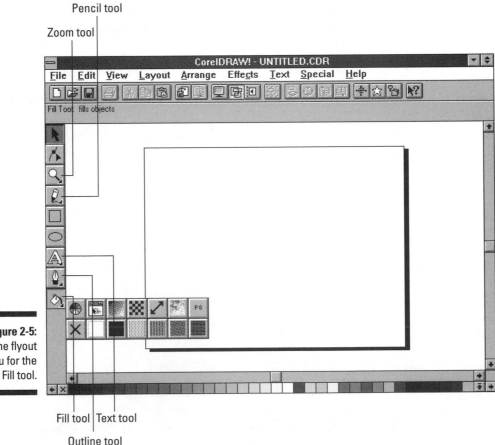

Figure 2-5:
The flyout menu for the Fill tool.

More technical stuff about flyouts

The flyout options for the Zoom, Outline, and Fill tools aren't really tools at all. They're just bogus graphical menus. Rather than allowing you to monkey around in the drawing area — a tool's right and responsibility — they perform immediate effects just like menu commands. The only exception is the Zoom In option, which looks like a magnifying glass with a plus sign in it. You have to click in the drawing area with that tool.

By contrast, the flyout options for the Pencil and Text tools are true tools that you can use to create shapes, lines, and text in the drawing area.

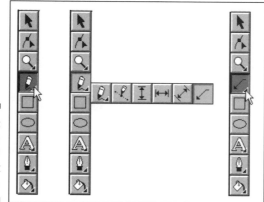

Figure 2-6: How to use the Pencil tool flyout menu.

More tool tricks

Usually, tool icons adhere to the left side of the CorelDraw interface as if they were stuck there with Polygrip. But you can change that by choosing View⇨Toolbox⇨Floating. The tools suddenly appear in a separate window called a *toolbox* (like maybe you didn't figure that out already), as demonstrated in Figure 2-7.

Just for fun, here are some things you can do with the toolbox:

- ✔ You can move the toolbox by dragging that tiny bit of title bar in its upper-right corner, just above the Arrow tool icon.

- ✔ You can change the shape of the toolbox by pulling on any of the borders. Set up a 3 × 3 grid and you've got an instant tic-tac-toolbox.

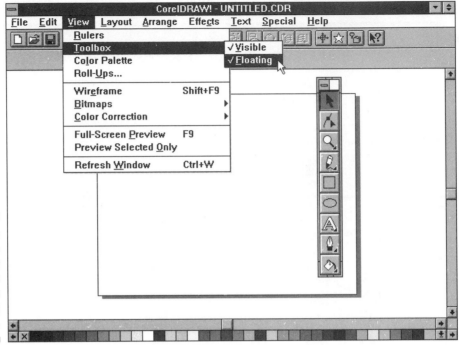

Figure 2-7:
Behold the
floating
toolbox
and its
corresponding
command.

✔ Another Draw 5-only feature: When you double-click on the control menu and deselect Grouped, all the hidden flyout tools really fly out. It looks like CorelDraw is now competing with Tetris (see Figure 2-8).

✔ Double-click on the control menu icon in the toolbox's upper-left corner, and the toolbox disappears. Panic! Quick, go to View⇨Toolbox and select Visible. Resume breathing now.

✔ If you get tired of the toolbox floating around, simply deselect the Floating option from the toolbox's control menu, and it snaps back to its traditional spot on the left. I think that Corel should have renamed the toolbox the *Power-Tool Box*.

✔ When the toolbox is anchored on the left side, hold the Shift key down and then click and drag down on any icon in the toolbox. As you drag, the toolbox detaches and follows your cursor until you release the mouse button.

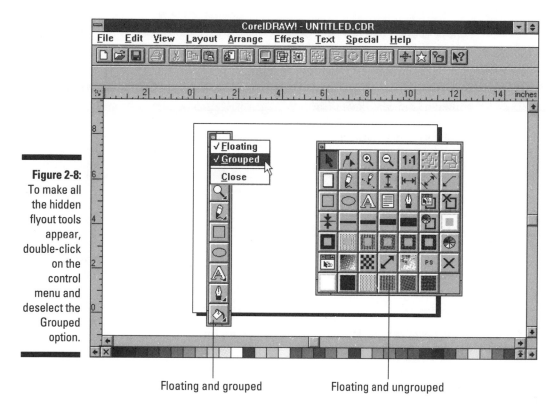

Figure 2-8:
To make all
the hidden
flyout tools
appear,
double-click
on the
control
menu and
deselect the
Grouped
option.

Floating and grouped   Floating and ungrouped

Les Menus sans Soup du Jour

Rather than listing hors d'oeuvres and other tasty morsels, CorelDraw's menus let you do stuff like open a drawing, abuse the drawing until it's no longer recognizable, and save it to disk under the name *Mud*.

To choose a command from a menu, click on the menu name and then click on the command name. For example, if you want to choose File⮞Open, click on the File menu name to display the File menu and then click on the Open command.

Les equivalents du keyboard

In the case of File⇨Open, there's no reason to go to all that effort. You can simply press Ctrl+O — that is, press and hold the Ctrl key, press the O key, and then release both keys — to achieve the same results. This combination is called a *keyboard equivalent.*

Most keyboard equivalents are listed along the right side of a menu. Some keyboard equivalents select tools and perform other functions. Either way, I'll keep you apprised of them throughout this book. If you take the time to memorize a few here and there, you'll save a heck of a lot of time and effort.

Alt, ma chère amie, oui?

Not satisfied? Well, there's yet another way to access commands from the keyboard that is common to all Windows programs. Windows provides special Alt+key equivalents. The following steps demonstrate one scenario for exploiting Alt:

1. **Press the Alt key to activate the menu bar.**
2. **If you want to browse through the menus, press the down-arrow key to display the current menu.**

    Then use the left- and right-arrow keys to change menus. Use the up- and down-arrow keys to highlight command names.

3. **Press Enter to choose the highlighted command.**
4. **To abandon the whole menu bit, press Esc twice, once to hide the menu and again to deactivate the menu bar.**

Alternatively, after pressing Alt, you can press the key for the underlined letter in the menu name, followed by the key for the underlined letter in the command name. For example, to choose File⇨Open, press Alt, then F, and then O. These are called *hot keys* or *shortcut keys.*

The Incessant Chatter of Dialog Boxes

Some menu commands react immediately. Others require you to fill out a few forms before they can be processed. In fact, any command that's followed by an ellipsis (three dots, like so: . . .) displays a *dialog box* or a *roll-up.* Roll-up commands are easy to identify because they actually say *Roll-Up* in the command name, as in Envelope Roll-Up and Text Roll-Up. Any command that doesn't say *Roll-Up* but still sports an ellipsis displays a dialog box.

Figure 2-9 shows a sample dialog box. As the figure demonstrates, a dialog box can contain any of five basic kinds of options. But thanks to the fact that none of CorelDraw's dialog boxes are kind enough to contain all five, Figure 2-9 is partially fabricated. Well, *largely* fabricated. Okay, it's totally made up. Be that as it may, the options work as follows:

- ✔ An option in which you can enter numbers or text is called an *option box.* Double-click on an option box to highlight its contents and then replace the contents by entering new stuff from the keyboard. Or if you prefer, use the arrow icons to the right of an option box to incrementally raise or lower a numerical value. All without hydraulics, mind you.

- ✔ To conserve space, some multiple-choice options appear as *drop-down lists.* Click on the down-pointing arrow icon to display a menu of option choices. Then click on the desired option in the list to select it, just as you would choose a command from a standard menu.

- ✔ You can select only one diamond-shaped *radio button* from any gang of radio buttons. To select a radio button, click on the button or the option name that follows it. The selected radio button is filled with a black dot; all deselected radio buttons are hollow.

- ✔ Unlike radio buttons, you can select as many *checkboxes* as you want. Really, go nuts. To select a checkbox, click on the box or the option name that follows it. Clicking on a selected checkbox turns off the option.

- ✔ Not to be confused with the radio button, the normal, everyday variety of *button* allows you to close the current dialog box or display others. For example, click on the Cancel button to close the dialog box and cancel the current command. Click on OK to close the dialog box and execute the command according to the current settings. Click on Display to display another dialog box.

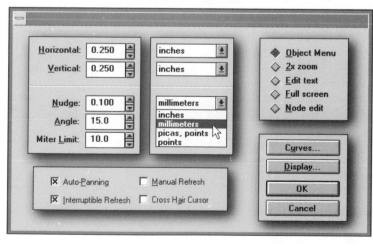

Figure 2-9:
The anatomy of an imaginary dialog box.

✔ As with menus, you can select options and perform other feats of magic inside dialog boxes by using the keyboard. To advance from one option to the next, press the Tab key. To back up, press Shift+Tab. To select any option, press Alt and the key for the underlined letter (or you can press the letter by itself when no option box is highlighted). Press Enter to select the button surrounded by a heavy outline, such as OK. Press Esc to select the Cancel button.

Roll-Ups, Now in 20 Fruity Flavors

Roll-ups, like the one shown in Figure 2-10, are basically dialog boxes that can remain on-screen while you work with other functions in CorelDraw. They float above the surface of the drawing area, just like the toolbox. In Draw 5, there are a total of 20 roll-ups that you can display on-screen at once or a few at a time or whatever. Each roll-up provides so many individualized kinds of options that there's no point in running through them all. Suffice it to say that they let you do some pretty amazing stuff.

The roll-up in Figure 2-10, for example, lets you add depth to an otherwise two-dimensional shape. You can stretch the shape off the page, much like you'd . . . well, frankly, there's no real-life equivalent. It's way cool, and I describe it in Chapter 9.

Roll-ups are called roll-ups (I bet you were wondering about this one) because you can roll them up. There's a shocker. Click on the up-pointing arrow icon in the upper-right corner (or double-click on the title bar) of the roll-up window to hide everything but the title bar. Click on the icon again — now it's a down-pointing arrow — to restore the full window (or double-click on the title bar). This way, you can have several roll-ups on-screen at once without cluttering up the interface. Because a cluttered interface — repeat after me — gets in your face. (The third time for that lame joke — and not the last.)

Figure 2-10:
Roll-ups
float above
the drawing
area like
clouds. Flat,
rectangular,
non-rain-
bearing
clouds.

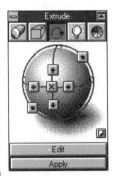

Quite Frankly, You Need Help

We all get lost inside software from time to time. Especially inside a program that packs a punch like CorelDraw. That's why you need help. And CorelDraw's got it on-line.

How to get help

The most effective way to find help about a topic is to press Shift+F1 (or choose Help⇨Screen/Menu Help if you like to do things the hard way). Your cursor changes to an arrow with a question mark. Use the cursor to select a tool, choose a command, or click on some screen item that bewilders or intrigues you. (The term *intrigues* has a certain ring to it, doesn't it? Makes the situation seem less desperate.) After you select, choose, or click, CorelDraw displays a screen chock full of information about that exact topic.

Want some other ways to access help? Fair enough. Check these out:

TIP

✔ Highlight a command in a menu by using the Alt and arrow keys and then press F1 to display information about that command without having to perform any additional clicking or choosing, as the Shift+F1 technique requires.

✔ Without a command highlighted, press F1 or choose Help⇨Contents to open the Contents screen shown in Figure 2-11. This screen is your guide to the entire help system.

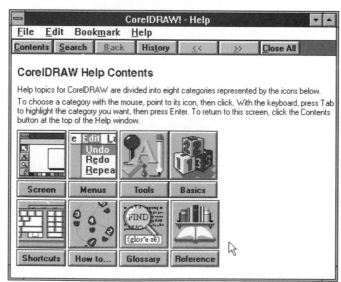

Figure 2-11:
The
CorelDraw
Help
Contents
screen.

> ✔ Can't really find what you're looking for? Press Ctrl+F1 or choose Help⊅Search For Help On to search the help system for a specific word or phrase. You can enter your own word or select one from a list. You may be able to uncover information you can't seem to find any other way.

More help, please

Nearly all Windows programs — including the Windows Program Manager itself — provide help systems that you can access by pressing F1. Shift+F1 frequently initiates a program's *context-sensitive help,* in which you select a bewildering — er, sorry, *intriguing* — screen item. So no matter where you go in Windows, you have a constant support system at your fingertips. And don't worry that it's some kind of codependency thing. To my knowledge, nobody's gotten hooked on help.

You did WHAT to my manual?

Here's something new that Corel put into Draw 5: The entire manual is electronic! Using Adobe's Acrobat reader technology, Corel dumped the technical manuals of all the applications onto one of the CDs in the box. You can wallow through the table of contents and simply click on the word that intrigues you (there's that word again). The reader program uses what's called a *hypertext* function to transport you to the right page ("Scotty, beam me up two paragraphs"). It also allows you to print any page in case you encounter one of the following typical scenarios:

> ✔ Your neighbor borrows the manual and then moves to South America.

> ✔ Your dog eats Chapter 3.

> ✔ Your spouse complains about your curling up to a good monitor in bed.

> ✔ Your new neighbor asks to borrow your manual.

This fancy hypertext, on-line, context-sensitive, save-the-trees, politically correct, kinder, gentler manual may signal the beginning of the end for printed manuals. It's tempting for software companies to make the traditional manual extinct; it'$ very co$tly to print and $hip these dead Dougla$ fir$ (money talk$). Besides, the programs are getting so fancy and complex that you have to remember to pick up the manual by using your legs, not your back.

If manuals do go electronic, you may be reading my next book on-screen as well (heck, I wrote it that way!). Personally, I still like real books — dog-eared pages, coffee stains, and highlighters look terrible on a monitor.

Chapter 3

Ladies and Gentlemen, Insert Your Pocket Protectors!

*T*his chapter covers creation, navigation, and storage. To put it slightly differently, I tell you how to get into CorelDraw, get around, and get out of the program without losing your stuff. To put it differently still, this chapter tells you how to prevent a CorelDraw session from turning into some kind of computer nightmare.

Spanking the Baby

You probably don't remember this, but when the doctor whisked you out of your mom, the doctor smacked your rump to make you take in that first lungful and bellow like a stricken, well, baby. Now here you are, a scant 10,000 or so days later, wondering why I'm bringing up such a painful subject. The truth is, you have to perform a similar maneuver before you can begin drawing in CorelDraw. You don't have to spank any babies — but you do have to give CorelDraw the equivalent of the welcoming paddle.

How do you do that? Well, here's your chance to see whether you've learned anything at all about computers so far. Which of the following actions do you suspect results in a new CorelDraw document?

A. Gently but firmly slap the disk drive. There's no time like the present to teach your computer who's boss.

B. Taunt the computer mercilessly until it cries and gives in.

C. Choose File⇨New or File⇨Open.

Four out of five computer scientists agree that B is the best way to humble your computer into producing a new document. But recently, a significant minority of dissenting scientists have come out in support of answer C. In the interest of fair and unbiased journalism, I test this strange theory on the following pages.

The new document

When you first start CorelDraw, the program produces an empty drawing area. This blank space is your new document. It has no preconceived notions of what a drawing is or what it should be. You can mold it into anything you want. You are master of the page.

Problem is, an empty drawing area can be terrifying. It's like looking inside the deepest recesses of your soul and seeing nothing, except not nearly as profound. Suffice it to say that a new document is the surest formula for performance anxiety.

The Chihuahua scenario

Fortunately, the empty drawing area isn't the only route available. You can approach your drawing from a different angle, namely by opening an existing drawing that can serve as a starting point. Suppose that you want to draw a Chihuahua. Where are you going to find a yippy little dog on the third floor of an air-conditioned building located in an office park surrounded by shopping malls? And even if you had a Chihuahua on your desk, baring its teeth at you in domesticated terror, you wouldn't have a hope of drawing it because the degree of difficulty for creating a realistic Chihuahua from scratch in CorelDraw is somewhere in the neighborhood of 13 on a 10-point scale. (For that very reason, there are no Chihuahuas in this book.)

So what's the solution? Well, in and amongst CorelDraw's vast library of clip art, you'll find a drawing of a small animal that is generally accepted as the direct ancestor of the Chihuahua. I am referring, of course, to the rat. All you have to do is shorten the tail, snip the claws, enlarge the ears, remove some whiskers, bulge out the eyes, reduce the size of the brain cavity, and add a little balloon above its head that says, "Yip yap," the extent of the Chihuahua's vocabulary.

Opening an existing drawing

Before you can do any editing, you have to open the rat file by using the File⇨Open command. The following steps tell you how to access the rat or any other drawing from inside CorelDraw:

1. **Choose File⇨Open or simply press Ctrl+O.**

   The Open Drawing dialog box appears, as shown in Figure 3-1. (The steps that point to items listed in the dialog box correspond to the following steps.)

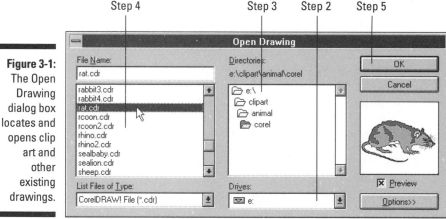

Figure 3-1: The Open Drawing dialog box locates and opens clip art and other existing drawings.

2. **Select a disk drive from the Drives drop-down list box.**

   Click on the down-pointing arrow icon on the right side of the Drives option to display a pop-up menu. Then click on the drive in which you believe your file is stored. In Figure 3-1, I selected drive E, which is my system's CD-ROM drive. But you can select any drive you want.

3. **Open the desired directory in the Directories list.**

   Double-click on a directory name to open it. The list then displays all the directories inside that directory. Double-click on another directory to open it, and so on.

4. **Select the drawing that you want to open from the File Name list.**

In my case, I clicked on the RAT.CDR file. A preview of the drawing appears on the right side of the dialog box so that you can see what it looks like.

5. **Click on the OK button or press Enter.**

That's all there is to it. Your drawing is now open and ready to abuse.

I wish I could tell you how to change a rat into a Chihuahua in five easy steps, but I can't. Instead, I devote Chapters 4 through 9 to the topics of drawing and editing in CorelDraw. I don't specifically address Chihuahua illustrations, but you can tell that they're constantly in the back of my mind.

In the meantime, here are a few additional notes on opening drawings to carry you through your working day:

✔ To close a directory in the Directories list, double-click on the directory name above it.

✔ Use the Preview box to help you identify drawings. For example, if you or someone you work with has gone and named a drawing GT12_RR.CDR (or something equally meaningless), you can click on the box and view a really tiny version of the drawing that may or may not be identifiable. Hey, it's better than nothing.

✔ The File Name list usually shows only those drawings that end in .CDR, such as RAT.CDR or RATDOG.CDR. But if you work in a setting in which several people get their grubby hands on a single drawing, the filename can get so messed up that CorelDraw doesn't recognize it. To see all the files in a directory, enter ***.*** in the option box above the list and then press Enter.

✔ If CorelDraw can't open a file, there's a slim chance that the file is damaged and no longer usable. But it's more likely that the file was created in some program other than CorelDraw. Ask around and see whether anyone knows anything about the file, including where it came from.

✔ CorelDraw doesn't let you open more than one drawing at a time. This means that every time you try to open a drawing, CorelDraw must close the one that's already open. If you've made changes to that drawing since the last time you saved it, CorelDraw asks whether you want to save the changes to disk. Click on the Yes button to save the changes; click on No to dump the changes; or click on Cancel or press the Esc key to return to the drawing in question and cancel the Open command.

TECHNICAL STUFF

Word search

There's more than one way to smell out a rat. A great way to pilfer through CorelDraw's mountains of clip art is to search disks according to keywords. First, click on the Options button in the Open Drawing dialog box. A variety of new options appear at the bottom of the dialog box, as shown in the following figure. Click on the Find button, enter the keyword for which you want to search (in this case, *rat*), and press Enter. In a matter of minutes, CorelDraw locates all files that contain that keyword. What a time-saver!

You can add keywords to drawings from the Open Drawing dialog box by entering text into the Keywords option box. As soon as you close the dialog box or select a different drawing from the File Name list, CorelDraw asks whether you want to save the new keywords. You can answer Yes or No based on your preference. It's a free world, after all.

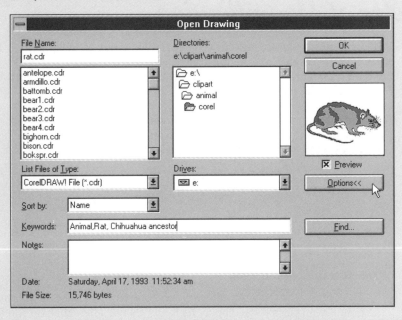

Getting Around in the Drawing Area

Ah, getting around. The favorite pursuit of the Beach Boys. Of course, we all know that in reality the Beach Boys were about as likely to get around as a parade of go-carting Shriners. I mean, it's not like you're going to confuse a squad of sandy-haired Neil Bush look-alikes with the Hell's Angels. John Denver, Richie Cunningham, and James Watts could play kazoos on "The MacNeil/Lehrer Report" and come off more streetwise than the Beach Boys.

Now that I've offended everyone who ever surfed or enjoyed falsetto harmonies, I will say two things in the Beach Boys' defense. First, "Help Me, Rhonda" and "Good Vibrations" are crankin' tunes. And second, even a bunch of squares like the Beach Boys can get around in CorelDraw (nice tie-in, huh?).

Miracles of Magnification

When you first open a drawing, you see the full page, as in Figure 3-2. To fit the page entirely inside the drawing area, CorelDraw reduces the page so that it appears considerably smaller than it prints. It's as if you're standing far away from it, taking in the big picture.

Although the big picture is great, it lacks detail. Imagine trying to edit the claws, the eyes, or some other minute feature from this vantage point. That's why CorelDraw lets you zoom in to magnify the drawing and zoom out to make it smaller.

Zoom In

To get up close and personal with your drawing, do the following:

1. Select the Zoom In tool.

To magnify the drawing, click on the Zoom tool — the one that looks like a magnifying glass — to display its flyout menu. Then click on the first icon in the menu, which represents the Zoom In tool.

To get to the Zoom In tool even faster, press F2. The F2 key selects the Zoom In tool without hassling with the flyout menu.

2. Click in the drawing area with the Zoom In tool.

CorelDraw magnifies the drawing to twice its previous size, as demonstrated in Figure 3-3. The program centers the magnified view about the point at which you click. In Figure 3-4, for example, I clicked the eyeball to center the view about the eyeball.

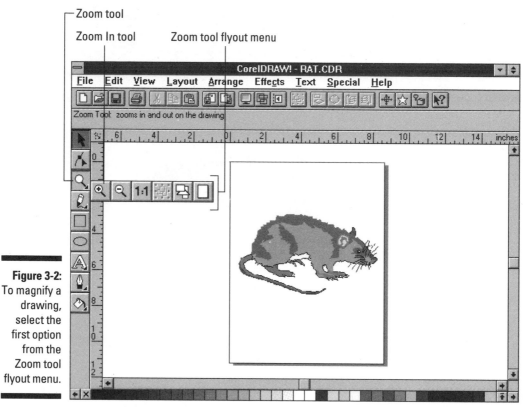

Figure 3-2:
To magnify a
drawing,
select the
first option
from the
Zoom tool
flyout menu.

Alternatively, you can drag with the Zoom In tool to surround the area that you want to magnify with a dotted outline. Using this technique, you can zoom in to more than twice the previous level of magnification.

3. Repeat Steps 1 and 2.

The Zoom In tool is a one-time deal. After you click with it, the program reverts back to the Arrow tool. If you want to magnify the drawing further, you have to press F2 and click again.

Figure 3-4 shows the result of pressing F2 and clicking a total of three times. The magnified rat is 800 percent as large as its counterpart in Figure 3-2 and 400 percent as large as that in Figure 3-3.

Zooming doesn't change the size at which your drawing prints. It just affects the size at which you see the drawing on-screen. It's like looking at an amoeba under a microscope. The creature doesn't actually grow and shrink as you vary the degree of magnification, and neither does your drawing.

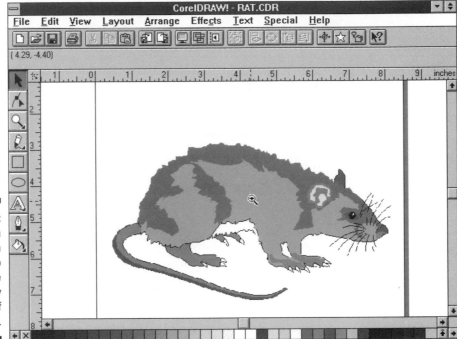

Figure 3-3:
Click with
the Zoom In
tool to
magnify the
drawing by
a factor of
200 percent.

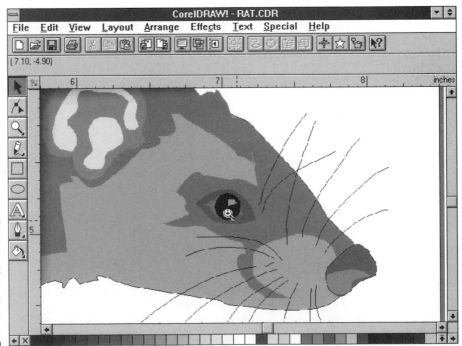

Figure 3-4:
The closer
you inspect
a rat, the
more it looks
like a
Chihuahua.

Make your right mouse button zoom in for you

Want another way to access the Zoom In tool? Wouldn't it be great if you could zoom in by right-clicking? Well, you can; otherwise, I wouldn't have brought it up. To access this feature, choose Special⇨Preferences or press Ctrl+J. After the Preferences dialog box appears, look for the section called *Right Mouse Button* (make sure that the *General* tab along the top is on top — you're looking at five screens in one). Click on the down arrow on the Action drop-down list and select the 2x Zoom option, shown in the next figure. Then click on the OK button in the dialog box. Now right-click. CorelDraw magnifies the drawing to twice its previous size.

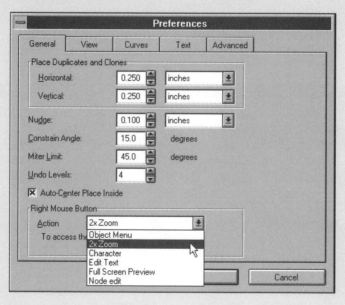

Zoom zooma zooma zoom

Magnification is only half the zoom formula. After all, that which zooms in must ultimately zoom out. CorelDraw also offers several automatic zoom controls that zoom in and out at predefined intervals. Here's the scoop:

- ✔ To zoom out, select the Zoom Out tool — the magnifying glass with the minus sign — from the Zoom tool flyout menu. No clicking, soaking, or whittling is required. CorelDraw automatically reduces the drawing to 50 percent of its former glory.

✔ Select the Actual Size tool — the one that reads 1:1 — to view your drawing at the size at which it will print.

 ✔ The Zoom to Selected tool enables you to zoom in to a selected object. For example, if you click on the rat's nose and then click on the Zoom to Selected tool, Draw zooms in to give you a close-up look at the nose.

 ✔ To reduce the view so that every line, shape, and character of text is visible, select the Fit in Window tool, as demonstrated in Figure 3-5.

 ✔ To see the entire page again, select the Show Page tool, located last in the flyout menu.

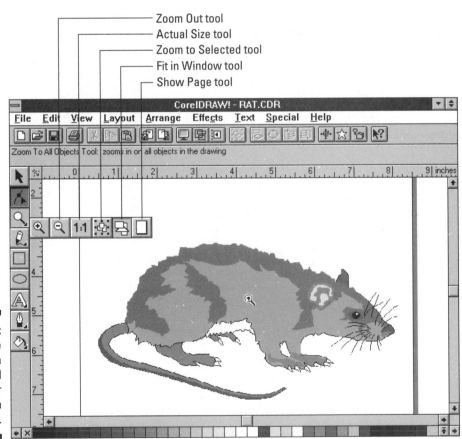

Figure 3-5:
Select the
Fit in
Window tool
to see your
drawing in
its entirety.

Scroll and Crossbars

Scrolling is an ancient navigational craft thought to be developed by prehistoric Cro-Magnons for the breeding and conveyance of domesticated animals. Abandoned entirely by the Iron-Age Villanovans and Classical Greeks, scrolling was rediscovered by the Roman Emperor Flavian — himself a devout sheep enthusiast — as a means of charting the boundaries of territory won in battle. It remained a favorite throughout the reign of Constantine and spread as far north as modern-day Britain and as far east as Mongolia, where scrolling replaced that society's fascination with snorting gunpowder.

Scrolling turned reckless and violent in the 12th century, when Byzantine pirates roamed the seas scrolling whomsoever they pleased in appalling rituals. Their symbol, the scroll and crossbars (see Figure 3-6), became synonymous with terror and cross-dressing. Only after American revolutionary Thomas Paine, in a moment of supreme fatigue, adopted the symbol as a sign of self-determination, did scrolling eventually regain its good name. Now a favorite of Little League teams and heavy metal bands, the scroll and crossbars symbol has lost much of its meaning. But the spirit of scrolling lives on in CorelDraw and other Windows software.

Figure 3-6:
The infamous scroll and crossbars, the universal symbol for navigation.

Accessing zoom tools with keyboard shortcuts

As shown in the figure to the right, CorelDraw lets you access most of its zoom tools from the keyboard. For some reason, the folks over at Corel left out the Actual Size tool, which is one of the most useful. Dang! Incidentally, the keyboard equiva-lent to bring up the Show Page tool, Shift+F4, is finally documented in CorelDraw's documentation after five versions. It works in previous versions too, but only now does Corel fess up to this undocumented feature.

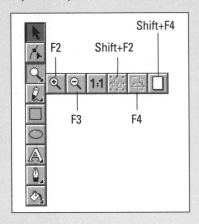

Real Scrolling

Having gotten that off my chest, I have only a few words to add on the subject of scrolling. As you may have noticed already, you can see only bits and pieces of your drawing when it is magnified. The scroll bars allow you to control which bits and pieces are visible.

Suppose that you can only see the nose of the rat, as shown in Figure 3-7. You want to view the animal's tail, which is several inches to the left. To do so, drag the *scroll box* on the *horizontal scroll bar* to the left, as shown in Figure 3-8. The process is so remarkably straightforward that it's hardly worth explaining. With a little experimentation, you'll find yourself scrolling with ease. Those Cro-Magnons — what'll they think of next?

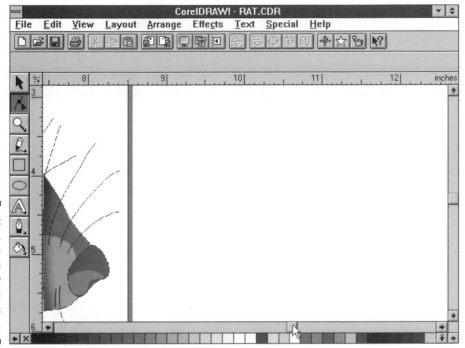

Figure 3-7:
In this view, only the rat's strangely formed snout is visible.

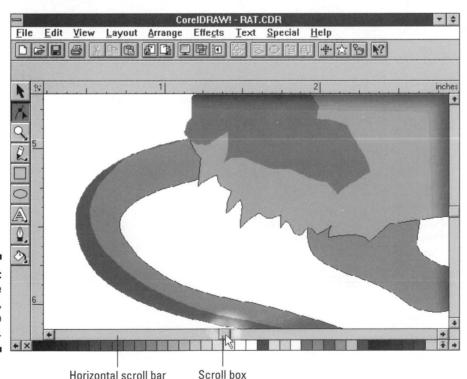

Figure 3-8:
To view the tail instead, just scroll to the left.

Horizontal scroll bar   Scroll box

The Screen Is What You Make It

You can also change the way CorelDraw shows you a drawing on-screen by switching *display modes*. Normally, you see the drawing in full, glorious color with all fills and outlines intact. This is called *Editable Preview mode*. This mode is excellent in that it shows the drawing as it will look when printed. The only problem with this mode is that it can be slow, especially when you're viewing a complex drawing.

String art revival

To speed things up, choose View⇨Wireframe or press Shift+F9. In *Wireframe mode*, CorelDraw displays each shape in your drawing as if it were transparent and defined only by a thin black outline, as shown in Figure 3-9. Compare this figure to Figure 3-5, which shows the rat at the same zoom ratio in the Editable Preview mode.

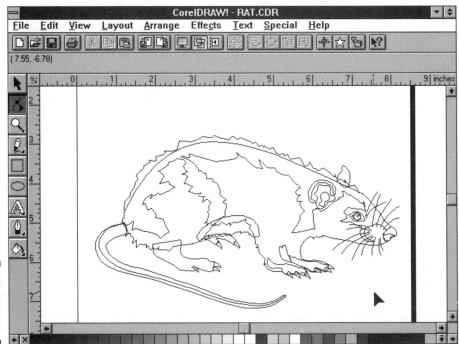

Figure 3-9:
The rat in Wireframe mode.

Wireframe mode speeds things up considerably because CorelDraw can display a bunch of black outlines much faster than it can display colors, gradations, arrowheads, and other attributes that you'll learn about in Chapter 7. But Wireframe mode also makes it more difficult to edit the drawing. It's like trying to imagine how a house will look when it's still in the framing stage. It's like reconstructing the *Venus de Milo* out of toothpicks and tissue paper. It's like removing your skin and going out in public with your bones showing. I could come up with many more analogies, but suffice it to say that it's an underlying structure kind of thing that takes some getting used to.

You only need to use Wireframe mode if CorelDraw is running exasperatingly slowly. Even then, you will probably want to switch back and forth regularly between it and Editable Preview mode to keep track of what's going on.

To return to Editable Preview mode, press Shift+F9 or choose View➪Wireframe, just as you did to enter Wireframe mode. A single command that switches you back and forth like this one is called a *toggle*.

Die, you gravy-sucking interface

Although absolutely essential in communicating with CorelDraw, the interface can occasionally prove distracting. To temporarily hide everything but the drawing itself, press F9 or choose View➪Full-Screen Preview. Even the cursor disappears. Whether you were previously working in Wireframe or Editable Preview mode, CorelDraw shows the drawing in full color (actually, shades of gray in this book), as in Figure 3-10.

This mode is called *Hands-Off Preview mode* because you can't do anything in it besides look at the drawing. The second you click the right mouse button or press a key on the keyboard, CorelDraw exits the Hands-Off Preview and restores the interface. Clicking the left mouse button forces CorelDraw to refresh the screen, but that's the extent of it. The Hands-Off Preview is just a means of looking at your drawing without having to print it.

Occasionally, new users become panicky when the interface disappears and assume that the only way to return to CorelDraw is to turn off the computer and start over again. I don't want this to happen to you. So at the risk of sounding repetitive, I'll repeat myself: Just press *any* key on the keyboard and the interface returns.

Figure 3-10: Unencumbered by the CorelDraw interface, the rat appears perceptibly more at ease with its surroundings.

Just as you can set the right mouse button to magnify your drawing, you can set the button to switch in and out of Hands-Off Preview mode. Because I already explained how the basic process works a few pages back (in the Technical Stuff sidebar in the section "Miracles of Magnification"), I'll run through it very quickly. All you have to do is press these keys:

Ctrl+J, Alt+A, F, Enter

Now right-click. Zowie, you're in Hands-Off Preview mode. Right-click again and you're out.

Previewing bits and pieces

CorelDraw provides one additional method for previewing a drawing. Its benefits become more apparent as you become more familiar with the program. When you're working with a complex drawing, some shapes can get in the way of other shapes. You may be tempted to delete shapes just to get them out of your way. But don't, because there's a better way. Follow these steps:

1. Select the lines, shapes, and text that you want to preview.

 I don't explain how to select stuff until Chapter 4. But to get you started, you can select a single object by clicking on it with the Arrow tool. You select multiple objects by clicking on one and then Shift+clicking on the others.

2. Choose View⇨Preview Selected Only.

You need to choose this command only once because it stays on until you choose the command again to turn it off.

3. Press F9.

Only the selected objects appear on-screen. The rest temporarily vanish.

Figure 3-11 shows the result of selectively previewing a few shapes that make up the rat. The poor animal looks like a gang of field mice stripped it down to its underwear.

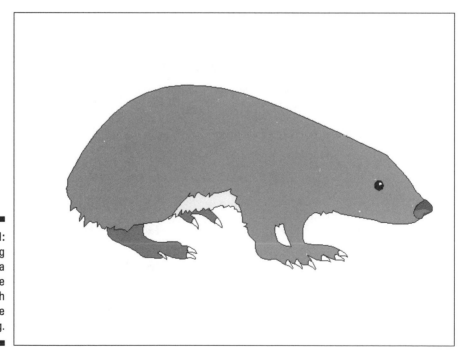

Figure 3-11:
Transforming
a rat into a
mole
through
selective
previewing.

Save or Die Trying!

Saving your drawing is like locking your car. After you get in the habit of doing it, you're protected. Until then, life can be traumatic. A stereo stolen here, a crucial drawing lost there. During my formative desktop publishing years, I managed to lose so many drawings that I finally taped the message *Save or die trying* to the wall above my computer. If you're new to computers, I suggest that you do something similar. You look up, you save your drawing, and you live happily ever after.

After all, there's nothing like spending an hour or so working on a complex drawing that you've neglected to save only to be greeted by a system error, power outage, or some other electronic tragedy. It makes you want to beat your fists on the top of the monitor, strangle the thing with its own power cord, or engage in other unseemly acts of computer terrorism.

To avoid the trauma, save your document to disk early and update it often.

Saving for the very first time

The first time you save a new drawing, you have to name it and specify its location on disk. Here's how:

1. **Choose File⇨Save or press Ctrl+S.**

   The Save Drawing dialog box appears, as shown in Figure 3-12.

2. **Enter a name in the File Name option box.**

   The name may contain up to eight characters and should be followed by a period and the suffix .CDR. RAT.CDR, RAT01.CDR, and RAT_DOG.CDR are all fine. CHIHUAHUA.CDR is too long (although CHIHUAHU.CDR is perfectly acceptable).

3. **Select a disk drive from the Drives drop-down list.**

   Use the drop-down list to select the drive to which you want to save your drawing. Incidentally, you can't save a drawing to CD-ROM. If you opened a piece of CorelDraw's clip art, you need to save it to your hard drive or some other disk.

4. **Select a directory from the Directories list.**

   Double-click on a directory name to enter and exit it just as you do when opening a drawing.

5. **Add keywords and notes according to taste.**

   You can enter 200 characters of text in the Keywords option box and more still in the scrolling Notes option. Keywords are especially useful because they allow you to search for drawings from the Open Drawing dialog box.

6. Click on the OK button or press the Enter key.

Your drawing is now saved! Come hell or high water, you're protected.

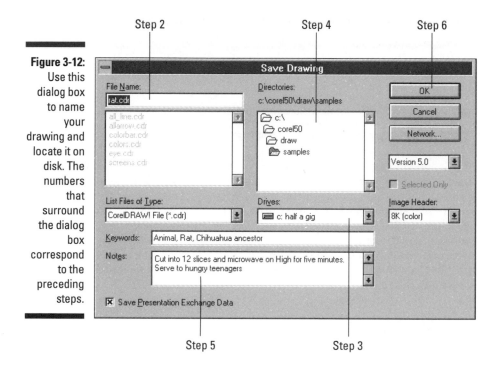

Figure 3-12: Use this dialog box to name your drawing and locate it on disk. The numbers that surround the dialog box correspond to the preceding steps.

Step 5 mentions that you can attach notes to drawings, sort of like electronic sticky notes. Just in case you're a little vague on their potential, here are a few great ideas for notes:

- ✔ **Document history:** For example, *Created 2-14-92; lost 2-15-92; re-created 6-18-93; last edited 3-26-94.*

- ✔ **Instructions:** *Anne, that thing in the upper-left corner is a hydroplane. I know it looks like a duck with porcupine quills, but it's not. If you can make it look any better, go for it.*

- ✔ **Reminder:** *Murray, will you please make some coffee?*

- ✔ **Fortune:** *Aries: Your sunny disposition will win out over your complete lack of common sense in today's financial negotiations. Best to go home early.*

- ✔ **Gossip:** *I'm pretty sure Burt cut his own hair again. Either that or he took a match to it. You should see it!*

- ✔ **Warning:** *Stay away from this drawing. I didn't spend hours on it so that you could come along and mess it up. Don't even look at it, buster.*

Updating the drawing

After you name your drawing and save it to disk, press Ctrl+S every time you think of it.

This automatically updates your drawing on disk, without dialog boxes, options, or any other interface artifacts. When something goes wrong — notice that I said *when*, not *if* — you don't lose hours of work. A few minutes, maybe, but that comes with the territory.

Creating a backup copy

If you spend longer than a single day creating a drawing, you should create backup copies. That's not a hard and fast rule, mind you, but it is a sound principle of drawing management. When a drawing takes longer than a day, you're that much worse off if you lose it. By creating backup copies — for example, RAT01.CDR, RAT02.CDR, RAT03.CDR, and so on, one for each day that you work on the project — you're less likely to lose your work. If a disk error occurs or you accidentally delete one or two of the files, one of the backups will probably survive the disaster, further protecting you from developing an ulcer or having to seek therapy.

At the end of the day, choose File⇨Save As. The Save Drawing dialog box appears, as when you first saved the drawing. Change the filename slightly and then click on the OK button. Way to be doubly protected!

Auto Backup

Once in a while, the CorelDraw hourglass starts spinning on-screen for no apparent reason. Look carefully at the status bar and you see the phrase Doing Auto Backup. Relax; stop looking for your car keys or checking to see whether your Chevette is still in the driveway.

Every 10 minutes, CorelDraw saves your work in your COREL50\DRAW subdirectory (or whatever you named it during installation). When it does an Auto Backup, it creates an .ABK file, such as RAT.ABK. When you save the .CDR file, the .ABK file disappears from your PC.

Why all the fuss? Well, Windows is a multitasking environment, which means that you can run more than one program at a time. Something, through no fault of your own, may bring Windows — and all programs that you're running — crashing down. If you have never experienced this, knock on particle board. If it has, then you know what General Protection Fault (GPF) means — curse, hit the monitor, reboot, and start all over again.

CorelDraw's Auto Backup feature saves your file (and your hide) if a GPF occurs — and even if your dog yanks out the power cord, for that matter. You can go to the COREL50\DRAW subdirectory and use either DOS or the File Manager to rename RAT.ABK as RAT.CDR. You may have lost the last 10 minutes of work, but it's better than losing the entire file.

You can determine where the ABK file is created and the time interval between auto backups in the Preferences Window (press Ctrl+J). When you're in the Preferences Window, click on the Advanced tab along the top; the controls are very simple. You can even turn Auto Backup off, which you may want to do if you're working with a very large file or if you methodically practice "safe save."

There's one more feature of Auto Backup that you won't find in any manual. It knows precisely when you want to print or do a Full Screen Preview for your boss. It samples your brain waves to determine whether the above criteria are met and then starts Auto Backup, forcing you to sit around in anguish or embarrassment. After it starts Auto Backup-ing, it sends *you* brainwaves that make you stand up and get coffee.

In other words, you can't interrupt Auto Backup once it starts; you just have to be patient and wait for the computer to finish saving your work. Even so, Auto Backup is an invaluable safety net that you'll want to have around in most cases.

Don't confuse .ABK files with .BAK files. If you choose Ctrl+J, click on the Advanced tab, and turn on the Make Backup On Save option, Corel automatically makes a backup copy of your drawing and assigns the copy the .BAK extension. This backup copy isn't updated until the next time you save your file.

Putting Your Drawing to Bed

To leave CorelDraw, choose File➪Exit or press Alt+F4. I know that using Alt+F4 to close a document doesn't make anywhere near as much sense as using Ctrl+O to open and Ctrl+S to save, but it's not Corel's fault. Microsoft demands the Alt+F4 thing from all its Windows programs. Where Microsoft came up with Alt+F4 is anyone's guess. I think that they made it confusing on purpose. This is the same company that brought you DOS, so what can you expect?

Anyway, when you press Alt+F4, CorelDraw may say `RAT.CDR has changed. Save current changes?` or something to that effect. Unless you have some reason for doing otherwise, press the Y key or click on the Yes button. The program then quits and takes you back to the Windows Program Manager.

To exit Windows into the murky world of DOS, press Alt+F4 again. Windows always warns you that you're about to end your Windows session. It's as if even Microsoft knows how horrible DOS is. But like death and taxes, DOS is inevitable. May as well press Enter and be done with it.

Part II
Let the Graphics Begin

The 5th Wave   By Rich Tennant

PC DESCENDING A STAIRCASE

"THE ARTIST WAS ALSO A PROGRAMMER AND EVIDENTLY PRODUCED SEVERAL VARIATIONS ON THIS THEME."

In this part...

Traditional artist's tools are messy. Real-life ink, for
example, bleeds into the fibers of the paper; it goops
and glumps onto the page; and it stains if you accidentally
spill some on your clothes. Real-life pens clog; real-life
paintbrushes need washing; and real-life paintings flop over
accidentally and get dust and hairs stuck all over them. Real
life, in other words, is for the birds (which is only fitting
since birds are wholly unequipped to use CorelDraw, what
with their puny little brains and their sad lack of opposable
thumbs).

CorelDraw, being a figment of your computer's imagination,
is very tidy and orderly. There's nothing real to deal with.
The pencil draws a line that remains the same thickness
throughout. Whoever heard of such a thing? You can edit
lines and shapes after you draw them. Unbelievable. And if
you make a mistake, you can choose the Undo command.
There's no equivalent in the real world. CorelDraw provides
a flexible, forgiving interface that mimics real life while at
the same time improves on it.

In the next six chapters, I'll show you how to draw, how to
edit what you've drawn, how to apply colors, how to
duplicate portions of your artwork, and how to create
special effects. By the time you finish with Chapter 9, those
Number 2 pencils you've been storing all these years will be
history.

Chapter 4
The Secret Society of Simple Shapes

Ever try to draw a perfect square the old-fashioned way? Regardless of how many metal rulers, drafting arms, and absolutely 100-percent-square stencils you have at your disposal, you're liable to miss the mark to some extent, however minuscule. And that's if you kill yourself over every corner and use the highest-grade engineering pens and acetate.

If you want to keep the Euclideans happy — none of us wants to attract the wrath of an angry Euclidean — there's nothing like a drawing program for accuracy, simplicity, and downright efficiency. Suddenly, squares and circles are as easy to draw as those little smiley faces that little girls frequently use in their letters as punctuation at the end of jokes.

You know, like, "Sam caught a swordfish. It's so big and scary that I asked Sam if he was sure the fish didn't catch him!" followed by a smiley face. A semicircle mouth and two dots for eyes. Not even a circle to identify the boundaries of the head. Just a face in space, like some minimalist version of the Cheshire cat. Well, anyway, the point is that smiley faces are ridiculously easy to draw, and so is the stuff in this chapter.

Shapes from Your Childhood

Wow, is this going to be easy! In about five minutes, you'll be laughing out loud at the idea that you once viewed computers as cold-blooded machines.

Rectangles and squares

 Click on the Rectangle tool (fifth from the top, just below the Pencil tool) to select it, or press F6 if you prefer. Now drag it into the drawing area. A rectangle grows out of the movement of your cursor, as demonstrated in Figure 4-1. One corner of the rectangle appears at the point at which you begin dragging. The opposite corner appears at the point at which you release the mouse button. What could be simpler?

Rectangle tool

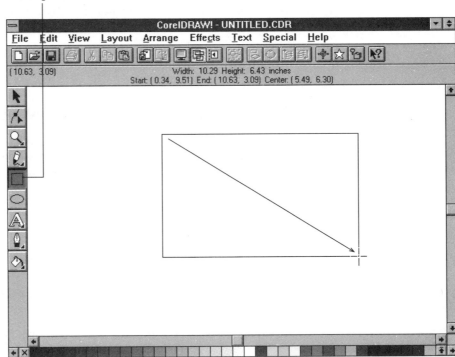

Figure 4-1:
Drag
with the
Rectangle
tool to draw
a rectangle.

Here's some more stuff you can do with this tool:

✔ Press and hold the Ctrl key while dragging with the Rectangle tool to draw a perfect square. The Ctrl key constrains the rectangle so that all four sides are the same length. Be sure to hold the Ctrl key until you release your mouse button.

✔ Shift+drag with the Rectangle tool — that is, press and hold the Shift key while dragging — to draw a rectangle outward from its center. CorelDraw centers the rectangle about the point at which you begin dragging. A corner appears at the point at which you release.

✔ Ctrl+Shift+drag to draw a square outward from the center.

Ovals and circles

The Oval tool, the sixth tool down, works the same way as the Rectangle tool. It even has a keyboard equivalent, which is F7. You drag inside the drawing area to define the size of an oval, as shown in Figure 4-2. As with the Rectangle tool, you can draw a perfect circle by Ctrl+dragging with the Oval tool. Shift+drag with the tool to draw an oval from the center outward.

Oval tool

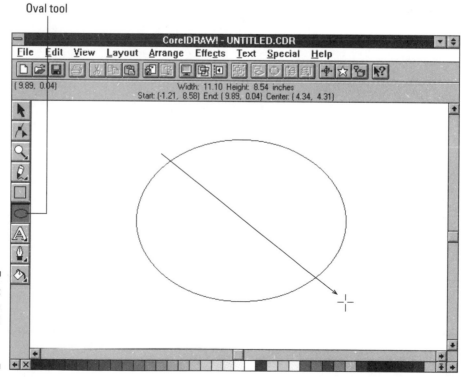

Figure 4-2:
Drag with the Oval tool to draw a perfect oval.

Within every oval lurks an ellipse

Euclideans call the oval an *ellipse*, which is a shape with an outline that travels at a fixed distance from two central points. You can draw an ellipse by hammering two nails into a board, tying a string between the two nails so that it has a lot of slack, and tracing the path of the string as shown in the following figure. The slack in the string determines the size of the ellipse.

Who cares? Well, technically, an oval is less structured than an ellipse. An oval can be any-

thing from oblong to egg-shaped to lumpy-bumpy; an ellipse is always perfectly formed and exactly symmetrical vertically and horizontally, just like shapes drawn with the Oval tool. And besides, I want to make sure that you appreciate the little things in CorelDraw. I mean, you wouldn't want to have to go back to board, string, and pencil, would you?

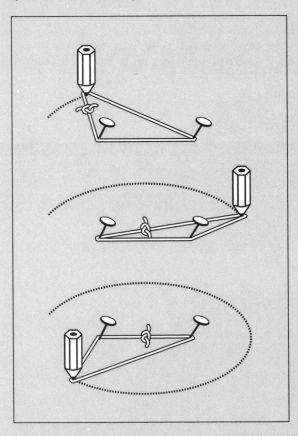

Changing Shapes

After you finish drawing a rectangle or oval, look at it. You see one or more tiny square *nodes* on the outline of the shape. At least that's what Corel calls them. *Webster's* says that a node is a "knotty, localized swelling." If I were you, I'd try not to think about that.

 As highlighted in Figure 4-3, a rectangle sports a node on each of its four corners, and an oval features just one node at the top. Although decorative and particularly festive during the holidays, these nodes perform a bona fide function. You can change the shape by dragging a node with the Shape tool (second in line just below the Arrow tool), which is CorelDraw's mysterious tool of a thousand faces. Were he alive today, Lon Chaney would undoubtedly sue.

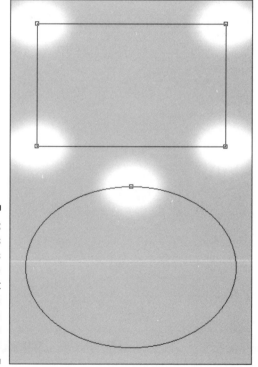

Figure 4-3:
Rectangles and ovals include nodes that you can drag with the Shape tool.

Sanding off the corners

When applied to one of the nodes of a rectangle, the Shape tool rounds off the corners of the shape as shown in Figure 4-4. Here's how it works:

1. Draw a rectangle.

You can't edit a rectangle until you draw it.

2. Click on the Shape tool to select it.

Or press the F10 key.

3. Drag one of the rectangle's nodes.

Regardless of which node you drag, CorelDraw rounds off all four of the shape's corners to the same extent. Notice that you now have eight nodes, which mark the transitions between the straight and curved edges of the shape. Release the mouse button when you have sufficiently rounded off the corners.

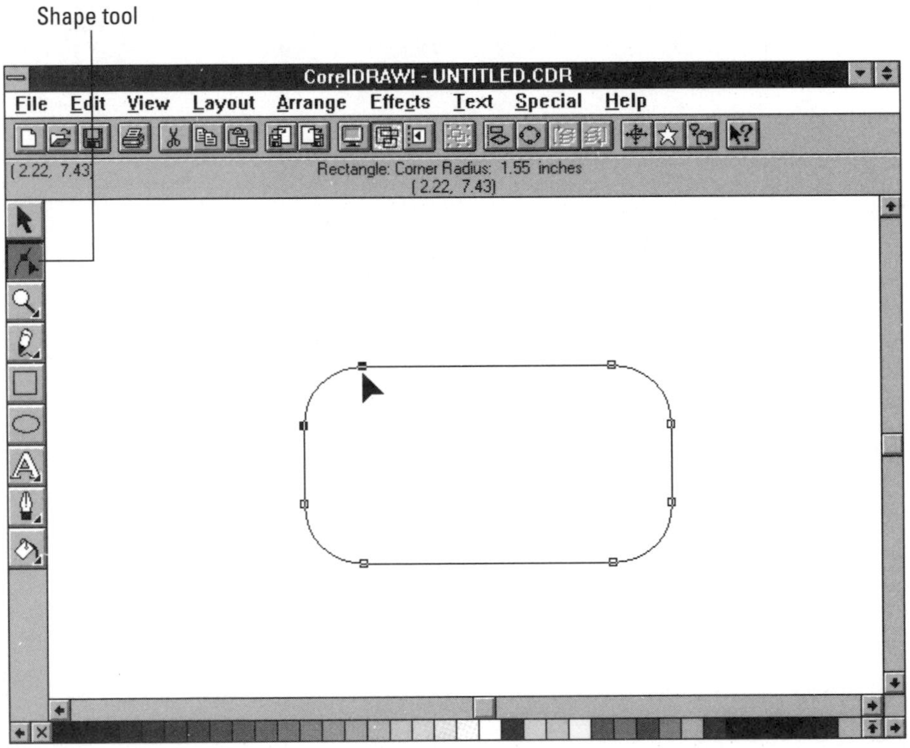

Shape tool

CorelDRAW! - UNTITLED.CDR

File   Edit   View   Layout   Arrange   Effects   Text   Special   Help

[2.22, 7.43]   Rectangle: Corner Radius: 1.55 inches
[2.22, 7.43]

Figure 4-4:
Drag any node of a rectangle with the Shape tool to round off the corners.

To restore the rectangle's original sharp corners, drag any of the eight nodes all the way back to the corner position. These corners should now be considered dangerous. Don't play too near to the rectangle or run around it with scissors in your hands.

Turning an oval into a tempting dessert

I speak, of course, of a pie. When you drag the node of an oval with the Shape tool, you change the oval into a piping hot pie with each of two nodes adorning either side of the wedge. Truth be told, you can actually create a pie or an arc, depending on how you drag the node, as illustrated in Figure 4-5.

✔ Move the Shape tool cursor inside the oval during your drag to create a pie shape (see the top two objects in Figure 4-5). Like any shape, the pie has an interior that you can fill with a solid color, gradation, or what have you. (See Chapter 7 for more talk about fills.)

✔ Move the cursor outside the oval during the drag to create an arc (see the bottom two objects in Figure 4-5). Notice that with an arc, the slice segments that form a V between the two pie nodes disappear. An *arc* is therefore a curved line with no interior.

✔ If you're left-handed like me, drag in a clockwise direction to draw a pie with a wedge cut out of it or a long arc (see the left two objects in Figure 4-5). If you're right-handed, drag in a counterclockwise direction.

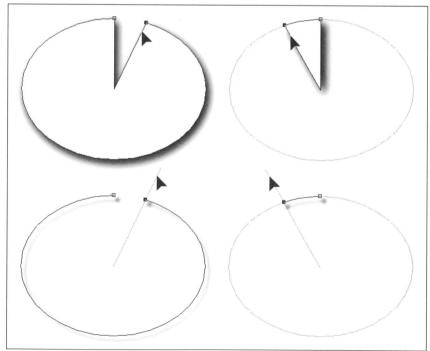

Figure 4-5:
The
different
ways to turn
an oval into
a pie or an
arc by using
the Shape
tool.

✔ Left-handers drag in a counterclockwise direction to draw a slim wedge or a short arc (see the right two objects in Figure 4-5). Right-handers drag clockwise.

✔ Your hand preference matters because it affects the way you originally create your oval, which in turn affects the way you edit it.

✔ Press the Ctrl key while dragging to constrain the wedge angle to the nearest 15-degree increment. Because a circle contains 360 degrees (I don't honestly know where Euclid got that number — maybe he had 36 toes or something), Ctrl+dragging produces 24 equal increments around the perimeter of the oval. 360 ÷ 15 = 24, in case you're interested.

After you change the oval to a pie or arc, you can continue to apply the Shape tool to either node and create all sorts of wedges and curves. To restore the pie or arc to a circle, drag one node exactly to the other while keeping the cursor outside the shape. Don't worry about positioning the cursor directly over either node during the drag; the two nodes automatically snap together when they get close enough to one another.

Give the pie a wedgie

Creating a pie is pretty straightforward. But because of the clockwise/counterclockwise thing, it's kind of hard to create the pie-and-floating-wedge effect shown in Figure 4-6. I mean, you drag one way for the pie and the other way for the wedge, so how are you supposed to get the pie and wedge to match?

Well, I'll tell you how, but it involves a couple of tricks that I haven't discussed yet. Assuming that you're willing to jump boldly into the unknown, here's how it works:

1. Draw an oval with the Oval tool.

As your mom used to say, if you don't draw your oval, you don't get any pie.

2. Click on the Shape tool to select it.

3. Ctrl+drag clockwise on the oval's node.

Here, I'm talking to left-handers. You right-handers should drag counterclockwise.

This action creates a slice in the pie. Because the Ctrl key constrains your drag in increments, it makes it easier to match the wedge to the slice in Step 5. Be sure to keep your cursor on the inside of the shape. Otherwise, it's all up to you. It doesn't matter how far you drag. You can create a thin slice or a big chunky one. Depends what you want to represent. Or how hungry you are.

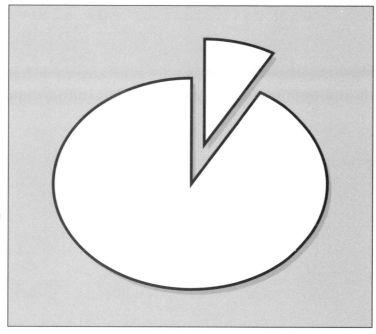

Figure 4-6:
The popular
pie shape
with a
floating
wedge.

4. **Press Ctrl+D.**

   Or you can choose Edit⇨Duplicate. The Duplicate command makes a copy of the shape (I discuss this command in Chapter 8).

5. **Ctrl+drag the right-hand node of the new shape around the circle until it becomes the left-hand node.**

   Your shape should look something like Figure 4-7.

6. **Now drag the right node clockwise until the direction of the slice line (the straight part) of the wedge matches its counterpart on the bigger pie. Do the same with the left node, dragging counterclockwise.**

7. **Click on the Arrow tool to select it.**

   I explain how to use the Arrow tool with rectangles, ovals, pies, and so on in the next section.

8. **Press the left-arrow key once and the down-arrow key twice.**

   The arrow keys move the shape incrementally (called a *nudge*). The wedge is now moved into place.

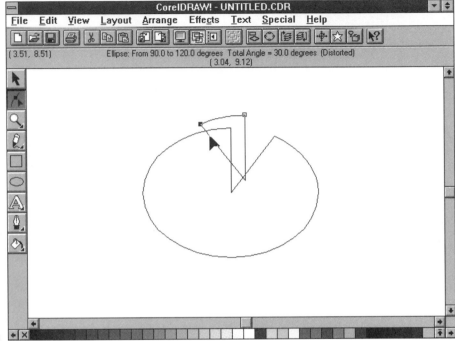

Figure 4-7:
Ctrl+drag
with the
Shape tool
to match the
wedge to
the slice.

Arrow Tool Tricks

 The Arrow tool, first tool among tools, is an editing tool much like the Shape tool. However, instead of allowing you to change details in an object like the Shape tool, the Arrow tool changes the object as a whole.

Maybe an analogy will help. In sculpture, the Arrow tool would be a hammer and chisel, and the Shape tool would be one of those little things dentists use to scrape plaque off your teeth. Okay, how about this instead: in the demolition business, the Arrow tool would be a big charge of dynamite, and the Shape tool might be a bug bomb. Oh, I have another one: in bricklaying, the Arrow tool would be a cement truck dumping liquified concrete all over the place, while the Shape tool would, uh . . . well, again, it's one of those little dental things, because they might need to clean the bricks off when they get dirty. . . . Just forget it.

 Here's how to use the Arrow tool:

1. Select the Arrow tool.

2. Click on a shape to select it.

Be sure to click on the outline of the shape because all the shapes you've drawn so far are transparent (unless you've been experimenting without me). If you just drew the shape or were editing it with the Shape tool, you don't need to click on it with the Arrow tool. It remains selected automatically.

When selected, the shape displays eight big black *handles* in a rectangular formation, as shown in Figure 4-8. The handles enable you to change the dimensions of the shape.

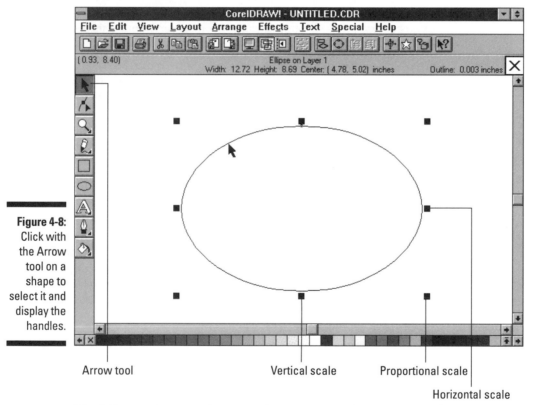

Figure 4-8: Click with the Arrow tool on a shape to select it and display the handles.

Arrow tool   Vertical scale   Proportional scale

Horizontal scale

The following items explain some basic ways to change a rectangle or ellipse with the Arrow tool:

- ✔ To move a shape, drag its outline.
- ✔ To scale the shape horizontally, drag the handle on the left or right side of the shape. Drag toward the center of the shape to make it skinnier, and drag away from the shape to make it fatter.

- To scale the shape vertically, drag the handle on the top or bottom of the shape. Drag in to make the shape shorter, and drag away to make it taller.

- You can also scale the shape proportionally so that the horizontal and vertical proportions remain equal. To do so, drag one of the four corner handles. Drag in to reduce, and drag away to enlarge.

- If you press the Shift key while dragging a handle, you scale the shape about its center. In other words, the center of the shape remains stationary throughout your drag. Normally, the opposite side is stationary. Try it out to see it more clearly.

- Ctrl+drag a handle to scale in 100 percent increments. You can scale a shape to twice, three times, or four times its previous size and even larger. You generally need a lot of extra room on-screen to pull this one off. Try zooming out a couple of times before embarking on a Ctrl+drag.

- Ctrl+drag a side handle past the opposite side to flip the shape. For example, if you Ctrl+drag the left handle to the right past the right handle, you flip the shape horizontally. Drag the top handle past the bottom handle to flip it vertically.

- If you click on the outline of a shape that is already selected, the handles change to double-headed arrow icons. These allow you to rotate and slant the shape. I discuss these operations in Chapter 9. To return to the big black handles, just click on the shape again.

Kiss It Goodbye

To delete a shape, just select it and press the Delete key. It doesn't matter whether you selected the shape with the Shape tool or the Arrow tool or you just finished creating it with the Rectangle or Oval tool. If you press Delete, it's a goner.

Don't press the Backspace key, by the way. It doesn't do anything but cause your computer to chirp at you. At least, that's what mine does. Your computer might beep.

Aaaugh, It's Gone!

Relax. Everything that I've discussed in this chapter can be undone. You can undraw a rectangle or oval, restore a shape that you change with the Shape tool, move a shape back to where it was, and return it to its original size. And, yes, you can even bring back a shape you've deleted.

To undo something, choose Edit➪Undo. Or better yet, press Alt+Backspace. These combinations restore your drawing to the way it was before your last operation. Try it out. Learn the keyboard equivalents. Believe me, you'll be using this feature a lot.

Raising the Undo ceiling until the rubble falls on your head

You can find out for sure how many operations you can undo in a row by pressing Ctrl+J (Special➪Preferences) and looking at the value in the Undo Levels option box in the General tab, highlighted in the next figure. If the value is more than 4, someone has changed it. You can change it to any number from 1 to 99, but be careful. Depending on your computer, CorelDraw may not function as well if you raise the value. It may crash more often or prevent you from using other Windows programs.

Unless someone who is familiar with the inner workings of your computer tells you otherwise, I recommend that you raise the Undo Levels value to no higher than 10. Ask for credentials before you change anything. It's always those computer know-it-alls who tell you to do something and then go on vacation when the entire system breaks down. Personally, I live by the credo, "If it ain't broke, don't fix it."

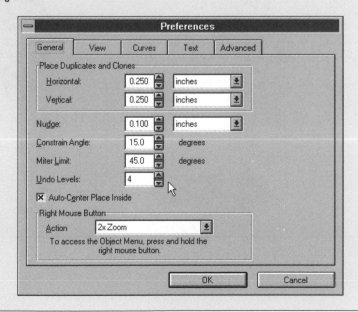

CorelDraw provides the option of undoing multiple operations in a row. For example, when you draw a rectangle, round off the corners with the Shape tool, and then scale it, you can press Ctrl+Z three times, first to return the rectangle it to its original size, then to restore its sharp corners, and finally to delete it.

If you want to retrace your steps, you can restore an operation that you "undid" by choosing Edit⇨Redo or by pressing Alt+Enter.

You can run into problems with Undo when you try to undo several sequential operations. By default, you can undo no more than four operations *in a row*. So if you deleted something five operations back, you probably won't be able to retrieve it.

The 5th Wave
By Rich Tennant

"This Corel color scheme is <u>really</u> going to give our presentation <u>style</u>!"

Chapter 5

Drawn It, Shaped It, Ready to Go Free-Form

● ●

In This Chapter

▶ Meet Shenbop, crazed adventure seeker

▶ Draw with the Pencil tool

▶ Learn about paths, segments, and control points

▶ Go on a rampage with the Shape tool

▶ Wake the neighbors with your endless curve bending

▶ Face the Node Edit roll-up without fear

▶ Hack away extraneous nodes

▶ Convert simple shapes to free-form paths

● ●

*I*f you've taken in a recent minute or two of MTV, ESPN, "Star Trek: The Next Generation," or anything else that appeals to the young male set, you've probably seen those Mountain Dew commercials. A bunch of guys poke their faces in front of the camera and express with virile bravado how they've "jumped it," "scaled it," yada yada yada, while visions of stunt men flinging themselves into and off of everything imaginable reel across the screen. Restless daredevils overcome nature. Fledgling Odysseuses indulge in dangerous doses.

I'm not a parent, but if I were, I'd be unnerved. These young men, juiced up on too much caffeine and confident beyond their levels of skill and endurance, are quite obviously destined to crack their skulls open during miscalculated bungee jumps, pound their kayaks into unyielding underwater boulders, smash their ultralights into low-flying crop dusters, or invite blood blisters when constructing spice racks without adult supervision. I mean, are we really comfortable handing over the leadership responsibilities of this great nation to a bunch of supercharged yahoos? Haven't we learned anything from the supercharged yahoos currently at the helm?

I'm not exactly sure where this introduction is leading, but it's definitely a cautionary note. Some of you, Mountain Dews in hand, are naturally pumped about the skills you have acquired so far. You're drawing rectangles with rounded corners and pies with flying wedges and bandying about terms like *ellipse* and *node* like a veteran CorelDraw hack. With the maddening rush of adrenaline surging through your veins combined with the dizzying sensation of newfound knowledge, you're itching to go free-form!

I see nothing wrong with that. Just don't overdo it the first time out. I think that Edgar Allan Poe said it best: "Quoth the raven, 'Chill, homeboy'."

Doodling with the Pencil

Figure 5-1 shows an amphibian of dubious heritage named Shenbop. Shenbop's most attractive quality is that he's ridiculously easy to draw. After selecting the Pencil tool by clicking on the tool's icon or by pressing F5, you can draw Shenbop in six steps, as demonstrated in Figure 5-2. Just drag with the tool as though you were doodling with a real pencil. Your lines may look a little shakier than mine — not that mine are all that smooth — but you can do it.

Paths, lines, and shapes

Before I go any further, I need to introduce a few basic concepts. First of all, anything you draw — whether it's with the Rectangle tool, the Oval tool, the Pencil tool, or some other tool that I haven't mentioned yet — is called a *path.*

Think of it this way: If you enlarge a rectangle to make it the size of a city block, the shape's outline becomes as wide as a sidewalk. Just as a sidewalk is a path around a city block, the outline serves as the path around the rectangle. The only difference is that paths in CorelDraw are for extremely small people.

In the first four steps shown in Figure 5-2, you draw an *open path,* in which the beginning and end of the path don't touch. An open path is therefore the same as a *line.* Steps 5 and 6 show *closed paths,* which are paths that loop around continuously with no apparent beginning or end. In layperson's terms, a closed path is a *shape.* It may seem condescending to define common words like line and shape, but they lie at the core of CorelDraw. In fact, everything you draw falls into one of these two camps.

Chapter 1 discusses the term *object,* which can be a line or shape. A block of text is also an object, but it cannot be a path. To qualify as a path, an object must have an outline that you can edit. Therefore, paths form a subset of objects that includes lines and shapes only. Figure 5-3 shows the family tree of CorelDraw objects.

Pencil tool

Shenbop (a frog)

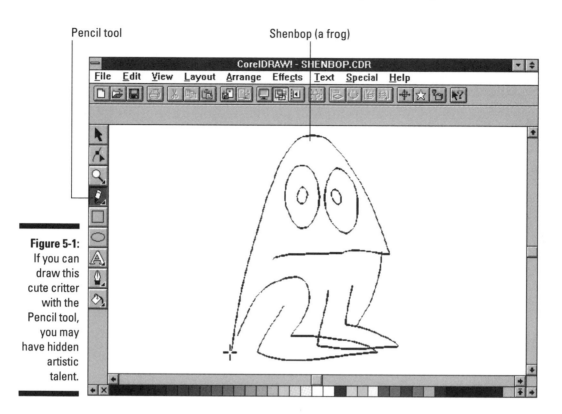

Figure 5-1:
If you can draw this cute critter with the Pencil tool, you may have hidden artistic talent.

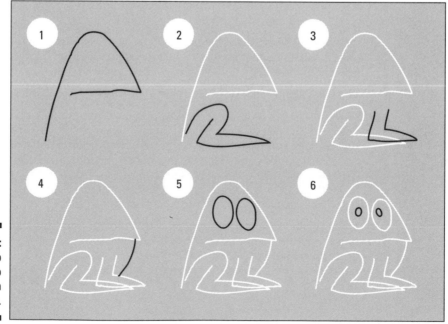

Figure 5-2:
The six-step Shenbop creation program.

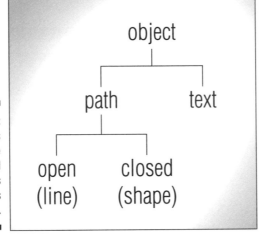

Dissecting a drawing

Now that I've completed the tiresome task of establishing the basics of CorelDraw's vocabulary, here are a few slightly more lively pointers for using the Pencil tool:

✔ Immediately after you draw a line or shape, CorelDraw performs some intense calculations and assigns nodes to the path automatically. The section of a path from one node to the next is called a *segment* (see Figure 5-4). And you thought we were finished with new vocabulary words.

✔ If the path is fairly simple — say, requiring ten nodes or fewer — Draw displays all the nodes. If the path is more complex, the program shows only the first and last nodes. It's just a display thing; all the nodes are present, but they're hiding. (If you were a node, wouldn't you be shy?)

✔ The total number of nodes for a path appears in the middle of the status line.

✔ CorelDraw has a habit of depositing nodes based on the speed at which you draw. When you draw quickly, it lays down one node here and another there. When you draw slowly, the program riddles the path with nodes because it thinks you're slowing down for emphasis. Unfortunately, densely concentrated nodes result in abrupt transitions and zigzags that make the path look jagged and irregular, as demonstrated in Figure 5-4. So try to maintain a quick and consistent drawing speed.

✔ If you're inexperienced at drawing with a mouse, nearly all of your first 100 or so paths will be jagged and irregular. What can I tell you? It takes time to get it down. But don't let it bother you. As long as you can draw approximately what you want, you can shape and mold it later.

Segment   Node

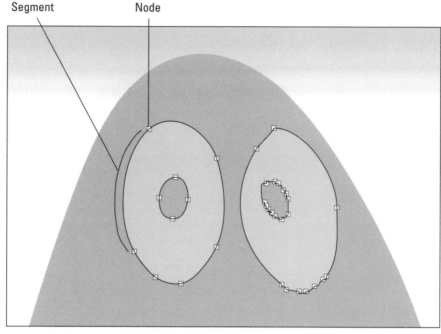

Figure 5-4:
Paths with
moderate
numbers of
evenly
spaced
nodes are
smooth
(left), while
paths with
densely
concentrated
nodes are
jagged
(right).

✔ To draw a straight line, click with the Pencil tool to establish the first node and then click at a new location to establish the second. CorelDraw automatically draws a straight line between the two.

✔ To draw a polygon, which is a shape with straight sides (such as a triangle or pentagon), click to create the first node, double-click at a new location to create the second, and continue double-clicking to establish additional nodes in the path. The program draws a straight segment between each pair of nodes. To complete the polygon, click only once.

✔ To draw a closed path, you have to connect the end point with the point at which you begin dragging or clicking. If you miss, the path doesn't close properly and the message `Open Path` appears in the upper-right corner of the status line (see Figure 5-5). An open path cannot be filled.

✔ If a path does not close as you want it to, you can press Delete and redraw it. But you can also close the path with the Pencil tool. Immediately after drawing an open path, drag from the first node to the last node to add a few more segments and close the path to form a shape. To close the path with a straight segment, click on the first node and then click on the last.

✔ You can extend any open path with the Pencil tool. After drawing the path, drag from the first or the last node. Or click on either node to add straight segments.

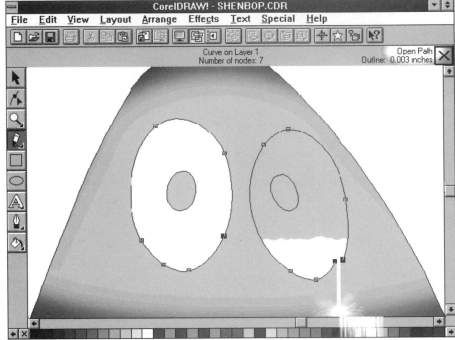

Figure 5-5:
A closed path (left) can hold its fill, but an open path (right) leaks, metaphor- ically speaking.

Nodes as You Never Knew Them

 As I said earlier, it's no big deal if you don't draw your paths correctly right off the bat. Even the best and most knowledgeable CorelDraw artists spend a significant portion of their time editing and rehashing paths with that tool of tools, the Shape tool. It helps you move nodes, change the curvature of seg- ments, add and delete nodes, close open paths, open closed ones, and change a haphazard scrawl into a gracefully sinuous line or shape.

Nodes: galactic wonders on the head of a pin

 To view and edit the nodes in a pencil path, select the Shape tool (second tool from the top) and click on the path. The nodes in the path light up like candles on a Christm . . . er, tree of ambiguous religious origin.

Click on an individual node in the path to select the node. It changes from hollow to black. You may also see one or two *control points* extending from the node, as shown in Figure 5-6. A purely decorative *lever* connects each control point to its node. Control points determine the curvature of segments. Yet unlike nodes, they don't actually reside on the path; they float above it like little satellites. In fact, a control point tugs at a segment in much the same way that the moon tugs at the ocean to create tides. It's like a detached, ethereal force with special gravitational powers.

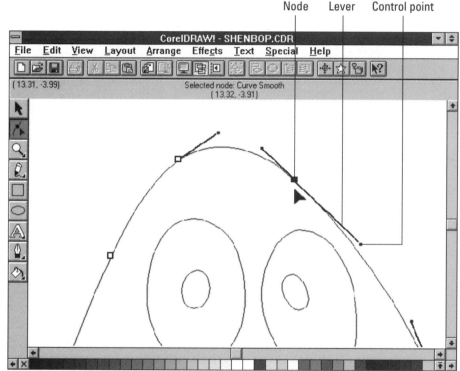

Figure 5-6:
Control
points flank
most nodes
in a path
drawn with
the Pencil
tool.

The Shape tool in action

The follow items explain how to use the Shape tool to select nodes and control points as well as to change the appearance of a path. I also toss in a few general notes and bits of wisdom to help you along your way:

- ✔ Click on a node to select it and display any control points associated with that node. A node can have no control points or as many as two, one for each segment.

- ✔ Segments need control points to be curved. If a segment is not bordered on either side by a control point, the segment is absolutely straight.

- ✔ Drag a node to move it and its control points. The segments that border the node stretch to keep up, as demonstrated in Figure 5-7. You can drag the node as far as you want; segments are infinitely stretchy.

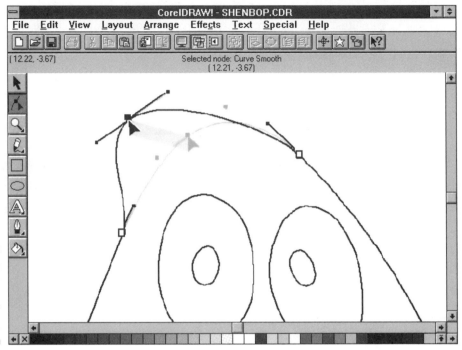

Figure 5-7:
Drag a node
to extend a
portion of
the path.

✔ Drag a control point to bend and tug at the corresponding segment, as shown in Figure 5-8. Notice that the node remains stationary, anchoring the segment.

✔ If the node is smooth (or symmetrical), the opposite control point also moves, bending its segment as in Figure 5-8. It's kind of like a seesaw, where the control points are kids on each end moving up and down. When you pull a control point away from the node, the other control point starts moving in the opposite direction. This keeps both line segments identical in size and keeps both kids happy, too. In a smooth node, the line segments still stay opposite, but one side can be larger than the other. This concept applies to seesaws when one kid is heavier than the other. If the node is a cusp node, you can move one control point independently of the other. The cusp node permits you to create corners in a path. A cusp also occurs in seesaws when one of the kids is way too heavy, snapping the seesaw in two.

✔ Still vague on the whole control point thing? It might help to envision a typical pencil path as a rubber band wrapped around a pattern of nails, as shown in Figure 5-9. The nails represent nodes in the path, and the rubber band represents its segments. A sample control point appears as a round knob. The rubber band is stretched to give it tension and prevent it from crimping. A path in CorelDraw similarly bends evenly in the direction of its handle.

Opposite control point   Smooth node

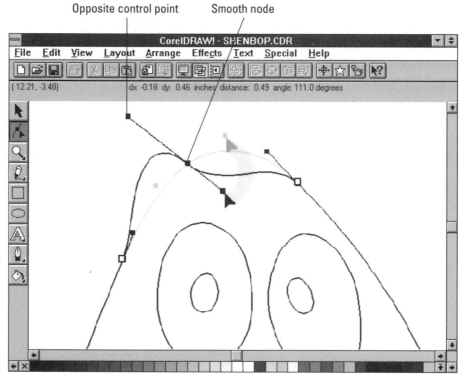

Figure 5-8:
Drag a
control point
to alter the
curvature of
a segment.

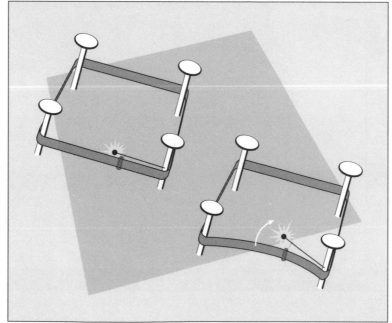

Figure 5-9:
By dragging
the control
point from
its original
position
(left), you
bend the
rubber band
segment
in that
direction
(right).

✔ If you don't want to deal with control points — believe me, everybody hates them — you can drag a curved segment directly. The segment bends and stretches, as shown in Figure 5-10.

✔ When you drag a segment bordered by smooth node, the segment on the other side of that node bends and stretches with your drag. In Figure 5-10, both bordering nodes are smooth nodes, so a total of three segments are affected.

✔ You can't drag a straight segment. Well, you can, but it doesn't do any good.

✔ To drag a node, control point, or segment in a strictly horizontal or vertical direction, press Ctrl while dragging.

✔ To select more than one node, click on the first node and Shift+click on each additional node. Then drag any one of them to move all the selected nodes at the same time.

✔ If the nodes that you want to select border each other, you can select them by dragging around them with the Arrow tool. As you drag, CorelDraw displays a dotted rectangle called a *marquee,* as shown in Figure 5-11. Draw selects every node within the marquee.

✔ Don't forget to choose Edit⇨Undo if you make a mistake. No change is irreparable if you catch it in time.

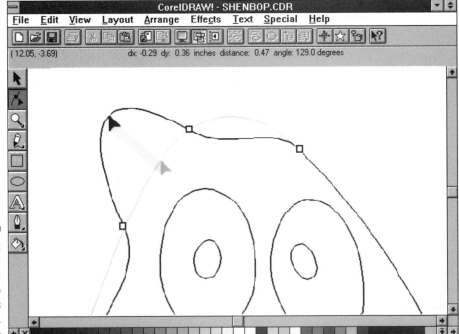

Figure 5-10: Drag a curved segment to change its curvature.

Marquee

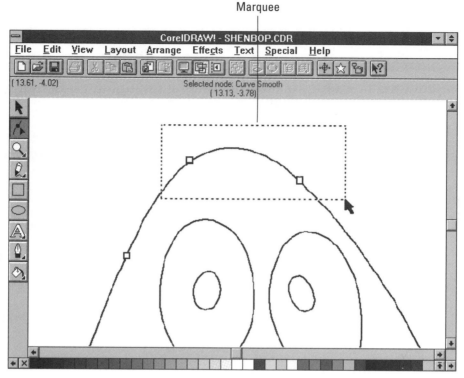

Figure 5-11:
Drag around
the nodes to
select them
with a
marquee.

Meet the Node Edit Thingie

To perform any other node-editing function, such as adding and deleting nodes or joining and splitting paths, you have to open up the trusty Node Edit roll-up. To display the roll-up featured in Figure 5-12, do either of the following:

✔ Double-click on a node with the Shape tool.

✔ Press Ctrl+F10.

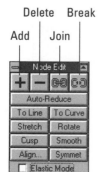

Figure 5-12:
The Node
Edit roll-up.

TECHNICAL STUFF

A little something you really don't need to know

When you draw with a real pencil, you smudge graphite directly onto the page. It's a cause/effect thing, a simple law of nature. When you draw with the Pencil tool, CorelDraw tries to imitate nature by using math. But because math isn't the natural state of anything except computer programs and high school calculus teachers, the line has to undergo a conversion. You can tweak this conversion by using the Preferences options.

Press Ctrl+J to display the Preferences dialog box and then click on the Curves tab along the top to activate the Curves screen. The ensuing dialog box features three options that have a bearing on pencil paths, which are highlighted in the following figure. Freehand Tracking controls how closely the path follows your drag. Corner Threshold controls CorelDraw's tendency to insert jagged

corners in a path. Straight Line Threshold determines the likelihood of straight segments in a path.

In all three cases, the values in the option boxes can vary from 1 to 10. If you develop uncanny dexterity with the mouse, you may want to test lower values, which, taken to their extremes, encourage the path to follow every nuance and jiggle of your drag. If your drags exhibit the kinds of tremors normally associated with small earthquakes, or if folks have a tendency to ask you why you write your letters in moving vehicles when you actually write them at a desk with optimal lighting during the stillest of evenings while listening to endless loops of Pachelbel's *Canon in D minor,* you may want to limit yourself to higher values, which result in smoother and less jagged (albeit less accurate) paths.

Preferences

| General | View | Curves | Text | Advanced |

Freehand Tracking: `5`   pixels

Autotrace Tracking: `5`   pixels

Corner Threshold: `5`   pixels

Straight Line Threshold: `5`   pixels

AutoJoin: `5`   pixels

AutoReduce: `0.004`   inches

Min. Extrude Facet Size: `0.125`   inches

[OK]   [Cancel]

I'm sick and tired of nodes!

Too bad, because more node information is on the way.

At least spare me the lists!

I knew you'd say that, which is precisely why I've cooked up four or five more lists for your reading pleasure. These items explain how to use the options in the Node Edit roll-up to add nodes, delete nodes, and otherwise wreak havoc on the whole node-oriented world. Get psyched, because this is about the most exciting list you'll ever read — short of the phone book, of course.

Oh, by the way, all these items assume that you've already displayed the Node Edit roll-up by double-clicking on any node with the Shape tool. It's a good thing to keep on-screen. If it gets in your way, click on the up-arrow icon on the right side of the title bar.

- ✔ To add a node to a path, click on the spot on the segment where you want to add the node. A round sort of blob appears. It's not a node yet; it's sort of a fetal node. Click on the plus-sign icon in the roll-up to spank the node and bring it into the world of the living.

- ✔ To delete one or more nodes, select all the nodes you want to delete and then press the Delete key. Why bother with the minus-sign icon when the Delete key is so much more convenient?

- ✔ You can press the + or – key on the keypad to respectively add or delete a node. These keys work even when the Node Edit roll-up is hidden.

Excuse me for interrupting, but I feel it my duty to come out in hearty support for the flagrant clearing of nodes. Verging on criminal overpopulation, CorelDraw invariably assigns too many nodes to pencil paths. It's not rare to see nodes stuck one right on top of the other like procreating cockroaches or wet Skittles. As a rule of thumb, you need a *cusp node* for every corner in a path, and you need a *smooth node* for every quarter circle's worth of curve. Anything beyond that is garbage. Figure 5-13 shows a path before and after deleting extraneous nodes.

Figure 5-13:
Bad
Shenbop's
nodes are
overcrowded.
Good
Shenbop's
nodes are
few and far
between.

Bad Shenbop   Good Shenbop

Opening, splitting, closing, and joining

To recap, I've explained how to add and delete nodes, which is super common stuff. If only for the sake of strip-mining paths, you'll be engaging in these operations frequently. The next functions I describe are slightly less common but nonetheless rank right up there in importance. You learn how to open closed paths, close open ones, slice and dice paths without the aid of a Vegematic, and put them back together as effortlessly as a supercollider bonds kernels of creamed corn back onto the cob:

✔ To open a closed path, select a node that you want to split into two nodes and click on the Break icon (far right) in the roll-up. If the closed path was filled with a color before you opened it, the color disappears.

✔ To split an open path into two independent paths, select the node at which you want the split to occur and then click on the Break button. The path splits but it remains a single unit in CorelDraw's mind. To finalize the divorce, press Ctrl+K or choose Arrange⇨Break Apart. The two paths can now go their separate ways.

✔ To close an open path, select both the first and last nodes in the line — by clicking on the first node and shift-clicking on the last node — and then click on the Join icon (second from right) in the roll-up. CorelDraw transforms the line into a shape.

Joining two completely independent open paths into a single, longer path is a little tricky. I'll explain it in steps:

1. **Select the Arrow tool.**

   See, it's tricky already.

2. **Click on the first open path you want to join.**

   Don't try this on a closed path. If you want to extend a shape, make sure to open it first (as described a few items back — you know, select a node with the Shape tool and click on the Break button).

3. **Shift+click on the second open path you want to join.**

   Now both paths are selected.

4. **Press Ctrl+L or choose Arrange⇨Combine.**

5. **Select the Shape tool.**

   Getting trickier.

6. **Click on the first or last node in one path and then Shift+click on the first or last node in the other path.**

   In other words, select the two nodes you want to fuse into one.

7. **Click on the Join icon.**

   The two short lines are now one long line.

Options you'll use once in a blue moon

I'm tempted to end my discussion of the Node Edit options right here. It's not that the rest of the options are useless (well, okay, some of them *are* pretty useless), it's just that they're more specialized. Most beginners and intermediates barely touch these options. But they do serve a purpose, so you may as well know about them. Besides, I'm afraid that if I don't explain them, a few of you will get so curious that you'll resort to reading the manual, and that could be fatal. So in the interest of keeping you alert, informed, and alive, here are the remaining options in the Node Edit roll-up, from most to least useful.

Before I get started, I want to explain why so many options seem to be dimmed all the time. In many cases, the option is already in effect. For example, if you select a cusp node, the Cusp button is dimmed because the cusp can't be any cuspier than it already is. Other times, the option is inapplicable. The Align button is dimmed if fewer than two nodes are selected because you can't align a single node to itself. Well, maybe you can, but what's the point?

✔ The To Line button straightens out a curved segment. To use this option, select the node that follows a curved segment and then click on the To Line button.

✔ To Curve fulfills the opposite function. Select the node that follows a straight segment and then click on the To Curve button.

How do you know which node follows a segment? Well, it depends on the direction in which you draw the path. But because no one should waste valuable brain space remembering such trivial details, I suggest experimentation. Select a node and click on a button. If you guess correctly, good for you. If not, press Ctrl+Z or Alt+Backspace and try the other node.

✔ To change a smooth node so that it represents a corner in the path, select the node and click on the Cusp button. You can then move the control points of the cusp independently of each other.

✔ To change a corner to a smooth arc, select the node and click on the Smooth button. CorelDraw locks the control points into alignment so that the transition between neighboring segments is seamless.

✔ The Align button aligns multiple nodes in horizontal or vertical formation. You'll learn more about alignment in Chapter 6, if you choose to read it. Otherwise, you'll remain ignorant.

✔ The Stretch and Rotate buttons are marginally useful. You can scale, rotate, flip, and slant individual segments in a path by selecting a node, clicking on one of these buttons, and dragging a handle. To learn about the standard object transformation functions, read Chapter 9. Then come back to these options and try them out.

✔ The Symmet button locks the control points of a node into symmetrical alignment so that the two levers are always the exact same length. This variation on the smooth node has almost no relevance in today's world. I think Peking Man used it in some sort of greet-the-dawn ritual, but nowadays, forget it.

✔ Don't worry about that Elastic Mode checkbox. It's a waste of time. People who know how to use this option are dumber for it. Still curious? Okay, the option changes the way segments react when you drag a node. They shrink and expand differently. Believe me, it's totally stupid and useless to boot. At best, it's an okay idea that was poorly implemented. Don't you feel dumber already?

✔ The Auto-Reduce option is supposed to remove extraneous nodes automatically. But think about it for a moment. If CorelDraw were smart enough to eliminate extraneous nodes, it wouldn't put them there in the first place. You can rearrange some settings in the Curves tab of the Preferences dialog box (see the Technical Stuff sidebar in this chapter) and get some remarkably disappointing results. But for the most part, the option doesn't do squat.

Upgrading Simple Shapes

This chapter has been devoted exclusively to stuff that you can't do to rectangles and ovals. You can't move the nodes in a rectangle independently of each other; you can't adjust the curvature of a segment in an oval; and you can't do much of anything to a flying wedge.

That is, not until you convert the simple shapes to free-form paths. Select the shape with the Arrow tool and then press Ctrl+Q.

That's all there is to it. By pressing Ctrl+Q or choosing <u>A</u>rrange⇨Con<u>v</u>ert To Curves, you convert the selected shape to nodes, segments, and control points, just like a path drawn with the Pencil tool. You can then edit the shape to any extent imaginable.

I guess Corel thought that having two ways of doing the same thing wasn't enough. You can also convert a selected shape to curves by selecting that funny button on the ribbon bar that looks like a circle with four nodes, a bisexual lady bug, or a happy face drawn by a small Klingon child.

Keep in mind, however, that by converting a simple shape to a path, you ruin all semblance of the shape's original identity. You can no longer use the Shape tool to add rounded corners to a rectangle or change an oval into a pie, as described in Chapter 4.

Chapter 6

Celebrating Your Inner Draftsman

• •

In This Chapter

▶ Corel's four tools of control

▶ Using rulers

▶ Setting up the grid

▶ Positioning guidelines

▶ Observing the status line

▶ Moving objects incrementally and numerically

▶ Aligning objects

▶ Amassing objects in groups

▶ Changing the stacking order (whatever that is)

• •

Do you have problems expressing your feelings? Are you critical of other people's driving? Do you insist on alphabetizing your guests at the dinner table? Do you distrust the government, yet at the same time harbor suspicions that Ross Perot is a certifiable loony? If you said yes to any of these questions — except the bit about Perot — you may be a closet control freak. And you know what? That's okay. Because, doggone it, people like you. A couple of them, anyway. Well, maybe *like* is too strong a word. *Know*, then. People scurry out of the room when you appear because they know you. Isn't that comforting?

This chapter is a call to arms for control freaks, a reawakening of the fuss-budget. You can muck around with rulers, guidelines, and other tightly structured features in an attempt to precisely arrange minuscule details. No one but you will ever notice, but that secret sense of pride you get makes it all worth it, doesn't it?

I don't want to cure your perfectionism. I want you to rejoice in it! By the way, is that a grease stain on your shirt? Ha ha, made you look.

Your Four Tools of Control

CorelDraw has four main control tools:

- *Rulers* appear along the top and left sides of the drawing area and serve as visual aids.

- The *grid* is a network of regularly spaced points that attract your cursor and prevent you from drawing crooked lines and other haphazard-looking stuff.

- *Custom guidelines,* which you set up between grid increments, align objects and generally ensure an orderly environment.

- The *status line* shows the location of your cursor, the dimensions of shapes, the distance and angles of movements, and a bunch of other stuff that I can't tell you right now because then I wouldn't have anything to talk about in the status line section.

Rulers with no power

Unlike grids and guidelines, rulers don't constrain your movements or make you draw better. In fact, they don't *do* much of anything. They just sit there. But rulers can be nice to have around because they show you the size of objects and the distance between them. It's like having a compass in the woods; with rulers, you know where you are.

To display the rulers, choose <u>V</u>iew⇨<u>R</u>ulers. As shown in Figure 6-1, one horizontal ruler and one vertical ruler appear along the edges of the drawing area. With a little luck and a lot of divine intervention, they may inspire you to create something as fantastic as the Roman Coliseum found in the \LANDMARK directory on the first of the two CorelDraw 5 CD-ROM disks. Here's how to exploit the rulers to the fullest:

- The rulers monitor the location of the cursor by using two tracking lines. At the same time, the status line displays the numerical coordinates of the cursor, which correspond directly to the tracking lines. In Figure 6-1, for example, the horizontal tracking line appears just to the right of the 5 mark, and the status line displays the coordinate 5.04.

- All measurements are made from the *zero point,* which is the point at which both rulers display the value 0. You can change the location of the zero point by dragging the ruler origin box, which appears at the meeting of the two rulers, as shown in Figure 6-2. The point at which you release becomes the new zero point, as Figure 6-3 demonstrates.

Cursor coordinates　　Rulers　Vertical tracking line　　Horizontal tracking line

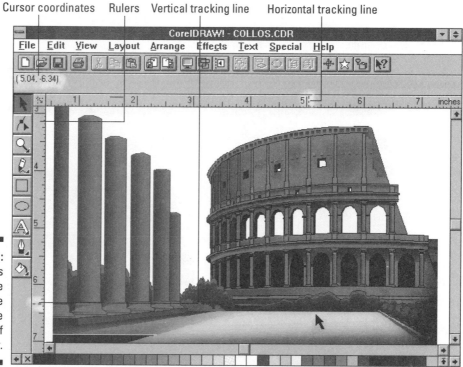

Figure 6-1:
The rulers
and the
status line
monitor the
location of
the cursor.

Ruler origin box

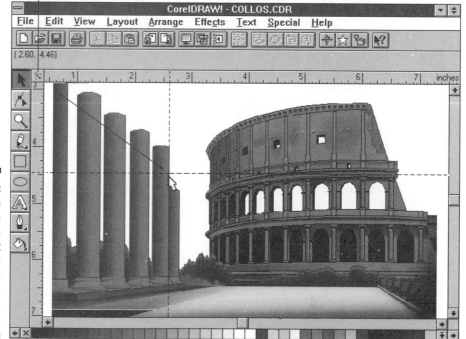

Figure 6-2:
Drag the
ruler origin
box to move
the point
from
which all
measure-
ments are
made.

New coordinates

New zero point

New zero point

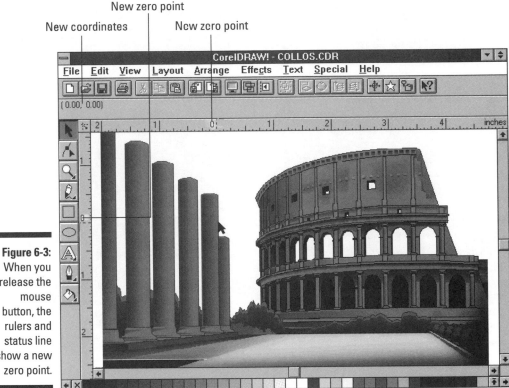

Figure 6-3:
When you release the mouse button, the rulers and status line show a new zero point.

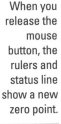

✔ Rulers generally display units in inches. If you prefer to work in a different measurement system, you can change either ruler by double-clicking on it. This action displays the Grid & Scale Setup dialog box shown in Figure 6-4. To change a ruler, select a different option from the Grid Frequency drop-down list boxes. The first list box controls the horizontal ruler, and the second controls the vertical ruler.

✔ The status line's coordinates always correspond to the units on the horizontal ruler (displayed on the ruler's far-right side).

✔ To get rid of the rulers, choose View⇨Rulers again.

Going downtown

Imagine a plan for the perfect city center — something like Washington, D.C. Every block measures ¹⁄₁₀ mile × ¹⁄₁₀ mile. No block has an alley. Exactly 11 East-

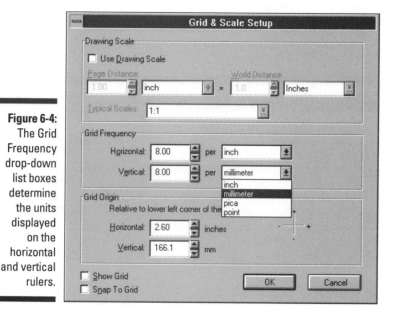

Figure 6-4:
The Grid
Frequency
drop-down
list boxes
determine
the units
displayed
on the
horizontal
and vertical
rulers.

West streets and 11 North-South avenues subdivide each square mile into 100 square blocks.

Oh, sure, it's a little formal. It lacks spontaneity and *joie de vivre,* but you're supposed to be getting work done, not sitting around enjoying the scenery. Besides, it's a grid, just like the one in CorelDraw.

In Draw, the grid affects the placement of nodes, control points, handles, and so on. Although a free-form path can snake along wherever it pleases, its nodes are constrained to precise grid increments. The same goes for rectangles, ovals, and blocks of text.

Here's how to set up a grid:

1. **Double-click on one of the rulers.**

   If the rulers are not available, choose Layout⇨Grid & Scale Setup. The Grid & Scale Setup dialog box appears (refer back to Figure 6-4).

2. **Enter the distance between grid points in the Horizontal and Vertical option boxes.**

   You specify the number of city blocks per mile or inch or whatever here. The number of points per unit of measure is called the *grid frequency.*

3. **Select the Show Grid checkbox so that you can see the grid points on the screen.**

4. **Select the Snap to Grid checkbox.**

   When this option is active, nodes, control points, and handles gravitate toward grid points. If you don't select this option, you see the grid, but it doesn't have any effect. This is the most important step. Don't skip it.

5. **Press Enter or click on the OK button.**

   The grid points appear in the drawing area, as shown in Figure 6-5.

To try out the grid, draw a rectangle with the Rectangle tool. Your cursor snaps from one grid point to the next, as demonstrated in Figure 6-5. Incidentally, CorelDraw doesn't always display all grid points. Depending on the grid frequency and zoom ratio, the program may hide every other grid point, for example, to reduce on-screen clutter. But whether or not you can see a grid point, the snapping is still in force.

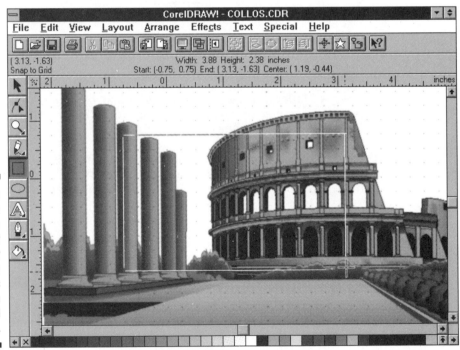

Figure 6-5:
When the grid is active, your cursor snaps to the grid points when you draw and edit paths.

After you establish your grid, you can turn it on and off by pressing Ctrl+Y.

Is the Coliseum really that small?

Well, not really. It seems a little bigger in real life. To compensate for that (especially if you're building the floorplans for the Coliseum), you can set up a scale in CorelDraw so that 1 inch equals 1 mile, or 1 millimeter equals 5 megameters, or 1 coupon equals 2 free Mountain Dews with any take-out item.

Here's how to set up a scale:

1. **If the rulers are not available, choose** Layout⇨Grid & Scale Setup. **The Grid & Scale Setup dialog box appears.**

   Double-click on one of the rulers.

2. **Select the checkbox for Use** Drawing Scale.

   Doing so activates the scale features.

3. **Select your base unit of measurement in the** Page Distance section.

   Are you going to use inches? millimeters? 1 inch? 3 inches? Pick 1 inch if you just don't know (or don't care at the moment).

4. **Select the** World Distance unit of measurement.

   In the example of 1 inch equals 1 mile, 1 mile is the world distance. Select feet for this example. Now you can change the numbers so that 1 inch equals, for example, 30 feet either by typing **30** or by scrolling through the Typical Scale list box.

5. **Press Enter or click on OK.**

When you finish and return to the normal CorelDraw screen, take a look at the ruler measurements (see Figure 6-6). Your rulers have taken on the scale that you've just plugged in.

Let the lines be your guide

If you live in or near a highly structured city center, you know that it's a mixed blessing. On the plus side, it's great for tourists and new residents who rely on predictability to get around. For example, anyone who can count can find Manhattan's Fifth Avenue. On the minus side, a network of streets and avenues can prove stagnant and limiting for commuters and longtime residents. You wish for a freeway to get you up over the traffic or a winding country road to break up the monotony.

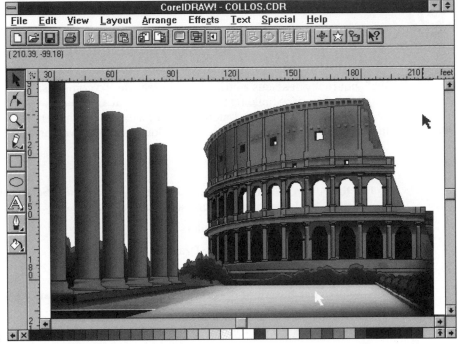

Figure 6-6:
The ruler
measure-
ments
reflect the
changes
you make to
the scale
options.

Similarly, CorelDraw's grid is great for novices but loses some of its attraction after you become moderately familiar with the program. It's not that you outgrow the need for structure; order is always helpful. What you need is increased flexibility.

That's where guidelines come in. Like the rulers, they come in two varieties, horizontal and vertical. Like the grid, they have gravitational attraction. However, you can create as many guidelines as you like and place them wherever you want:

✔ To create a guideline, drag from the ruler into the drawing area with the selection tool, as shown in Figure 6-7.

✔ Dragging the horizontal ruler produces a horizontal guideline; dragging the vertical ruler produces — everybody sing! — a bright red lobster in a green varsity sweater.

Actually, that last action produces a vertical guideline. I just made up the bit about the lobster. No lobsters were made to wear sweaters in the making of this book. One was encouraged to wear a high school letter

Vertical guidelines   Horizontal guidelines

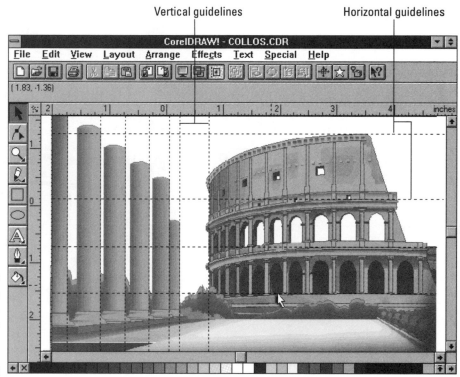

Figure 6-7:
Drag from a
ruler to
create a
guideline.

jacket, but only briefly. The lobster is now in a recovery program (see Figure 6-8). In fact, he and I are in the same ward.

✔ To move a guideline, drag it. But be careful. It's easy to accidentally drag an object when you're trying to drag a guideline (and vice versa).

✔ When the grid is active, it constrains the creation and movement of guidelines. There's no point in having a guideline that duplicates a line of grid points, so be sure to turn off the grid (by pressing Ctrl+Y) so that you can position guidelines freely.

✔ If both guidelines and the grid are active, a guideline takes precedence over the grid points near it. The guideline has a stronger gravitational force, in other words. It's as if Jupiter and Pluto were really close to each other and you were inside the gravitational fields of both planets. Jupiter has the more powerful gravitational force, so you'd fall toward it. Of course, Pluto would follow and come crashing down on your head, but that's strictly a function of planets.

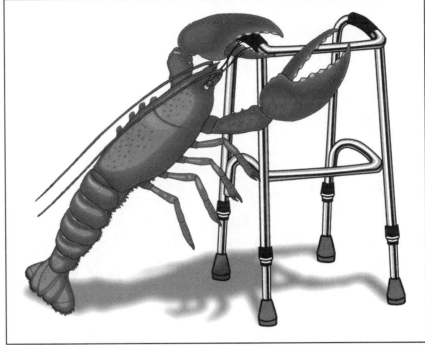

Figure 6-8:
The lobster
demonstrates
his
indomitable
will to
survive.

The status line tells all

Like the rulers, the status line doesn't affect the movement of your cursor.
Instead, it reports everything you do in CorelDraw. This information is organized into six basic reports, as illustrated in Figure 6-9 and explained here:

- Anytime your cursor is inside the drawing area, the status line lists the
  horizontal and vertical coordinates of the cursor in the upper-left corner.

- The lower-left corner states that the grid is on. When the grid is off, this
  spot is blank.

- The middle report varies, depending on the operation. When an object is
  selected, the status line lists what kind of object it is along with its dimensions and other information. When you transform an object by moving,
  scaling, or rotating it, the status line lists information about the transformation — the distance of the movement, the percentage of the scaling, the
  degree of the rotation, and so on.

✔ The upper-right corner lists the fill applied to the selected object. Alternatively, the `Open Path` message may appear, in which case the object cannot be filled. The fill report appears only when an object is selected.

✔ The lower-right corner lists the thickness of the outline. This report only appears when an object is selected.

✔ To the right of the fill and outline reports, a graphic display shows what a small square would look like according to the current fill and outline attributes.

Cursor Coordinates   Object or   Fill report
                                  transformation report

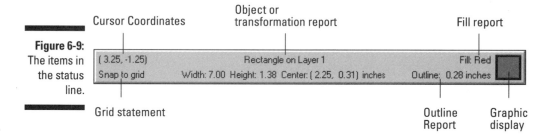

Figure 6-9:
The items in
the status
line.

Grid statement   Outline   Graphic
                                                                  Report   display

Even something as useful as the status line goes away if you want it to. If you need more space for the drawing area, for example, choose Special➪Preferences (or press Ctrl+J) and select the View tab along the top. Now click on the Show Status Line box, as in Figure 6-10. Choose the command again to redisplay the status line.

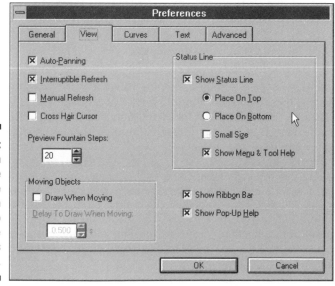

Figure 6-10:
You can
turn the
status line
on and off in
the View tab
of the
Preferences
dialog box.

Those of you who aren't dozing off — hey, wake up! — may have noticed that the Preferences dialog box offers a couple more features new to the CorelDraw 5 status line. They are as follows:

✔ **Place on Top, Place on Bottom:** If you've graduated from CorelDraw 2, 3, or 4, seeing the status line along the bottom of the screen may be a little unsettling, but you can now choose this option. (Those of you who have panicked, rotate your monitor back to its proper position. The Status line defaults to the bottom option when you first run CorelDraw.)

✔ **Small Size:** Aside from turning the status line on and off, you can make it thinner, and thicker, and thinner . . . just like Oprah. However, when you make the status line thinner, you can only see one line of information. The rest isn't displayed. Figure 6-11 shows the fit and trim version of the status line.

Figure 6-11:
Status line
lite contains
50 percent
less
information
at no extra
cost.

[0.38, -0.63]		Rectangle on Layer 1		Outline: 0.003 inches ☒

✔ **Show Menu & Tool Help:** The Tool Help function in the status line gives you a blow-by-blow description of what the commands, functions, and icons do. For instance, select View⇨Full Screen Preview, and the status line says: `Display a full-screen preview of the drawing.` I would never have guessed that.

Tool Help does come in handy, helping you discover what those fandangled buttons on the ribbon bar do. Unfortunately, you have to actually click on the button to get Tool Help, and clicking on the button makes the button do what it does. By that time, you figure out that you didn't want to do that.

The status line also tells you what color you're going to pick in the color palette. This feature can be helpful if you're still using an amber monitor or if your two-year old has discovered what the contrast control does.

Because CorelDraw is such an intuitive program, you may or may not find the Tool Help stuff helpful. It's up to you to decide whether you'd rather figure it out on your own.

Telling an Object Where It Can Go

In Chapters 4 and 5, I explained how to move whole objects and individual nodes by dragging them. But dragging isn't the only means for movement in CorelDraw. You can move objects in predetermined increments, in numerical distances, or in relation to each other.

Incremental shifts

The arrow keys put selected items in motion. Pressing the arrow keys moves the items — a few nodes selected with the Shape tool or one or more objects selected with the Arrow tool, for example — incrementally in the direction of the arrow.

By default, each arrow key moves a selected item ¹/₁₀ inch. However, you can change this increment by using the Preferences command. Press Ctrl+J to display the Preferences dialog box and click on the General tab. Then enter a value in the Nudge option box, shown in Figure 6-12. If necessary, select a different unit of measurement from the drop-down list box.

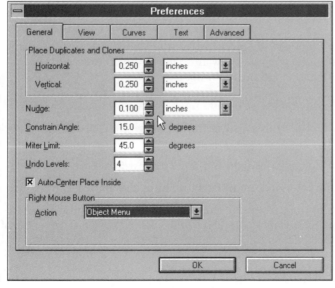

Figure 6-12:
The Nudge value determines the increment by which an arrow key moves a selected node or object.

Rather than pressing an arrow key again and again to move a selected node or object a random distance, you can press and hold an arrow key. The selection scoots across the drawing area until you release the key.

The big move

To move an entire object a numerical distance in CorelDraw , press Alt+F7 or choose Effects⇨Transform Roll-Up. The Transform roll-up menu, featured in Figure 6-13, appears. There are two ways to approach this menu. You can either move the object in relation to its current position or move it to an exact coordinate location.

Figure 6-13:
Use these options to move an object a specified numerical distance.

If you want to move the object to a specific coordinate, leave Relative Position unchecked. But if you instead want to move the object a certain distance from its current location, do the following:

1. **Check the Relative Position box.**

2. **Click on the little arrow button to the right of the Relative Position option.**

   This action rolls down the roll-down menu a little more, as shown in Figure 6-14.

3. **Select a reference point from the nine checkboxes.**

   These options represent the eight handles around the selected object and the object's exact center. So if you want to position the center of the object at a specific location, for example, select the Center checkbox. (Unlike other checkboxes, you can only select one at a time. These really ought to be radio buttons.)

4. **Enter the coordinates in the Horizontal and Vertical option boxes.**

   The coordinates are measured in relation to the rulers' zero point.

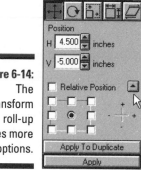

Figure 6-14:
The
Transform
roll-up
bares more
options.

Transform functions apply to whole objects only. If you select a node with the Shape tool and apply a function, CorelDraw doesn't do squat, mostly out of malicious spite. It really is a dumb limitation, but you can't argue with a computer program.

By the way, the Apply To Duplicate button creates a duplicate of the object at the new location. I discuss duplication in Chapter 8. In fact, Chapter 8 puts this Transform roll-up menu to shame.

Fall in line

The last way to move objects is to shift them in relation to each other. For example, suppose that you've drawn a series of silhouetted soldiers marching down the road, but you were so busy concentrating on making the shapes look like soldiers against an eerie twilight sky that you neglected to line them up properly. So instead of marching on a flat road, they bob up and down. To align their feet along a perfectly horizontal surface, select all the soldier shapes with the Arrow tool and press Ctrl+A or choose Arrange⇔Align.

Shown in Figure 6-15, the Align dialog box lets you align objects vertically in columns or horizontally in rows. You can select only one option from the Vertically group and one from the Horizontally group at a time. Figure 6-16 shows each of the Vertically options applied in tandem with each of their Horizontally counterparts.

You don't have to select an option from both the Vertically and the Horizontally groups. To align the soldiers along the road, for example, select the Bottom radio button without selecting any of the Horizontally options. In fact, you more often than not select only one radio button from the Align dialog box. Otherwise, the shapes bunch up on each other, as in Figure 6-16.

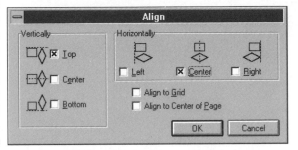

Figure 6-15: Use these options to align selected objects in columns and rows.

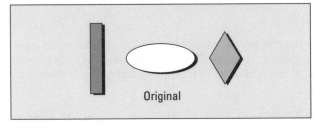

Original

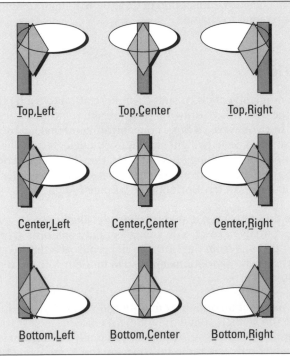

Figure 6-16: Test your spatial reasoning skills: three simple objects (top) subject to nine variations on the Align dialog box settings.

The following information falls into the gee-whiz-that-certainly-is-interesting camp of Align dialog box knowledge:

- ✔ If you select one of the Vertically or Horizontally options but then change your mind, you can deselect it by clicking on it again.

- ✔ The Align command keeps the last object you selected stationary and moves all the others into alignment with it. If you select the objects by marqueeing them rather than by Shift+clicking, the lowest object remains stationary.

- ✔ Select the Align to Grid checkbox to align objects to the nearest grid point according to the Vertically and Horizontally settings. For example, if you select the Top and Left radio buttons, Draw aligns the upper-left corner of each selected object to the nearest grid point.

- ✔ For mysterious reasons — I suspect extraterrestrials — the Align to Grid checkbox is dimmed until you select a radio button.

- ✔ Select the Align to Center of Page checkbox to align selected objects to the center of the page. See what $19.95 buys you? Eye-popping information, that's what. Do you feel smarter? You *look* smarter.

- ✔ The Align command works only on whole objects. To align nodes selected with the Shape tool, double-click on one of the nodes to display the Node Edit roll-up and then click on the Align button.

Gang Behavior

A moment ago I asked you to imagine drawing silhouetted soldiers. You probably thought that I was just trying to stimulate your interest by setting a mood. But there was a modicum of method to my madness that is normally entirely absent. See, you can create a silhouette using a single shape. If each of your soldiers is composed of *multiple* shapes, however, the Align command may present a problem.

Figure 6-17, for example, shows a soldier made up of 18 shapes (left). Because CorelDraw aligns the bottom of *each and every* shape when I align the shapes along the bottom, the soldier falls apart (right).

To prevent the soldier from falling to pieces, you need to make Draw think of all 18 shapes as a single object. To do so, select the shapes with the Arrow tool (click on the first shape and Shift+click on the other shapes) and press Ctrl+G or choose Arrange➪Group. All the shapes in the group now behave as a single, collective object.

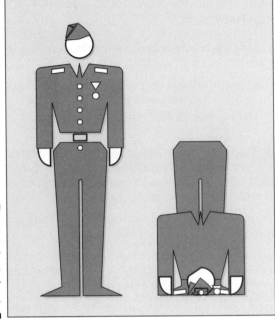

Figure 6-17:
It's sad to see a soldier crumble under pressure.

✔ To align several soldiers that are each composed of many shapes, group the shapes in each soldier — each soldier is its own group, in other words — and then apply the Align command.

✔ To split the group into its individual shapes, press Ctrl+U or select Arrange➪Ungroup.

✔ You cannot use the Shape tool on a group. You must first ungroup the shapes and then use the tool.

✔ You can include groups in other groups. For example, after grouping the shapes in each soldier, you can group all the soldiers together. If you want to restore the original shapes later, you have to press Ctrl+U twice.

Your Drawing Is a Plate of Flapjacks

Once again, I speak metaphorically. Don't go pouring maple syrup on the screen or anything. Most condiments *do* damage your computer.

I refer to flapjacks because of their typical arrangement in stacks. One flapjack is at the bottom of the stack, one flapjack is on top, and each additional flapjack is nestled between two others. Pretend that you're looking at the flapjacks from an aerial view like a hungry magpie. You can see the butter on the top, several flapjacks beneath that, and a plate at the bottom, as in Figure 6-18. Each flapjack obscures but does not completely hide the flapjack beneath it.

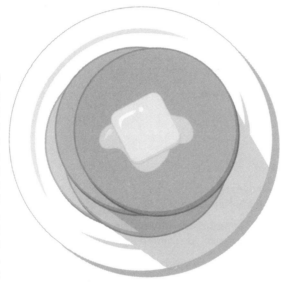

Figure 6-18:
Viewing objects in CorelDraw is like looking down at a stack of flapjacks, although not as appetizing.

CorelDraw stacks objects in the drawing area in a similar fashion. Every object in your drawing is in front of or behind another object. When it displays and prints artwork, Draw starts at the back of the drawing and works its way to the front one object at a time. If two objects overlap, the frontmost of the two partially obscures the other. This hierarchy of objects is called the *stacking order*.

When you leave CorelDraw to its own devices, the first object you draw appears at the back of the drawing and the most recent object appears at the front. But you can change the order of any object by selecting it and choosing one of the five commands in the CorelDraw 5 Arrange⇨Order submenu (press Alt,A,O).

✔ Press Shift+Page Up (or choose the To Front command) to bring one or more selected objects to the front of the drawing. Figure 6-19 shows the result of selecting the face and hands of the soldier drawing and pressing Shift+Page Up. Having moved to the front of the drawing, the face and hands conceal the portions of the shapes that make up the cap and jacket. In the last example of the figure, I select the jacket and press Shift+Page Up again, which covers up the buttons and medal.

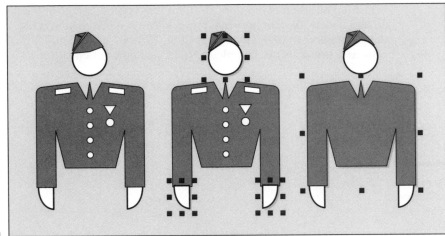

Figure 6-19:
The result
of moving
the face and
hands
(middle) and
the jacket
(right) to the
front of the
drawing.

✔ Press Shift+Page Down (or choose the To Back command) to send one or more selected objects to the back of the drawing.

✔ Press Ctrl+Page Up to nudge selected objects one step forward. Or, if you prefer, choose the Forward One command.

✔ Press Ctrl+Page Down to nudge selected objects one step backward. If you like to choose things, choose the Back One command.

✔ Last but not least, choose the Reverse Order command to reverse the stacking order of selected objects, as demonstrated in Figure 6-20. At least two objects must be selected to use this command.

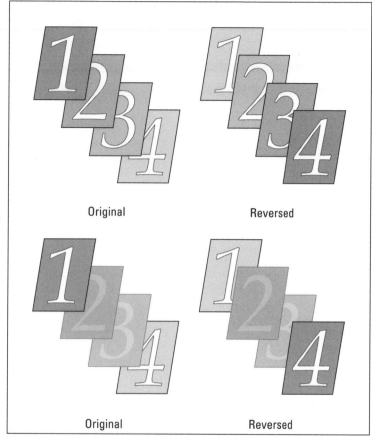

Original   Reversed

Figure 6-20:
Applying
the Reverse
Order
command to
four
selected
objects (top)
and two
selected
objects (1
and 4,
bottom).

Original   Reversed

Chapter 7

Making Your Shapes Look Like Something

*I*t was an ashen morning on the blanched desert. The dusty earth was pallid, the cacti were bleached, and even the lone coyote looked a bit pasty. Worst of all, I myself was entirely without pigmentation.

Suddenly, I spied a flash of color on the horizon. Big, billowy clouds of green, yellow, and purple were accompanied by the thunder of hoof beats. It could only mean one thing — the infamous Chromastazi tribe approached.

Moments later, the swiftest rider emerged from a poofy pink cloud and stopped dead in front of me. Fixing me with his terrible emerald gaze, he drew from his ceremonial paint bucket the biggest, most menacing brush I had ever seen. Before I had time to run, the warrior threw his weapon straight and true. The brush hit me full in the chest, releasing a fountain of colors. As I hit the ground, I couldn't help but notice the sky itself explode with fragments of deepest azure highlighted with streamers of pale blue and crystal white.

"Pale Shape is no more!" went up the rider's cry.

Looking at myself, I hardly believed my eyes. I was no longer transparent. Finally, I knew what it meant to be filled!

— excerpted from *Memoirs of a Pioneerin' Path*, 1875

Fills, Thrills, and Chills

Wasn't that thrilling? I remember when I first read that passage in art history class. The student body was so inspired that we spray-painted the professor.

Now that I have wads of computer experience under my belt, I can see the truth. Regardless of how paths look or act, deep down inside they want to be filled. It's in their nature. Take Figure 7-1, for example. On the left, we see an enhanced version of Shenbop, *primus inter amphibius.* Because all Shenbop's lines and shapes are transparent, it's nearly impossible to focus on the picture. The Shenbop on the right contains the exact same paths as its transparent neighbor, but its paths are filled, which gives the frog form, substance, and a mighty big sense of purpose.

Figure 7-1:
Shenbop's
paths as
they appear
when
transparent
(left) and
when filled
(right).

Filling the void

Newly drawn paths are transparent. To fill the interior of a path with a solid color, do the following:

1. **If any of the paths that you want to fill are open, close them.**

    You can fill closed paths only. Open paths are inherently transparent. You can close a path by using the Pencil tool or the Join icon in the Node Edit roll-up, described in Chapter 5.

2. **Select the shapes that you want to fill.**

    Draw a marquee around the shapes by using the Arrow tool or click on one shape and then Shift+click on the others.

3. Choose a shade to fill the paths.

If your monitor is a grayscale monitor, select a grayscale option. Click on the Fill tool — the one that looks like a spilling paint bucket — to display a flyout menu of fill options. The options on the bottom row (all except the X option, which deletes the fill) let you fill the selected shapes with white, black, or a shade of gray.

If you have a color monitor, click on one of the colors in the *color palette*. The color palette is the strip of colors along the bottom of the interface (see Figure 7-2). Click on the palette scroll arrows to scroll through the palette and display hidden colors.

If you'd rather not scroll, but want to see the entire palette, click on the Palette Expand arrow on the right end of the palette. It will temporarily expand the entire palette on the screen. Once you've chosen a color, the palette shrinks back to its original size.

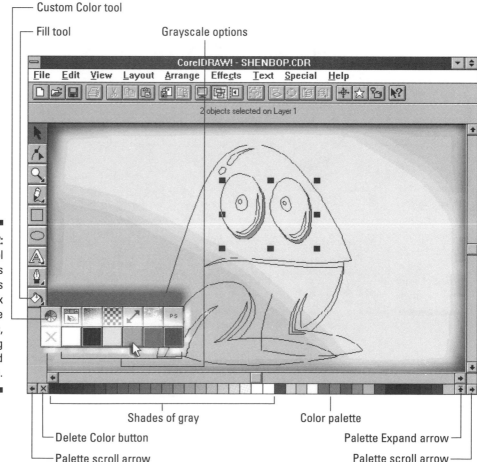

Figure 7-2: The Fill tool provides access to six grayscale options, including black and white.

The first options in the color palette are shades of gray, arranged from black to white in even increments. These shades include all those found in the Fill tool flyout menu and a few more.

If the Custom Color palette does not appear at the bottom of your screen in Draw 5, choose View⊏>Color Palette⊏>Custom Colors (Alt,V,L,C).

Making a new color from old favorites

 If you can't find the color that you want in the color palette, you can create your own color. I warn you: It gets kind of messy. After selecting one or more shapes in your drawing (they must be closed paths), click on the Fill tool. Then click on the first icon in the flyout menu (the one that looks like a wheel), which is called the Custom Color tool. In response, the Uniform Fill dialog box appears, as shown in Figure 7-3. (You can also access this dialog box by pressing Shift+F11.)

Color grid

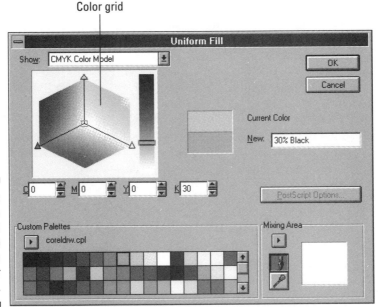

Figure 7-3:
Use the
Uniform Fill
dialog box to
create a
color of your
own.

If you get a dialog box that reads Nothing is currently selected, click on Cancel and make sure that you have selected a shape in the drawing.

Here's where things get tricky. In elementary school, you learned how to mix colors by using the three *primary colors:* blue, red, and yellow. Commercial printers also make colors by mixing primaries, but the primaries are different.

✔ Instead of blue, printers use a light green-blue color called *cyan* (C).

✔ In place of red, they use magenta (M), a purplish color.

✔ Instead of yellow . . . actually, they decided to hang on to yellow (Y).

✔ And because the science of color printing is about as reliable as reading tea leaves, commercial printers throw in black (K) to ensure uniform dark colors.

So there you have it — cyan, magenta, yellow, and black, better known as the *CMYK* (pronounced *C-M-Y-K,* not *simyk* or *kamick* or *ceemwac*) color model.

Applying the expanse of your color knowledge

Because too much color theory has been known to drive people stark raving mad, the following items seek to disseminate the abstractions of CMYK into the real world of the Uniform Fill dialog box:

✔ Primaries are measured in percentages. The more primary you toss in, the darker the color gets. For example, 100 percent cyan plus 100 percent magenta makes deep blue. If you add either yellow or black, you darken the color. Try entering values in the C (Cyan), M (Magenta), Y (Yellow), and K (Black) option boxes to get a feel for the way percentages work.

✔ To create a custom shade of gray, enter a value of 0 in the C, M, and Y option boxes, and then enter the shade of gray in the K option box. For example, 0% is white, 25% is light gray, 50% is medium gray, 75% is dark gray, and 100% is black.

✔ If you want to browse through CorelDraw's 16 million possible colors, check out the color grid on the left side of the Uniform Fill dialog box. The hexagon grid is essentially a graph of colors created by mixing magenta, cyan, and yellow. Remember that I said that cyan and magenta make deep blue? Magenta is the purply color on the left, and cyan is on the top. Now look at the corner between them — aha, deep blue! And red and green, too! If you're not getting these colors, you're probably looking at a grayscale picture in the book. Go ahead and get the Crayolas or turn on your CorelDraw program.

✔ Using your mouse cursor, click on a color region within the hexagon grid. Your color will be calculated in percentages of C, M, Y, and K along the bottom.

✔ To add your new color to the color palette, enter a name in the New box (along the right) and then click on the OK button.

Hasta la fillsta

 To return a shape to absolute transparency, select the shape, click on the Fill tool icon, and then click on the X icon (the Delete Color tool) in the flyout menu. Or easier still, click on the X icon in the lower-left corner of the screen, known as the Delete Color button (see Figure 7-2).

The Thick and Thin of Outlines

You can assign an outline to any path, open or closed. Whereas a fill has one property — color — an outline has two properties: color and thickness. Known as the *line width* or *line weight,* the thickness of an outline is traditionally measured in *points,* which are very tiny increments equal to $\frac{1}{72}$ inch. To put this measurement in perspective, a penny is 4 points thick, a typical pencil is 20 points in diameter, a business card is 254 points wide, a football field measures 259,000 points from one end zone to the other, Mount Everest is 25 million points above sea level, light travels at 850 trillion points per second, presidential elections occur every leap year, and a dozen eggs contain 12 yolks.

 Points are a useful system of measurement, because most outlines tend to be pretty thin. Nearly all the figures in this book, for example, feature outlines of widths one point or thinner.

Tracing the path

To assign an outline to a path, do the following:

1. **Select one or more paths with the Arrow tool.**

   Always the first step, eh?

 2. **Select a line width option.**

   Click on the Outline tool (also called the Pen tool — the one that looks like a pen nib) to display a flyout menu of outline options, as shown in Figure 7-4. The last five options in the top row control the thickness of the outline.

3. **Choose a shade for the outline.**

   If you have a grayscale monitor, select a grayscale option. Click on the Pen tool and then click on a grayscale option in the flyout menu.

   If you have a color monitor, right-click (that is, click with the right mouse button) on one of the colors in the color palette. Right-clicking changes the color of an outline just as left-clicking changes the color of a fill.

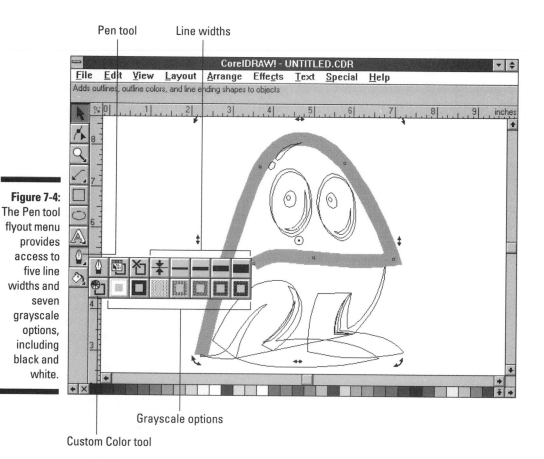

Figure 7-4:
The Pen tool
flyout menu
provides
access to
five line
widths and
seven
grayscale
options,
including
black and
white.

Customizing outline colors

 Outline colors work just like fill colors do. If you want to apply a custom color, make sure that something is selected and then click on the Custom Color tool in the Pen tool flyout menu or press Shift+F12. The Outline Color dialog box provides the exact same options as the Uniform Fill dialog box shown in Figure 7-3. (The Custom Color tool in the Pen flyout looks similar to the Custom Color tool in the Fill flyout.)

Useless line widths

Line width, however, is a whole different kettle of fish (or briar patch of bunnies or whatever rustic idiom happens to strike your fancy). As shown in Figure 7-5, the Pen tool flyout menu offers access to several predefined line widths as well as to the more functional Pen roll-up.

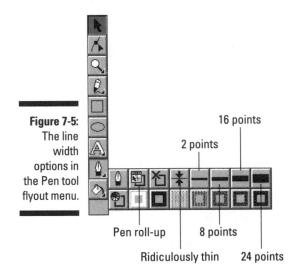

Figure 7-5:
The line
width
options in
the Pen tool
flyout menu.

16 points

2 points

Pen roll-up   8 points

Ridiculously thin   24 points

Each time you draw a line, the first line width option — appropriately labeled *Ridiculously thin* in Figure 7-5 — is in force. This option assigns the thinnest outline that your printer can print. On laser printers and cheaper printer models, the outline looks okay. But on professional-level typesetting machines, it can result in a nearly invisible outline that doesn't reproduce.

I know that some of you can't imagine that you'll ever in a billion years typeset your artwork. But you may as well prepare your drawings for typesetting no matter how remote a possibility you think it is. After all, you might win one of those Corel $1 million art contests only to have your drawing professionally printed with ridiculously thin outlines. Imagine having to describe the artwork to your grandma with her failing eyesight. "Lordy Lu," she'll cry, "If only you had used nice, hefty lines instead of these meager things!" Way to break an old woman's heart.

Figure 7-6 shows three line weight options from the Pen tool flyout menu applied to Shenbop. Compare this figure to the story of the three bears. The left example is too thin, the result of accepting CorelDraw's default outline. The right example is too fat. Only the middle example qualifies as acceptable.

Figure 7-6:
Being a
sensible
frog,
Shenbop
hates the
predefined
line weights
in the Pen
tool flyout
menu and is
highly
embarrassed
to appear in
this figure.

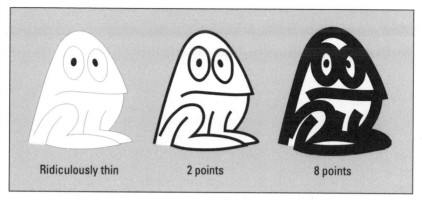

Ridiculously thin   2 points   8 points

Better line widths

 To access other line widths, select the Pen roll-up tool (labeled in Figure 7-5) to display the Pen roll-up shown in Figure 7-7. The Pen roll-up offers several options for changing the outline of a selected path.

 ✔ Click on the scroll arrows on the right side of the roll-up (labeled Thicker and Thinner in Figure 7-7) to increase or decrease the line width by ¹⁄₁₀₀-inch increments. The area to the left of the scroll arrows displays the line width in inches.

 ✔ If the line width is .003 inch (.2 point) or thinner, a cross fills the line width area, as in Figure 7-8. This cross indicates that your outline is too thin and may not reproduce well.

 ✔ To change the line width display from inches to points, click on the Edit button. The Outline Pen dialog box appears, which is discussed later in Figure 7-9. Select the Points option to the right of the Width drop-down list box using the down-arrow button. Then press Enter. From now on, clicking on a scroll arrow changes the line width by .7-point increments.

 ✔ Click on the Start arrow or End arrow button to display a drop-down list box of arrowhead options, as shown in Figure 7-8. Use the scroll bar on the right side of the menu to access any of 92 arrowheads that can appear at the beginning or end of an open path. (Arrowheads have no effect on closed paths.)

Line width

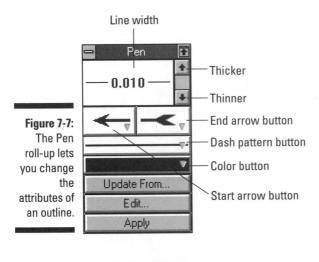

Thicker

Thinner

End arrow button

Dash pattern button

Color button

Start arrow button

Figure 7-7: The Pen roll-up lets you change the attributes of an outline.

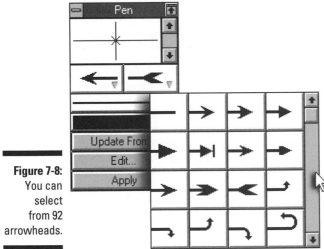

Figure 7-8: You can select from 92 arrowheads.

✔ Click on the Dash pattern button to display a drop-down list box of dotted-line patterns that you can assign to an open or closed path.

✔ Click the Color button to select a color for the outline.

✔ Click on the Apply button to apply the settings in the Pen roll-up to the selected paths in the drawing area.

If you get a dialog box that says that nothing is currently selected, click on Cancel and make sure that you have selected a shape in the drawing.

Someone else's outline

In CorelDraw, you can copy an outline from one path and assign it to another. For example, if you have two paths, Fred and Wilma, you can make Fred's outline look just like Wilma's. To perform this transformation, do the following:

1. **Select Fred and click on the Update From button in the Pen roll-up.**

   Your cursor changes to a horizontal arrow labeled `From?`.

2. **Click on Wilma.**

   The Pen roll-up now displays the outline settings assigned to Wilma.

3. **Click on the Apply button.**

   Now Fred and Wilma look the same (like so many other married couples).

Even better line widths

To recap, the Pen tool flyout menu offers five largely useless line widths. The Pen roll-up offers an unlimited number of line widths in .7-point increments. If you want to access an even wider array of line widths without weird or artificial constraints, select an object and click on the Edit button in the Pen roll-up or press F12, which opens the Outline Pen dialog box shown in Figure 7-9.

- ✔ Enter a value into the <u>W</u>idth option box from .1 to 288 points in ¹⁄₁₀-point increments or larger.

- ✔ When working in inches, you can enter any value from .001 to 4 inches.

- ✔ Don't go any thinner than .3 point or .004 inch. Line widths between .3 and .5 point are called *hairlines* because they're about as thick as (some) hairs.

  Personally, my hair rivals cotton candy for fortitude and manageability. Hairlines look like Corinthian columns compared to my hair. I suspect that my hair wouldn't reproduce well. If I were to photocopy my face, I'd doubtless look like a cue ball.

- ✔ To change the system of measurement, select an option from the drop-down list box to the right of the <u>W</u>idth option box. In addition to inches and points, the drop-down list box offers millimeters for you worldly, metric types and picas for you newspaper and magazine types.

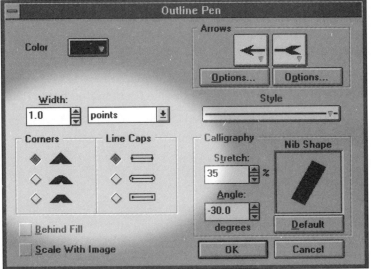

Corners and caps

In addition to the Width option, the Outline Pen dialog box offers a few other interesting items, which appear highlighted in Figure 7-9. These items fall into two categories: corners and caps.

Corners determine the appearance of the outline at corner nodes in the path:

- ✔ First among the Corners radio buttons, the Miter corner option ensures sharp corners in a path.

- ✔ When curved segments slope into each other to form a very acute angle, the Miter corner option can produce weird spikes that make your path look like it's covered with occasional bits of barbed wire. You may go your entire life without encountering this phenomenon, but if you do have a problem with it, select one of the other two Corners radio buttons.

- ✔ The Round corner option rounds off the corners in a path. I use this option a lot — it takes the edge off things. A real ice breaker at parties.

- ✔ The last option is called Bevel corner because it lops off the end of the corner as if the corner were beveled.

Figure 7-10 shows the three corners applied to fragments of Shenbop. The outlines appear black. I represent the paths with thin white outlines so that you can see how paths and outlines relate. Pretty insightful, huh?

The Line Caps options determine the way that lines look at the beginning and end of an open path. Caps have no effect on closed paths.

- ✓ The first Line Caps option is Butt cap. Honest, that's what it's called. I'm not trying to be offensive to inspire controversy and sell books. Which is funny, because that's exactly what I was trying to do when I wanted to use the word *butt* in my last book, and the editors wouldn't let me. Now they have to. After all, I didn't come up with the term Butt cap. Huge corporate forces beyond my control decided. I'm sure they giggled while they were at it. They must have been feeling very immature that day.

- ✓ Just in case you want to know what it does, the Butt (snigger) cap option ends the outline exactly at the end of the path. The outline butts up (hee hee) against the node, as it were.

- ✓ The Round cap does just that: It extends the outline slightly beyond the end of the path and rounds it off. Like Round corner, the Round cap option gives a path a friendlier appearance. Of course, if your path is inherently unfriendly, depicting, say, a slathering rottweiler chomping on a Chihuahua's skull, adding rounded caps isn't likely to do much good.

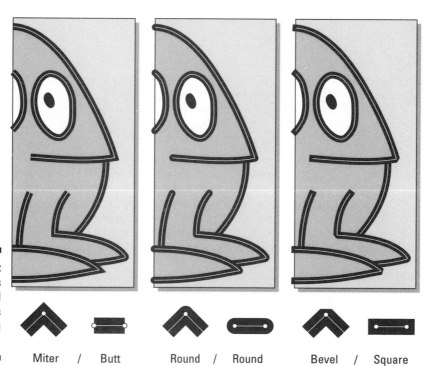

Figure 7-10: CorelDraw's Corners and Line Caps options in practice.

Miter / Butt   Round / Round   Bevel / Square

✔ Like the Round cap option, the Square cap extends the outline past the end of a path. But instead of rounding off the outline, it caps it off with a square. This option is useful when you want to prevent a gap between an open path and an adjacent object or when you're simply too embarrassed to use Butt caps, as when drawing in mixed company.

The vanishing outline

To remove a path's outline, select the path, click on the Pen tool and then click on the X tool in the flyout menu. Or you can right-click on the Delete Color button (also an X) in the lower-left corner of the color palette scroll bar.

✔ Generally speaking, you should only delete the outline of *filled* shapes. If you delete the outline of a transparent shape or open path, you make it entirely invisible. It's like losing your car keys. You know they're in the house, but you don't know where. Likewise, the outline isn't gone, but you can't see it, and it's hard to find.

✔ If you do lose the outline, here's how to find it. Press Shift+F9 (View⇨Wireframe) to go into Wireframe mode. Then you can change the outline and fill. Press Shift+F9 again to return to Preview mode. The outline is visible once more.

Changing the Default Settings

If you select an option from the Fill or Pen tool flyout menus or click on the Apply button in the Pen roll-up when no object is selected, CorelDraw assumes that you want to change the default attributes that affect each and every future path or fill that you create. To confirm this assumption, the program displays the message shown in Figure 7-11. If you don't want to change the defaults, click on the Cancel button. If you want to change the default settings for all future paths or fills, select the Graphic checkbox and press Enter.

The Artistic text and Paragraph text options affect varieties of CorelDraw text blocks discussed in Chapter 11.

Fill and Outline Join Forces

If you paid much attention to the fully filled and outlined version of Shenbop shown in Figure 7-1, you may have noticed something unusual. Namely, that a few *open* paths, such as the main body and the legs, appear to be filled. The interior of the body covers up the background behind it, the interior of the front leg covers part of the body, and the interior of the hind leg covers part of the front leg. There's no question about it — these paths are filled.

Figure 7-11:
This
message
appears
when you
try to apply
a fill or
outline
setting
when
nothing is
selected.

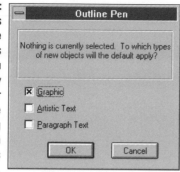

How can that be? After all, I specifically said that you can't fill an open path. I wouldn't lie — my mom told me *never* to lie — so there must be something else going on.

Actually, the body and the legs are made up of two paths apiece: one closed path with a fill and no outline; and one open path with an outline and no fill. Figure 7-12 demonstrates how the pairs of paths are stacked. The filled version of the path is situated behind the outlined version of the path, creating what appears to be a single shape.

Figure 7-12:
A filled,
closed path
with no
outline (first
column)
behind an
outlined,
open path
with no fill
(second
column)
creates the
appearance
of a filled
open path
(last
column).

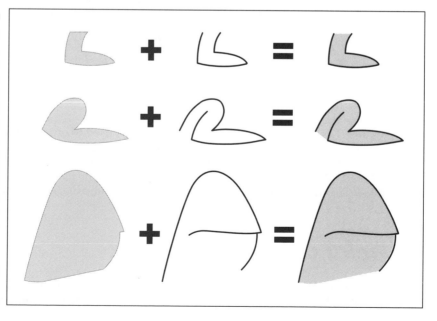

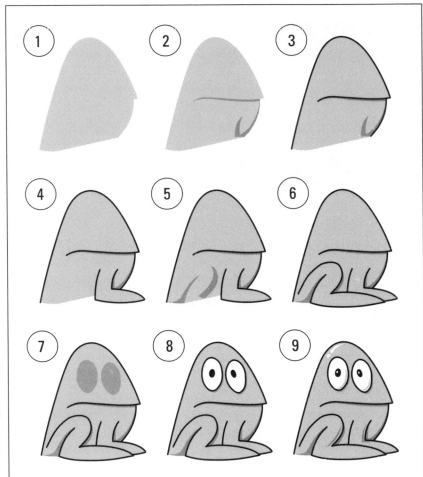

Figure 7-13:
The bits and pieces of Shenbop from back to front.

Figure 7-13 shows the stacking order of the paths used to create Shenbop from back to front. The paths that make up the body and legs are either strictly filled or strictly outlined. In fact, only the whites of the eyes are both filled and outlined. All outlines are one point thick. If you're in the mood for trivia, you'll be interested to know that the border around the figure is .5 point thick.

The Wacky World of Fills

If you're sensitive to detail, you've no doubt noticed that I skipped an option or two along the way. For example, I described the Pen roll-up but did not mention the Fill roll-up.

The Fill roll-up is devoted exclusively to advanced fill effects, including grada-tions, geometric patterns, and textures. Each of these effects can prove ex-tremely complicated. So rather than delve into tiresome lists of options and obscure settings, I'll just introduce each effect in the most basic terms possible.

Each of the buttons along the top of the roll-up duplicates a function in the Fill tool flyout menu, as Figure 7-14 demonstrates. The difference is that the options in the Fill roll-up are easier to use, as described in the following list. (As with any fill effect, each of these options is applicable exclusively to closed paths.)

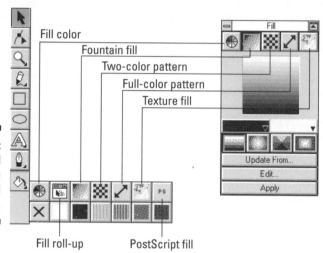

Figure 7-14:
The Fill tool flyout menu vs. the Fill roll-up.

Fill color
Fountain fill
Two-color pattern
Full-color pattern
Texture fill

Fill roll-up   PostScript fill

 ✔ Click on the Fill Color button to fill a selected path with a solid color. The Fill roll-up will show you the color palette, which is identical to the one on the bottom of your screen.

 ✔ Click on the Fountain fill button to fill a selected path with a gradual blend from one color to another, called a *gradation*. Select a beginning color and an end color from the drop-down lists below the gradient display. Specify the type of gradation by clicking on one of the icons directly above the Update From button. Finally, drag inside the gradient display in the upper-right portion of the roll-up to determine the direction or center of the gradation.

 ✔ The Two-color vector pattern button allows you to fill a shape with a pattern of vectors or shapes in any two colors. Specify the colors by selecting options from both of the Color drop-down list boxes. To change the pattern, click on the pattern display in the upper-right portion of the roll-up to show a drop-down list box of options. Select the desired pattern and click on OK.

✔ The Full-color pixel pattern button fills a shape with a pattern of pixels in any of 256 colors. To change the pattern, click on the pattern display, select the desired pattern from the resulting drop-down list box, and click on the OK option.

✔ Click on the Texture fill button to fill selected shapes with photographic-quality pixel images. To change the texture, click on the texture display in the upper-right portion of the roll-up, select the desired pattern from the resulting drop-down list box, and click on OK. Alternatively, you can select options from the two drop-down list boxes below the texture display.

✔ Click on the PostScript fill button to select a predefined PostScript texture fill. These fills are actually PostScript codes that the printer reads to create its own printed pattern. These fills only print on PostScript printers; if you don't have a PostScript printer as your current printer, you can't access this option. Also, there's no way to preview these fills on-screen; Corel just displays a little tile pattern with the characters *PS.* You might just want to experiment and see if there are any that you like. But be aware that the fills print a little differently each time you print them out. For example, if you draw a rectangle and fill it with the Cracked pattern, you'll get a square that looks something like cracked glass. But each time you print, the cracks will appear very differently. In other words, unless you really are in a mood to play around, leave these fills alone.

✔ Click on the Apply button to apply the specified gradation, pattern, or texture to the selected paths in the drawing area.

Chapter 8
The Fine Art of Cloning

*W*hat was the big deal about *Jurassic Park*? Okay, lawyer-eating dinosaurs — obviously I'm all for that. And if I were a poison-spitting dilophosaurus, I couldn't imagine a tastier treat than a well-fed computer programmer. Those guys spend so much time glued to their chairs that they make veal calves look active. But how hard can cloning be? CorelDraw's been able to do it for years. You don't need a mosquito trapped in amber with DNA squirting out its thorax. Give me a velociraptor, and I'll make as many duplicates as you like. And even before CorelDraw, there were photocopiers. Rubber stamps have been around forever — I'm pretty sure the Neanderthals used them. Don't believe everything you see — cloning is much easier than Hollywood would have you believe.

Mom, Dad, Is There Really a Clipboard?

Windows has this thing called the *Clipboard,* in which you can store one collection of objects at a time. Using the Clipboard, you can make copies of these objects and transfer them to other drawings. Three Edit menu commands — Cut, Copy, and Paste — provide access to the Clipboard.

Although you see a *group* of objects, the Clipboard treats them as a single item.

Here's how the three Clipboard commands work from the <u>E</u>dit menu:

✔ The Cu<u>t</u> command (Ctrl+X) removes all selected objects from your drawing and places them in the Clipboard. When you choose Cu<u>t</u>, Draw replaces the Clipboard's previous contents. So if you cut Object A and then later cut Object B, Object B knocks Object A off the Clipboard into electronic oblivion.

✔ The <u>C</u>opy command (Ctrl+C) makes a copy of all selected objects in your drawing and places the copy on the Clipboard. Like Cu<u>t</u>, this command replaces the Clipboard's previous contents.

✔ The <u>P</u>aste command (Ctrl+V) makes a copy of the contents of the Clipboard and places them in your drawing. Unlike Cu<u>t</u> and <u>C</u>opy, the <u>P</u>aste command leaves the contents of the Clipboard unaltered. You can choose the <u>P</u>aste command as many times as you want and make copy after copy after copy.

Snap, crackle, paste

Here's a typical example of how you can use the Clipboard:

1. Select one or more objects that you want to duplicate.

If you have a herd of dinosaurs handy, please select it now.

2. Choose <u>E</u>dit⇨<u>C</u>opy.

Figure 8-1 shows this step in progress. CorelDraw makes a copy of every selected object and places the copy on the Clipboard. Sometimes this process takes a long time, so a message appears to tell you that Draw is working on it.

3. Toodle around.

Perform scads of operations. Work for hours and hours. Wait several weeks if you like. Time has no effect on the Clipboard as long as you don't touch the Cut or Copy commands, exit CorelDraw or Windows, or turn off your computer.

4. Have a sandwich.

Make me one, too. A BLT, if you have the ingredients.

5. Choose <u>E</u>dit⇨<u>P</u>aste.

Bazoing! (That's a sound effect, in case you didn't recognize it.) CorelDraw makes a copy of the objects on the Clipboard and places them at the exact location in the drawing area at which they appeared when you chose the <u>C</u>opy command.

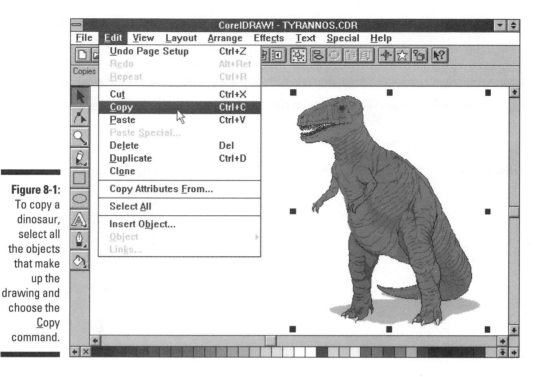

Figure 8-1:
To copy a
dinosaur,
select all
the objects
that make
up the
drawing and
choose the
<u>C</u>opy
command.

If you never move the original objects, you won't notice any difference in
your drawing because the copied objects sit directly on top of the originals. Drag the copied objects slightly off to the side to see that you do
indeed have two identical versions of your objects, as shown in Figure 8-2.

Clipboard keyboard capers

New computer users generally have problems remembering the
keyboard equivalents for Clipboard commands. Granted, Ctrl+C makes
sense as a shortcut for <u>C</u>opy. Although Ctrl+X is a stretch, it sort of
brings Cu<u>t</u> to mind. But where did Ctrl+V for <u>P</u>aste come from? The
answer resides in the lower-left corner of your keyboard: The keys read
Z, X, C, and V. That's <u>U</u>ndo (the first command in the <u>E</u>dit menu), Cu<u>t</u>,
<u>C</u>opy, and <u>P</u>aste.

Then again, if you think of <u>E</u>dit⇨<u>P</u>aste as regurgitating the contents of
the Clipboard, Ctrl+V takes on new meaning. Just trying to help.

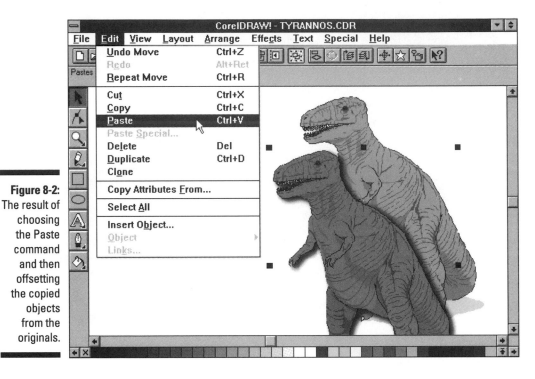

Figure 8-2:
The result of
choosing
the Paste
command
and then
offsetting
the copied
objects
from the
originals.

You can also press these keys, which apply to all Windows programs:

- ✔ Shift+Delete for Edit⇨Cut
- ✔ Ctrl+Insert for Edit⇨Copy
- ✔ Shift+Insert for Edit⇨Paste

I can't give you any advice for remembering these keyboard equivalents because, frankly, they're bizarre. Okay, I suppose that because the Delete key deletes objects, it makes sense for Shift+Delete to go one step further by scooping them up and sending them to the Clipboard. But then Copy should be Shift+Insert instead of Ctrl+Insert. Go figure. I can't blame Corel; Microsoft built these weird keyboard equivalents into Windows. And according to Strunk and White, the words *Microsoft* and *logic* don't ever belong in the same sentence.

A few Clipboard facts

Here are a few random bits of information about the Clipboard that you may want to stash away for future use:

✔ The most common purpose of the Clipboard is to cut or copy objects from one drawing and paste them into another. For example, to create Figure 8-3, I copied the tyrannosaur object, closed the tyrannosaur drawing, opened the stegosaur drawing, and pasted the tyrannosaur. They should be great friends; they have so much in common. One is a tasty, crunchy dinosaur, and the other likes to eat tasty, crunchy dinosaurs.

✔ If the current document contains more than one page (see Chapter 12), you can use the Clipboard commands to transfer objects from one page to another.

✔ You can also cut, copy, and paste objects within a single-page drawing. But it's generally easier to duplicate the objects by using the Duplicate or Clone command, as I describe later in this chapter.

✔ You can't see the Clipboard. You just have to have faith that it's there, like life after death or sea monkeys. As a result, you can't edit objects on the Clipboard, add or subtract them selectively, or do anything else except cut, copy, and paste them as a single unit.

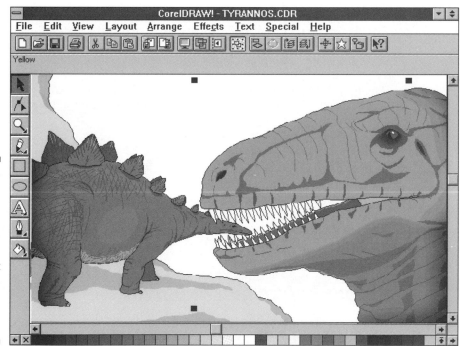

Figure 8-3: The Clipboard lets you combine objects from different drawings in cruel and unusual ways.

Why I Hate the Clipboard

Well, I don't really *hate* it. It's useful every once in a while. But I think that you should be aware of the following three problems with the Cu<u>t</u>, <u>C</u>opy, and <u>P</u>aste commands:

- ✔ Depending on the complexity of your drawing, Clipboard functions can be very slow. Inside the tyrannosaur drawing, for example, copying a simple rectangle takes . . . well, here, I'll do it right now. I select a rectangle by clicking with the Arrow tool. Now I choose the <u>C</u>opy command and start the old stopwatch. The message `CorelDraw is Copying` sits there for a while like the machine is frozen up. Dum dee dum. Still just sitting there. I'll twiddle my thumbs a little. Ah, now something's happening. It's wrapping up, almost finished. Done, and in just under 25 seconds! And that's on a 486 machine, mind you. That's what I call a waste of time.

- ✔ You have to choose two commands to pull off Clipboard actions: first Cu<u>t</u> or <u>C</u>opy and then <u>P</u>aste. That's what I call a waste of effort.

- ✔ Every time you choose Cu<u>t</u> or <u>C</u>opy, the previous contents of the Clipboard go up in smoke. If you want to use the objects on the Clipboard over and over again, you can't go around upsetting them every time you want to duplicate something. That's what I call a waste of status quo.

The moral is that you should avoid Clipboard commands whenever possible, which is almost always. The following sections explain how.

The Gleaming Clipboard Bypass

The easiest way to bypass the Clipboard is to choose <u>E</u>dit➪<u>D</u>uplicate or press Ctrl+D. CorelDraw creates an exact copy of all selected objects and offsets them a quarter inch up and to the right, as demonstrated in Figure 8-4.

Group before you duplicate

When you duplicate several paths at a time, Draw places each duplicated object directly in front of its respective original object. The paths weave in and out of each other, creating an indecipherable mess, as shown in Figure 8-5. Oh sure, it's great if you're buzzing on caviar and aperitifs at a local gallery and are willing to call anything you spy the highest of art forms — "Don't you just love it, Madge? It's like *Dino Descending a Staircase!*" — but it's hardly acceptable for the nine-to-five crowd.

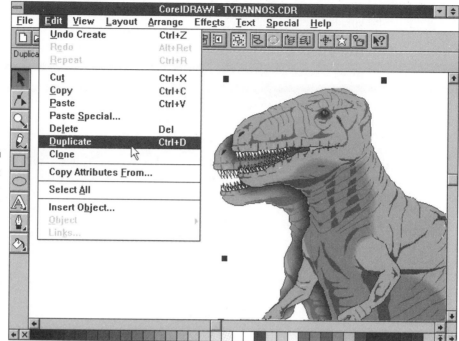

Figure 8-4:
Choose the
Edit⇨
Duplicate
command to
create a
copy of an
object
without
using the
Clipboard.

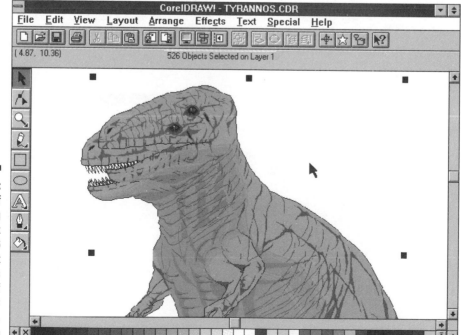

Figure 8-5:
The result of
duplicating
the T. Rex
as 526
independent
paths
instead of
one tidy
group.

To remedy this situation and group the objects, press either of the following key sequences:

> Shift+PgUp
>
> Alt+Backspace, Ctrl+G, Ctrl+D

The first Quick Step combination brings the duplicated objects neatly to the front and creates an effect like that shown in Figure 8-4 — assuming, of course, that in your panic you haven't gone and clicked randomly in the drawing area and deselected the paths prior to pressing Shift+PgUp. If you have, you're still okay. The second Quick Step groups the original selected objects first and then reapplies the Duplicate command.

The Group (Ctrl+G) command is an ideal prerequisite to the Duplicate command. By choosing Group, you ensure that all your objects stay together after you duplicate them. Generally speaking, I recommend that when you want to duplicate five or more objects, you group them first. If you want to edit the objects, you can always Ungroup them later.

Duplication distance

By default, the Duplicate command offsets the copied objects ¼ inch from the originals. You can change the offset by pressing Ctrl+J (or by choosing Special⇔Preferences), clicking on the General tab, and editing the values in the first two option boxes, as shown in Figure 8-6. Positive values offset the duplicate up or to the right; negative values move it down or to the left.

Figure 8-6:
The
Horizontal
and Vertical
values
determine
the
increment
by which the
Duplicate
command
offsets a
copied
object from
its original.

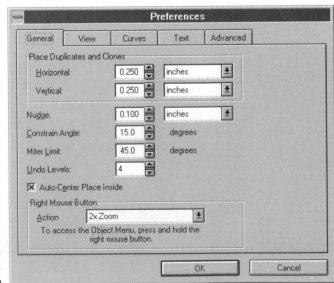

I recommend that you make these values an even multiple of the Nudge value. (The *Nudge value* is the distance a selected object moves with one press of an arrow key.) Better yet, make them equal to it. This way, if you want to align the duplicated objects with the originals, you only have to press the down-arrow key once and the left-arrow key once.

Duplicate in place

In addition to Ctrl+D, the Duplicate command has a secret keyboard equivalent that only I know. Well, you'll know about it in a moment. Actually, it's in the manual, but who reads the manual? Here goes:

Press the + key on the keypad to duplicate a selected object without offsetting it. Then drag it to a new location.

Pretty hot stuff, huh?

They Look Alike, They Act Alike — You Could Lose Your Mind

Imagine that every time Patty Duke changed her clothes, her identical cousin changed her clothes, too. Or that every time Patty missed a question on a test, her cousin entered the same wrong answer. Or that every time Patty locked braces with her boyfriend, so would her cousin. You'd have a couple of couplings. *That's* cloning.

Uh, what's cloning?

Allow me to elucidate. Available since CorelDraw 4, the Clone command creates a true twin of an object. Like the Duplicate command, Edit⇨Clone bypasses the Clipboard, creates an immediate copy, and offsets the copy the distance specified in the Preferences dialog box. But unlike the Duplicate command, the Clone command creates a link between copy and original. Any change made to the original also affects the clone.

For example, suppose that I clone the group of objects that make up the T. Rex. After waiting approximately half my life for Draw to complete that operation, I move the cloned group over a little so I can see what the heck I'm doing. Then I select the *original* T. Rex and drag one of its corner handles. Instead of scaling just the original tyrannosaur, CorelDraw scales them both. Let's see *Jurassic Park* do that!

Links on the brink

The link between a clone and its original object works in one direction only. For example, if you select a clone and apply a new fill, Draw fills the clone only, as demonstrated in Figure 8-7. But if you select the original and fill it, Draw fills the clone as well, as in Figure 8-8.

Changing the original also changes the clone, but changing the clone doesn't change the original.

Altering a clone damages the link between the cloned and original objects. You can think of the Clone command as providing four links: one governs the fill of the objects; another controls the outline; a third covers all transformations (scaling, rotating, and so on); and a fourth applies to Clipboard functions.

Each link is independent of the other three. So even if you apply a different fill to the clone, Draw retains the link between outline, transformations, and Clipboard functions.

Original   Clone

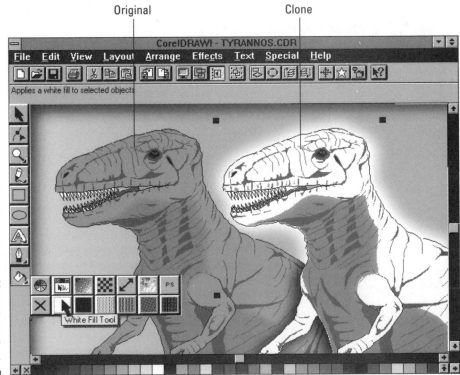

Figure 8-7:
When you fill a clone, you leave the original object unfilled and break the fill link between the two objects.

Original   Clone

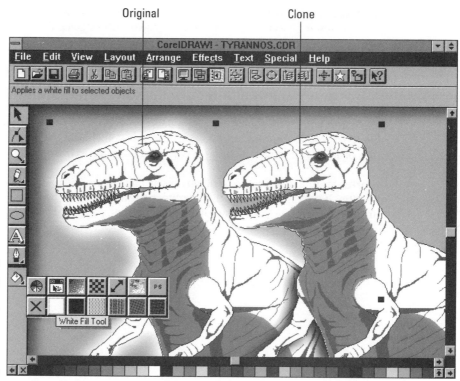

Figure 8-8:
To retain all
links, apply
changes to
the original
object only.

Feeding and caring for your clones

Here's some more stuff you should know about clones:

✔ Any transformation applied to a clone severs the transformation link completely. If you scale the clone, for example, you also prohibit rotating, skewing, and all other options described in Chapter 9.

✔ If you cut the original object, you cut the clone as well. The same holds true for the Copy command. However, whereas the Cut command destroys the Clipboard link, you can copy a clone as many times as you want with no detrimental effects.

✔ Although grouping and duplicating go hand in hand, grouping limits the functionality of the Clone command. If you have a group of objects, for example, and you want to be able to change the fill and outline of individual objects in the group later, be sure to ungroup them before choosing Edit⇔Clone. Then press Shift+PgUp (or Arrange⇔Order⇔To Front) to bring the objects to the front of the drawing area and proceed from there.

> ✔ If you apply the <u>G</u>roup or <u>U</u>ngroup command to cloned objects, you sever all four links between the original objects and their clones.

> ✔ If you clone a group, you cannot ungroup the original object until after you ungroup the clone, which totally wipes out the links. So if you're going to clone a group, be sure that you want it to remain a group.

Some operations do not affect clones. For example, the clone remains deselected when you select the original. When you move the original object, the clone remains stationary. And when you change the stacking order of an original object, nothing in particular happens to the clone.

Unfortunately, I was unable to discover the answer to one nagging question. If you scratch the original object's tummy, does the clone purr? Or does it bite your head off? Experiment at your own risk.

Chapter 9

The Twisty, Stretchy, Bulgy World of Transformations

In the movie *The Blues Brothers,* original "Saturday Night Live" cast member John Belushi does a series of back flips in a church. When you see it, you think, "Wow, that's amazing! Despite the fact that he's verging on obesity, high on nonprescription inhalants, and obviously completely out of shape (he spends half the movie breaking out in sweat), this guy is so gonzo that he's capable of performing complex floor exercises when sufficiently inspired."

Well, at least that's what I thought when I saw the movie in high school. Later, I learned the sad truth that it wasn't *really* John Belushi doing the back flips, but rather a padded stunt man. That fateful day, I promised myself that I would somehow make John's dream of gymnastic excellence come true. (I didn't really do anything of the kind, of course, but stay with me on this one. The whole introduction to this chapter hinges on your temporary suspension of disbelief.)

Today, I make good on that promise. In this chapter, you don't just see John do flips, although he performs quite a nice one in Figure 9-1. You see him undergo

Figure 9-1:
Belushi
finally does
his own
stunts.

a series of elaborate transformations that would cause any rational Olympic athlete at the peak of his or her career to shrink with terror. By the end of the chapter, you'll swear that the guy is some kind of inhuman shape-shifter who can assume any form at will. Either that, or he's just a drawing that's been subjected to CorelDraw's vast array of transformation functions.

The Belushi caricature comes from a company called Image Club, which offers a huge variety of celebrity and historical caricatures, almost all of which are splendid (in stark contrast to the general-purpose Image Club cartoons, which are pretty awful).

Like the rat, Coliseum, and dinosaurs from previous chapters, Mr. Belushi is included on the CorelDraw 5 CD-ROM.

Scaling, Flipping, Rotating, and Skewing

Scaling, flipping, rotating, and skewing are the big four transformations, and they've been available to CorelDraw users since our ancestors crafted the first version of the program out of twigs and iron-ore filings in the early 5th century. Just so that you know what I'm talking about — in approximate terms, anyway — here are a few quick definitions:

- ✔ To *scale* (or *stretch*) an object is to make it bigger or smaller. You can scale an object vertically, horizontally, or both.

- ✔ To *flip* an object is to make a mirror image of it, which is why CorelDraw calls this process *mirroring* and other programs call it *reflecting*. In the second example in Figure 9-1, I flip Mr. Belushi vertically, making the top the bottom and the bottom the top. You also can flip an object horizontally, making the left side the right side and vice versa.

- ✔ To *rotate* an object is to spin it around a central point like a top. Rotations are measured in degrees. A 180-degree rotation turns the object upside down. A 360-degree rotation returns it right back to where it started.

- ✔ To *skew* (or *slant*) an object is to incline it to a certain degree. Like rotations, skews are measured in degrees. Just to give you some perspective, a 45-degree skew applied to a rectangle slants the shape so that its sides are perfectly diagonal.

The objects must be in a group!

Well, they don't *have* to be in a group. But it's a good rule of thumb to group all objects before you transform them. For example, to transform the Belushi cartoon, I selected all the shapes that made up the drawing and pressed Ctrl+G. (You also can choose Arrange⇨Group.) Then I could scale, flip, rotate, and skew with a clear conscience. Grouping prevents you from accidentally missing an object — like an eye or an ear — while transforming its neighbors.

Scaling and flipping

 If you read the "Arrow Tool Tricks" section of Chapter 4, you're already familiar with how to use the Arrow tool to scale and flip an object. But just in case you missed that chapter, I'll quickly explain how it works:

1. **Select one or more objects that you want to scale or flip.**

   Eight square handles surround the selected objects.

2. **Drag one of the handles to scale the objects.**

   Drag a corner handle to scale the objects proportionately so that the ratio between the horizontal and vertical dimensions of each object remains unchanged. Drag the left or right handle to scale (enlarge or reduce) the objects horizontally only, as in Figure 9-2. Drag the top or bottom handle to scale the objects in a vertical direction only.

Status line   Stretch cursor

Figure 9-2:
The result
of dragging
the side
handle with
the Arrow
tool.

3. Drag one handle past the opposite handle to flip the objects.

In Figure 9-3, for example, I drag the right handle leftward past the left handle to flip John B. horizontally so that he looks exactly as if he were rehearsing an episode of "Samurai Pastry Chef" in front of a mirror . . . except, of course, that he's regrettably facing the wrong direction.

Notice that in both Figures 9-2 and 9-3, the status line measures the transformation in percentage points. A value below 100 percent indicates a reduction, and a value above 100 percent indicates an enlargement. A negative value, like that in Figure 9-3, indicates a flip.

The Transform roll-up

You also can scale or flip selected objects by using the Transform roll-up. This feature is new to CorelDraw 5. Versions 1, 2, 3, and 4 gave you different dialog boxes for different transformations; these dialog boxes are all dead now, having been rolled into the Transform roll-up, shown in Figure 9-4.

Status line

Figure 9-3:
By dragging
the right
handle way
the heck
leftward, I
create a
reflection of
Belushi.

The Transform roll-up looks pretty, but that's about the only plug I can give it. Everything that the roll-up can do, you can do yourself on-screen with your mouse. The fact that you can stretch, scale, rotate, skew, and whip up a nasty mocha java on-screen without entering dialog boxes or even touching the keyboard is what makes CorelDraw one of those ooh-wow-I-gotta-have-it programs.

If you use the roll-up, you're a Corel-wanna-be. I'll show you how to be a Corellian. Heck, you may even get invited to parties.

Figure 9-4:
The
Transform
roll-up.

Rotating and skewing

To rotate or skew one or more objects, do the following:

1. **Select one or more objects to rotate or skew.**

   As always, you see eight square handles.

2. **Click on one of the selected objects a second time.**

   When you do, CorelDraw changes the square handles to a series of double-headed arrows, as shown in Figure 9-5. These arrows are the alternate *rotate and skew handles,* or R&S handles for short. (The curved handles are rotation handles, and the straight handles are skew handles.)

   To return to the square stretch and mirror handles, click a third time on a selected object. Each time you click, you toggle between S&M and R&S.

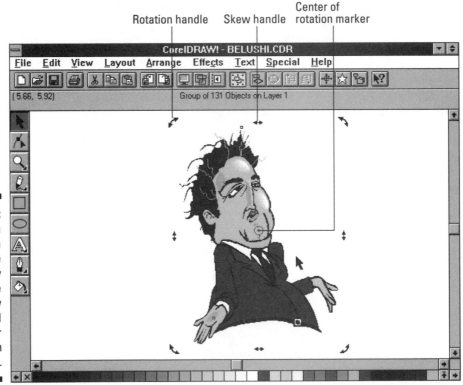

Figure 9-5:
Click on a selection a second time to display the rotate and skew handles and the center of rotation marker.

3. Move the center of rotation marker as desired.

The circle in the middle of the selection is the *center of rotation marker,* which indicates the point about which the rotation takes place. Make sense? No? Well, think of the marker as a nail in a piece of cardboard. If you flick the cardboard, it whirls around the nail, right? In the same way, a selection rotates around the center of rotation marker. You can move the marker by dragging it.

4. Drag a rotation handle to rotate the selected objects.

Drag any of the four corner handles to rotate the selection around the center of the rotation marker, as shown in Figure 9-6.

5. Drag a skew handle to slant the selected objects.

Drag the top or bottom handle to slant the selected objects horizontally, as in Figure 9-7. To slant the objects vertically, drag one of the two side handles.

Rotate cursor

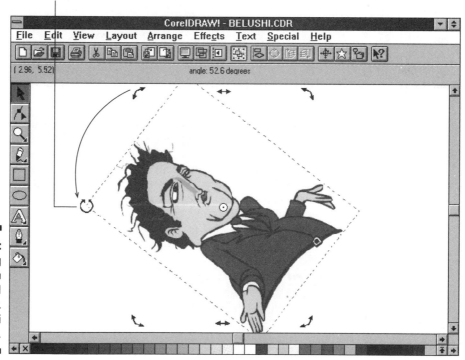

Figure 9-6:
By dragging a rotation handle, I send Mr. Belushi spinning.

Skew cursor

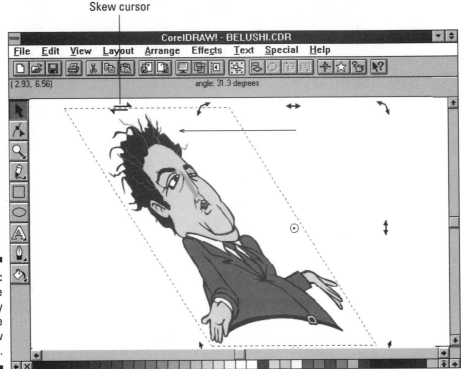

Figure 9-7:
I slant the
cartoon by
dragging the
top skew
handle.

As it does when you scale and flip objects, the status line measures rotations and skews, but in degrees instead of percentage points. When you are rotating an object, a positive value indicates a counterclockwise rotation, as in Figure 9-6; a negative value means that the rotation is clockwise. When you are skewing an object, a positive value slants the object to the left (see Figure 9-7) or up; a negative value slants it to the right or down. In other words, a positive value slants an object backward and a negative value slants it forward, which is just the opposite of what most people expect.

Degrees of transformation

Keep the following things in mind when you're rotating and skewing objects:

✔ I don't know how much you remember from geometry class, but here's a quick refresher. Think of degrees as measures on a clock. A clock measures 60 seconds; a geometric circle comprises 360 degrees. Each clock second is equal to 6 degrees, which means that the hour markers on a clock are 30 degrees apart. So a quarter turn — the distance from 12:00 to 3:00 — is 90 degrees in CorelDraw.

✔ Ctrl+drag a handle to rotate or skew in 15-degree increments. For example, you can rotate a selection by 30 degrees, 45 degrees, and so on. All major turns — ¼ turns, ⅛ turns, all the way down to ¹⁄₂₄ turns — are multiples of 15 degrees.

✔ If you don't like 15 degrees, you can change the angle by pressing Ctrl+J (Special➪Preferences). In the Preferences dialog box that appears, enter a new value into the Constrain Angle option box of the General tab. After you press Enter, Ctrl+drag a rotation handle to effect your change.

Ctrl+drag the center of rotation marker to align the center point with one of the eight handles. You can also Ctrl+drag to return the marker to the exact center of the selection.

Distortions on Parade

If scale, flip, rotate, and skew were the extent of CorelDraw's transformation capabilities, the program would be a real snoozer. It would be flexible, certainly, but hardly capable of inspiring the fanatical loyalty that accompanies this vast program. The remainder of this chapter covers three other amazing transformations you can perform with CorelDraw:

✔ Imagine a drawing that's printed on a sheet of flexible plastic in a rectangular frame. If you grab a corner of the plastic and stretch it, the drawing stretches in that direction. That's what it's like to distort objects in CorelDraw using the *perspective* function. Corel calls it perspective because it simulates the effect of viewing a two-dimensional drawing in 3-D space, sort of like an image on a billboard.

✔ If perspective is like viewing a drawing on a billboard, *enveloping* is like viewing its reflection in a funhouse mirror. You can bow the edges of objects inward, outward, or even along the edges of complex paths.

✔ *Extruding* an object gives it real depth by attaching sides to the shape. A square turns into a cube, and a circle turns into a cylinder. CorelDraw accentuates the appearance of depth by automatically lighting the extruded shape and rotating it in 3-D space.

Special effects you can ignore

If you take a look at your Effects menu, you'll notice that I left out blending, lens, contour, powerclip, and powerline.

✔ *Blending* creates intermediate shapes between two selected paths. For example, if you blend between a white square and a black circle, CorelDraw creates a series of shapes that become increasingly circular as they progress from light gray to dark gray. It's a cool concept, but so is an on-screen digital clock on your TV. Its practical uses are limited. But to appease the blendaholics in the crowd, I've included a somewhat useful blend concept in the chapter "Ten Way-Cool Special Effects."

✔ *Lens* lets you apply a change of color to the parts of objects that are overlapped by the *lens object,* just like looking through a magnifying glass. Lens lets you change the color, grayscale, tint, and other boring concepts.

✔ The *contour* function is easily the least useful function in CorelDraw. It fills a path with concentric versions of itself. Theoretically, you can use the contour function to create gradations that follow the contour of a path, but you generally end up with patterns that look for all the world like shooting targets.

✔ The *powerclip* function is a *framing* feature. It lets you put a big object inside a little object. The little object acts like a window, letting you see only a partial view of the big object. You can, for example, put a rectangular bitmap inside an ellipse to create an effect sort of like those goofy photos you have taken at the fair — you know, when you stand behind a piece of cardboard that's painted with some silly scenery and has oval-shaped cutouts that you stick your face through. The only part of you that is visible is what peeks through the oval — your "I survived the MonsterCoaster" T-shirt is hidden. The powerclip is a feature that Corellians have been screaming for since Version 1, mainly because it was the only thing that the competition offered that CorelDraw didn't.

✔ The *powerline* function lets you draw calligraphic lines that really are closed paths. I don't discuss powerlines in this chapter for the obvious reason that they have nothing to do with transformations. As a matter of fact, I don't discuss the powerline function in this book, period. For all its complexities and variations, it ultimately performs less aptly and less predictably than a quill dipped in ink. If you want calligraphy, go to a drugstore and buy a 95-cent fountain pen.

Ouch! How's that for stinging commentary? Sounds good, but the truth, of course, is graft. The Pencil tool bribed me generously to ignore the powerline function, and I was more than eager to accept.

A Lesson in Perspective

Before I go any further, I want to caution you against thinking of CorelDraw as a three-dimensional drawing program just because It provides a few wacky effects that simulate 3-D. In a true 3-D program — the kind used to create effects for movies like *Terminator 2* and *Jurassic Park* — you actually build a 3-D structure called a *model* that you can walk around and view from any angle imaginable. Then you wrap surface maps around the model, specify the reflectivity of the surfaces, light the model, apply ray tracing, and perform a lot more operations that would very likely sound like Greek to you.

The point is, CorelDraw is solidly rooted in two dimensions. Its tiny supply of 3-D-like effects are pure mockery and flimflam. All in the name of good fun. Something to do on a rainy night.

Viewing your 2-D drawing in 3-D space

Now that I've diplomatically sorted out that tender issue, allow me to show you how to distort one or more objects so that they look like they've been plastered on a billboard — providing that the viewer concentrates and uses a lot of imagination.

1. **Select some random objects.**

2. **Press Ctrl+G or choose Arrange⇨Group.**

   If you don't group the objects, CorelDraw assumes that you want to distort each object individually, which can prove more than a little messy.

3. **Choose Effects⇨Add Perspective.**

   CorelDraw converts the group to a *perspective object* and automatically selects the Shape tool, as shown in Figure 9-8. Perspective objects are a unique kind of object in CorelDraw and require a special editing approach.

4. **Drag any of the four corner handles.**

   CorelDraw stretches the selection to keep up with your moves. (The following section gives extra instructions for dragging handles in different directions.)

You can drag the handles for as long as you want. It's hard to predict how perspective objects will behave at first, so be prepared to spend some time editing. If dragging a handle produces an unwanted effect, just drag the handle back or press Ctrl+Z or Alt+Backspace to undo changes.

When you finish editing the selection, click on the Arrow tool. You then exit Perspective mode and can perform other operations.

Shape tool   Perspective object

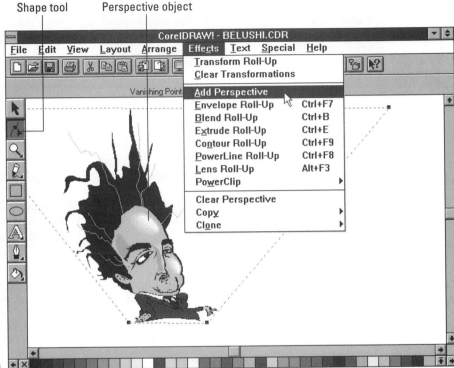

Figure 9-8:
Choose the
Effects⇨Add
Perspective
command to
convert a
group of
objects to a
perspective
object.

Putting perspective in perspective

Editing a perspective object is pretty straightforward stuff. But just in case, the following list offers a few items to bear in mind along with a few avenues for experimentation:

> ✓ Ctrl+drag a handle to drag it in a horizontal or vertical direction.

> ✓ Ctrl+Shift+drag a handle to move two handles at once. The handle you drag moves either horizontally or vertically; a neighboring handle moves the same distance in the opposite direction. When you Ctrl+Shift+drag horizontally, the handle to the left or right of the handle you drag also moves. When you Ctrl+Shift+drag vertically, the handle above or below the current handle moves.

> ✓ Imagine that the dotted outline that surrounds the perspective object extends forever in all directions. Instead of four straight sides, you have four straight lines extending across your screen. CorelDraw marks the two locations at which each pair of opposite imaginary lines meet — that is,

the point at which the left side meets the right side and the point at which the top side meets the bottom — with Xs that are called *vanishing points.* Unless you're far away from your object, you probably can't see the vanishing points because they're off-screen. But if you zoom out by pressing F3 or move two opposite sides at an extreme angle to one another (see Figure 9-9), one or both of the vanishing points comes into view.

The reason I even bring up this complicated topic is that you can drag a vanishing point to further distort the perspective object. Try it to get a feel for how it works.

Vanishing point

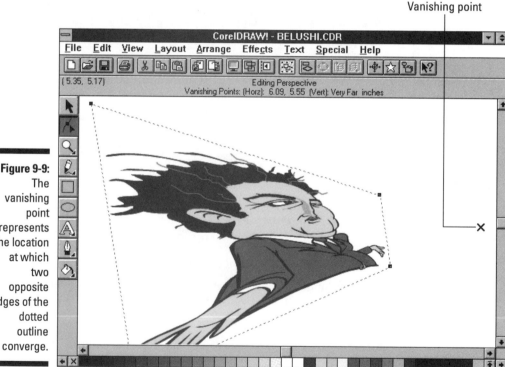

Figure 9-9: The vanishing point represents the location at which two opposite edges of the dotted outline converge.

✔ To restore the dotted outline to a rectangle and take a new stab at a perspective object, choose Effects⇨Add Perspective.

✔ To remove the most recent round of perspective edits from a selected object, choose Effects⇨Clear Perspective.

✔ To edit an existing perspective object, just select the Shape tool and click on the object.

✔ To edit the individual nodes and segments in a perspective object, you have to convert it back to paths. First press Ctrl+U (Arrange⇨Ungroup) to ungroup the object if necessary. Then select the object and choose Arrange⇨Convert to Curves (Ctrl+Q).

Envelope of Wonders

Corel's envelope function lets you bend and twist objects as if they were printed on a piece of Silly Putty. You know how you'd smoosh a piece of Silly Putty on the comics page of the newspaper and then wrap it around your little brother's face? As for why Corel calls it enveloping, I can only guess that someone in engineering or development received a pretty gnarly package from UPS.

If you've taken a look at CorelDraw's envelope feature, you probably said something like, "What the . . . ?" or perhaps more appropriately, "Duh." At least, that's what I did. But have faith. If I — king of the short attention span — could learn it, you can too. And believe me, it's worth the effort.

The ultimate distortion

Here's how it works:

1. **Select those objects (click and Shift+click).**

   There's a shocker.

2. **Group them by choosing Arrange⇨Group.**

   The envelope function works on only one object at a time. If you want to distort several objects, you need to group them into one.

3. **Press Ctrl+F7 or choose Effects⇨Envelope Roll-Up.**

   CorelDraw displays the Envelope roll-up, as shown in Figure 9-10.

4. **Click on the Add New button.**

   It's right there at the top of the roll-up. CorelDraw automatically selects the Shape tool and surrounds the selection with a dotted rectangle. The rectangle has eight handles — four at the corners and four on the sides.

5. **Select an editing mode.**

   The four icon buttons in the middle of the roll-up represent *envelope-editing modes*. For now, it's not important which one you select. (I explain how each mode works later.)

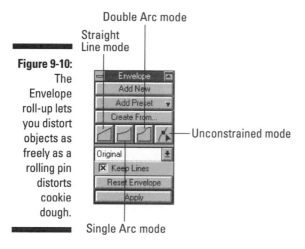

Double Arc mode

Straight
Line mode

Figure 9-10:
The
Envelope
roll-up lets
you distort
objects as
freely as a
rolling pin
distorts
cookie
dough.

Unconstrained mode

Single Arc mode

6. **Drag the handles to the shape of the distortion you want for your selected object.**

7. **Click on the Apply button in the Envelope roll-up.**

That's it! The program applies your envelope changes to your selected object.

The envelope-editing modes

The envelope-editing mode icons in the Envelope roll-up work like tools. Each one distorts the selected object in a unique and progressively more dramatic way:

- In *Straight Line mode,* CorelDraw maintains a straight side between each of the eight handles, as illustrated in Figure 9-11. It's rather like the perspective distortion, except for two things: 1) you have some additional handles to play around with; and 2) you can move the handles horizontally or vertically only. The left- and right-side handles move horizontally only; the top and bottom handles move vertically only. The corner handles move both ways.

- In *Single Arc mode,* CorelDraw permits a single arc to form between each pair of handles, as shown in Figure 9-12. Again, you can only drag the handles horizontally or vertically. Single Arc mode works best for distorting objects into hourglass and balloon shapes.

- *Double Arc mode* allows a wave to form between each handle, as illustrated in Figure 9-13. You can create rippling distortions, as if you were viewing your object under water. As with the Straight Line and Single Arc modes, you can drag the handles horizontally or vertically only.

Figure 9-11:
Dragging a
handle in
Straight Line
mode.

✔ In *Unconstrained mode,* the sky's the limit. You can edit the outline exactly as if it were a free-form path drawn with the Pencil tool. You can drag the handles — they're really nodes in this case — any which way you please. To determine the curvature of the segments between handles, CorelDraw provides you with control points, as shown in Figure 9-14.

You can add or subtract nodes by using the Node Edit roll-up. Just double-click on one of the handles to make the roll-up appear on-screen. You can even select multiple nodes at a time. In short, if you can do it to a pencil path, you can do it in the Unconstrained mode. (Chapter 4 talks more about nodes and pencil paths.)

Figure 9-12:
Single Arc
mode can
create a
slenderizing
effect.

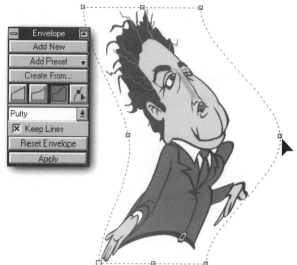

Figure 9-13:
You can create waves in Double Arc mode.

Figure 9-14:
For the distortion aficionado, there's no substitute for Unconstrained mode.

Pushing the envelope

That's as complicated as enveloping gets. If you don't read another word, you'll be able to distort your drawing to the point that its own mother wouldn't recognize it. But just in case you're hungry for more, here are a few tricks you may find helpful:

- ✔ You can use envelope-editing modes in tandem with each other. For example, you can select the Straight Line icon and drag one handle and then select the Double Arc icon and drag another handle.

- ✔ In the Unconstrained mode, the Shift and Ctrl keys behave just as they do when you're editing a pencil path. Shift+click on a node to select it without deselecting other nodes. Ctrl+drag a node to move it horizontally or vertically.

- ✔ In the other modes, Ctrl+drag a handle to move the opposite handle the same distance and direction as the handle you're dragging.

- ✔ Shift+drag to move the opposite handle the same distance as the handle you're dragging, but in the opposite direction.

- ✔ Ctrl+Shift+drag a side handle to move *all* side handles the same distance but in opposite directions. Ctrl+Shift+drag a corner handle to move all corner handles.

- ✔ If you don't feel up to editing the outline on your own, Draw can help you out. Click on the Add Preset button in the Envelope roll-up to display a menu of outline shapes, as shown in Figure 9-15. Select the outline you want to apply and then click on the Apply button.

- ✔ You can cancel an envelope distortion at any time before you click on the Apply button. Just click on the Reset Envelope button or select the Arrow tool.

- ✔ After you apply a few distortions, the dotted outline may become prohibitively wiggly. To restore the dotted outline to rectangular and take a new stab at enveloping an object, click again on the Add New button in the Envelope roll-up.

- ✔ To remove the most recent round of envelope edits from a selected object, choose Effects⇨Clear Envelope.

Well, Extru-u-ude Me!

In future years, brilliant minds no doubt will argue the merit of discussing extruding, which is one of CorelDraw's most complex functions, in a . . . *For Dummies* book (yeah, right). But I figure, what the heck — it's a fun feature, and

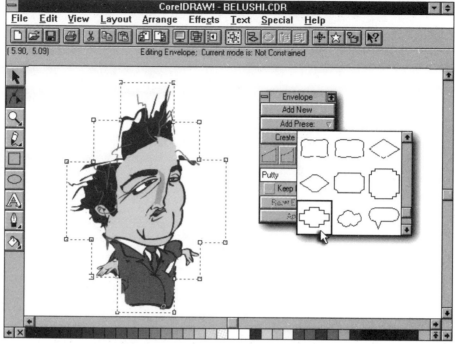

Figure 9-15:
Using Draw's predefined enveloping outlines, I managed to create a southwestern Belushi effect.

with enough effort, you may even figure out something useful to do with it. In the meantime, it's a great way to waste several hours being antisocial and playing with your computer.

Extruding in the real world

First, what is extruding? Simply put, *extrusion* is the act of assigning depth to a 2-D shape by extending its sides into the third dimension. Naturally, that doesn't make any sense, so perhaps an example is in order.

Did you ever play with one of those things that lets you crank Play-Doh through a stencil to create snaky geometric forms, as shown in Figure 9-16? Cut off the snaky bit with a plastic knife, and voilà! You have a 3-D star, polygon, or other useless piece of gook.

If this is your idea of a fond childhood memory, you are an extruder. Pasta machines extrude noodles. Sausage makers extrude columns of beef and pork by-products. Life is filled with examples of extruding.

Figure 9-16:
Play-Doh
oozing
through a
stencil in an
example of
extrusion.

Extruding in the workplace

For time immemorial, the Extrude roll-up served as the central headquarters for CorelDraw's extruding functions. Ever since the Big Bang (or thereabouts), CorelDraw users have been able to access this roll-up by choosing Effects⇨Extrude Roll-Up or pressing Ctrl+E.

As is the case when you use the enveloping feature, you can't extrude more than one object at a time. Furthermore, extruding is not applicable to groups. You can extrude a single path — open or closed — or a block of text. Sadly, I'm afraid that rules out any more transformations for John.

To extrude an object, follow these steps:

1. **Press Ctrl+E (or choose Effects⇨Extrude Roll-Up) to display the Extrude roll-up.**

2. **Select a path.**

   For now, keep it simple. Select a basic shape like a circle or a star.

3. Click on Edit in the Extrude roll-up.

A dotted *extrusion outline* representing the form of the extruded object appears on-screen, as shown in Figure 9-17. Click on the second icon along the top of the roll-up, which allows you to edit the shape of the extrusion perspective using the options in the roll-up.

4. Drag the vanishing point to change the direction of the extrusion.

Labeled in Figure 9-17, the vanishing point represents the point from which the extrusion emanates. If the star were a bullet rushing toward you, the vanishing point would be the gun.

5. Enter a value in the Depth option box.

This value determines the length of the sides that stretch away from the object toward the vanishing point. If you enter the maximum value, 99, the extrusion outline touches the vanishing point. The minimum value, 1, creates a very shallow extrusion. Figure 9-18 shows some examples.

Extrusion outline   Vanishing point

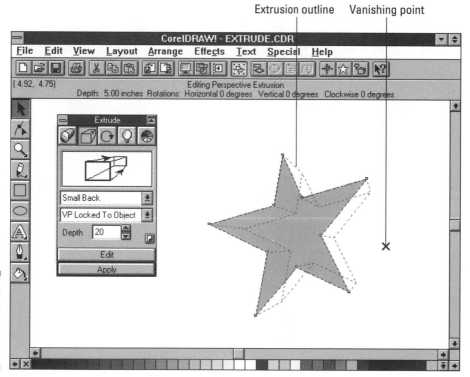

Figure 9-17:
A shape in the process of being extruded.

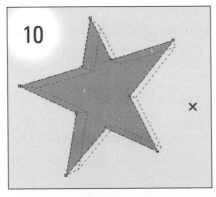
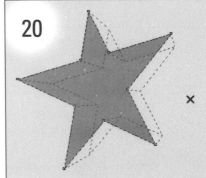
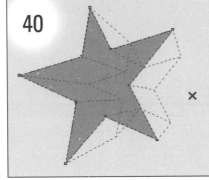
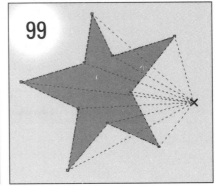

Figure 9-18:
The effect
of various
Depth
values
on the
extrusion
outline.

 6. Click on the 3-D Rotation icon.

The 3-D Rotation tool is the third icon in the Extrude roll-up.

7. Use the arrow icons in the Extrude roll-up to spin the selected object in 3-D space.

The arrows are labeled in Figure 9-19. The clockwise and counterclockwise arrows rotate the object in 2-D space, just like options in the Rotate & Skew dialog box. The left and right arrows rotate the object like a globe around a vertical axis. And the up and down arrows rotate the object like a . . . well, like a pig on a spit. Each click on an arrow icon rotates the object 5 degrees.

If you want to unrotate the object, click on the X icon.

8. Take a breather.

Maybe get some exercise. Now's a good time to work on those biceps.

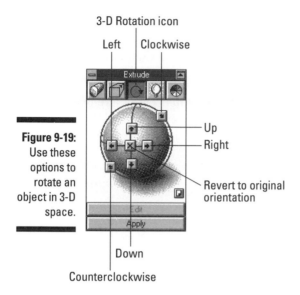

3-D Rotation icon

Left   Clockwise

Up
Right

Figure 9-19:
Use these
options to
rotate an
object in 3-D
space.

Revert to original
orientation

Down

Counterclockwise

 9. **Click on the Light Source Direction tool in the roll-up.**

The Light Source Direction tool is the fourth icon on the top of the
Extrude roll-up.

 10. **Click on the first light bulb to turn on the automatic lighting function.**

The *light bulbs* are labeled 1, 2, and 3 in the roll-up, as shown in Figure 9-20.
This means that you can generate three different light sources. I can see
the light!

Light Source Direction tool

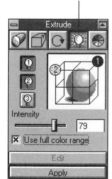

Figure 9-20:
The three
light bulbs
new to
CorelDraw 5.

11. Click on light bulb #1 to put it on the placement grid.

You should then see a circled number 1 on-screen. The 1 represents light bulb #1 and its location relative to the object. You can place the bulb on top of the object, below it, in front of it, behind it, and so forth. As you push the bulb around, the shading on the sphere changes, giving you an approximation of how your object will look subject to different light source placements. You can create additional light sources by putting light bulbs #2 and #3 on the grid as well; just click on each bulb and place it wherever you want. Don't overdo it, though — having too many light sources removes the dramatic effect of shading.

12. Drag the Intensity slider to increase or decrease the amount of light.

Alternatively, you can enter a value between 0 and 100 in the option box. Values below 50 get darker, and 0 is black; values above 50 get lighter, and 100 is white.

Keep in mind that small changes to the Intensity value make a big difference in how CorelDraw colors the object. Any value below 25, for example, almost guarantees an entirely black object.

13. Click on the Extrusion Coloring tool in the Extrude roll-up.

The options shown in Figure 9-21 appear.

Extrusion Coloring tool

Figure 9-21:
Click on the
Extrusion
Coloring tool
to color the
3-D object.

14. Select the Shade radio button to fill the partially lighted portions of the object with continuous gradations.

There's no reason *not* to select this option.

15. Select the desired colors from the From and To menus.

For the best results, select a light and dark shade of the same color.

16. Click on the Apply button.

CorelDraw automatically draws and fills the object to your specifications. Figure 9-22 shows the star from Figure 9-17 after I rotated and illuminated it.

Figure 9-22:
A three-dimensional star created in a two-dimensional drawing program.

Extruding is a long process, but it's not particularly complicated. The only place where you might get hung up is in the light-source direction settings. Your object may turn completely white or completely black, and very small changes to the Intensity value may produce ridiculously dramatic effects. As I said earlier, Draw is no 3-D drawing program; in its defense, it was never meant to be.

The point is, don't sweat it too much. After you finish creating and lighting your object, you can break the 3-D object apart and fill it as you please by taking the following steps:

1. Choose Arrange➪Separate.

This command separates the original object from its extruded sides.

2. Shift+click on the original object with the Arrow tool.

Doing so deselects the object, leaving only the sides selected.

3. Press Ctrl+U or choose Arrange➪Ungroup.

CorelDraw automatically creates the sides as a group, so you need to ungroup them before you can edit the fills of the extruded sides.

After you ungroup the individual paths that make up the extruded object, you can fill each path in the extrusion independently to create a better looking 3-D drawing.

Avoid applying any of these steps to extruded curved objects because they can have more than 100 extruded sides.

Presets and VPs

CorelDraw 5 has two unique extrusion features not included in previous versions: Presets and Vanishing Point control. You control both by clicking on the second icon at the top of the Extrude roll-up.

Presets

In case the coloring and shading processes are a little hairy for you, CorelDraw 5 includes built-in extrusion effects, which are placed in two different locations. *Presets* are prebuilt extrusions and coloring schemes that help you get closer to achieving the effect you're trying to build. The first button on the Extrusion roll-up gets you to the preset screen shown in Figure 9-23 — the preset even gives you a cute little commentary on what it's going to do. It's kinda like a chef telling you how he's gonna turn eggs into omelets. The presets may save you time in delivering the right look and feel to your extrusion. If you can't find the appropriate preset, you can make your own preset after you build it for the first time.

Figure 9-23:
The preset
screen that
you access
through the
Extrude
roll-up.

Preset roll-up

You can find this roll-up under Special⇨Presets Roll-Up or by pressing Alt+F5. How does the Preset roll-up differ from the Preset function in the Extrusion roll-up? Beats me. It appears that the extrusion-based presets can be found here, too . . . along with other nonextrusion presets. You can almost call these presets macros.

With this roll-up, you can add 3-D concepts and nifty design ideas to your text or objects. The presets can add extrusions, blends, shading, and even other objects to your screen. Take a look at Figure 9-24 to see how you can modify simple text into gosh-cool-how'd-ya-do-that stuff.

This roll-up contains quite a library of special effects and quasi-clip art. You can instantly build 3-D buttons from circles, bars of gold from rectangles, and beveled sign-plates from a chunk of text. I suggest that you take a look at some of them, take them apart, and see how they were built. You may want to modify them or build your own as well. After you build your effects, you can save them in the library for later use. Creating your own preset effects is a great time-saver because you don't have to build complicated effects from scratch every time you want to use them — you just call them up from the library and apply them to selected objects.

Figure 9-24:
You can add a variety of prebuilt effects through the Preset roll-up.

Vanishing Points

These features give you better control of vanishing point behavior, as follows:

- ✓ **VP Locked to Object:** When you move the object, the vanishing point follows along, staying at the same distance and direction. This option is always the default.

- ✓ **VP Locked to Page:** When you move the object, the extrusion is recalculated; the vanishing point is locked to the location where you placed it. Architects and others making drawings of buildings and railroad tracks love this one to death.

- ✓ **Copy VP from . . . :** This option lets you copy the vanishing point attributes of an already built extrusion and apply them to the new object. It's a great time-saver.

- ✓ **Shared Vanishing Point:** This option is a built-in Copy and Clone in the same shot. When you move the vanishing point, the program recalculates the extrusions of all objects that share that vanishing point.

Part III
Getting the Message Out There (Wherever There Is)

The 5th Wave   **By Rich Tennant**

"These kidnappers are clever, Lieutenant. Look at this ransom note, the use of 4-color graphics to highlight the victims photograph. And the fonts! They must be creating their own—must be over 35 typefaces here...."

In this part...

*1*f all there was to CorelDraw was drawing, this book would be over by now. But as luck would have it, CorelDraw — particularly Version 5 — is equally adept at creating documents, such as fliers, newsletters, and those little wrappers that cover your hangers when they come back from the dry cleaners.

Like most desktop publishing programs, CorelDraw lets you enter and edit text, apply special formatting attributes, specify the size and orientation of a page, and print your document to paper. Unlike most DTP programs, however, Draw also lets you drag letters independently of each other, create text on a circle, and actually edit the shape of characters of type. Few other pieces of software provide such a wide gamut of publishing capabilities.

At the risk of sounding like the crowned king of hyperbole, there's never been a tool like CorelDraw for slapping words onto a bit of sliced timber, not since Johann Gensfleisch — who mostly went about using his mom's maiden name, Gutenberg — decided to smack some letters on a particularly abbreviated version of the Bible.

Chapter 10
The Care and Planting of Text

. . . .

In This Chapter

▶ Creating artistic text that's truly artistic

▶ Adding text to a text block

▶ Moving, scaling, and rotating text

▶ Creating and editing paragraph text

▶ Pouring characters from one text block to another

▶ Converting artistic text to paragraph text and vice versa

▶ Assigning formatting attributes

▶ Getting to know PostScript and TrueType fonts

▶ Checking the spelling of your text

▶ Looking for synonyms

▶ Inserting symbols

. . . .

*T*here's more to creating text than whacking your fingers against the keyboard in a hysterical frenzy. Remember all that stuff you learned in typing class? Forget it. Yesterday's news. I, for example, can't type — not a word — yet I write professionally, I format like a champ, and I don't have any wrist problems. Knock on wood . . . aaugh, I knocked too hard! I think I'm going numb!

Had you going again, didn't I? And you know why? It's not that the text is lucid and gripping. Surely you figured that out by now. It's because the text *looks good*. The pages in this book appear professional — granted, in a sort of goofy way — so you naturally assume that a professional is behind them, not some crackpot like me.

The fact of the matter is, in the world of corporate communications, text is judged as much by its appearance as its content. Not to put too fine a point on it, text is art. Simply entering thoughtful and convincing text with a hint of Hippocrene genius is not enough. But don't panic — knowing what to do with text after you enter it is what this chapter is all about. (You were beginning to wonder, huh?)

A Furst Luk at Tekst

Unless you already know a thing or two about word processing and desktop publishing, this chapter is going to seem like a trip through the dictionary. You're going to learn so many terms that your brain will very likely swell up and pop. To prepare, you may want to tie a bandanna around your head and set a squeegee near your monitor.

For starters, text is made up of letters, numbers, and various symbols such as &, %, $, and, my favorite, §, which is meaningless to most of Earth's inhabitants. If § crops up in your documents, it's a sure sign that either a lawyer or an extraterrestrial has been using your machine.

Together, these little text elements are called *characters.* A collection of characters is called a *text block* or, in deference to its path cousins, a *text object.* A text block can contain a single word, a sentence, a paragraph, multiple paragraphs, or an odd collection of §s arranged in the shape of a crop circle.

In CorelDraw, you work with two kinds of text blocks:

- ✔ *Artistic text* accommodates logos, headlines, labels, and other short passages of text that require special treatment.

- ✔ *Paragraph text* is suited to longer passages, such as full sentences, paragraphs, pithy quotes, encyclopedia entries, epic poems, works of modern fiction, and letters to Grandma.

CorelDraw also offers access to specialized symbols, which — although they're not technically text — you can use as independent objects to highlight text objects or adorn your drawing. Symbols are organized thematically into categories, such as animals, furniture, medicine, and semaphore. No smoke signals yet, but I hear that's in the works.

Using the Text Tools

You create different kinds of text by using different tools, which are all accessible from the Text tool flyout menu, shown in Figure 10-1. To display the flyout menu, click and hold the mouse on the Text tool — which may appear as an *A* or as a small page — or double-click on the icon. Then select the desired tool from the menu.

After you select the Artistic Text tool or Paragraph Text tool from the flyout menu, the tool occupies the Text tool slot in the toolbox. This setup means that you can return to the tool without hassling with the flyout menu.

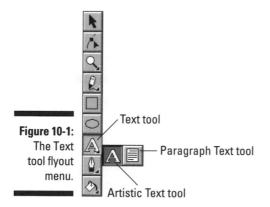

Figure 10-1:
The Text
tool flyout
menu.

Text tool

Paragraph Text tool

Artistic Text tool

The Artistic Text tool

Creating text with the Artistic Text tool is as easy as drawing a rectangle or oval:

 1. Select the Artistic Text tool.

If the *A* icon is available in the toolbox, click on it. If not, select the Artistic Text tool from the flyout menu.

Better yet, just press F8.

2. Click in the drawing area at the point where you want the text to begin.

After you click, a vertical line called the *insertion marker* appears on-screen. The thick, black insertion marker indicates the location where new text will appear.

3. Type away.

As you type, the corresponding characters appear on-screen. The insertion marker moves rightward with the addition of each character (see the upper example in Figure 10-2), indicating the location at which the next character will appear.

 4. When you finish, select the Arrow tool.

As illustrated in the lower example in Figure 10-2, eight square handles surround the text to show that it is selected.

Nearly every computer program in existence lets you change text after you create it. CorelDraw is no exception. To add more characters, select the Artistic Text tool and click inside the text block at the location where you want the new characters to appear. In Figure 10-3, for example, I first clicked in front of the *a* in *antiquated* and entered the word *an*. Next, I clicked between the *d* and the period and entered *piece of garbage*.

Figure 10-2:
Artistic text
as it
appears
when you
enter text
(top) and
after you
select the
Arrow tool
(bottom).

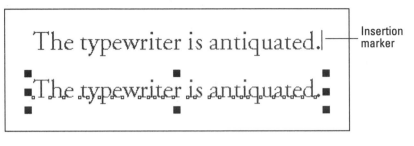

The typewriter is antiquated.| ——— Insertion marker

The typewriter is antiquated.

Figure 10-3:
Adding text
to an
existing text
block.

The typewriter is an|antiquated.

The typewriter is an antiquated
piece of garbage|.

Here are a few more ways to enter and edit artistic text:

✔ Unlike text you create using a word processor, artistic text does not *wrap* to the next line on its own. You have to manually insert line breaks by pressing the Enter key, just as you have to press the Return key to start a new line when you use a typewriter.

✔ To move the text block to a new location in the drawing area, drag it with the Arrow tool.

✔ You also can move a text block by selecting it with the Arrow tool and then pressing an arrow key to nudge the block to a new location.

When you drag the handles of an artistic text block with the Arrow tool, you change the size of the characters. Drag a corner handle to scale the characters proportionally.

✔ Drag the top or bottom handle to make the text tall and skinny, as in Figure 10-4. This kind of text is called *condensed*.

✔ Drag the left or right handle to make the text short and fat. This kind of text is called *expanded* text.

✔ Click a second time on a text block to access the rotation and skew handles, which you can use to create rotated and slanted text. The rotation and skew handles work just like those described in Chapter 9.

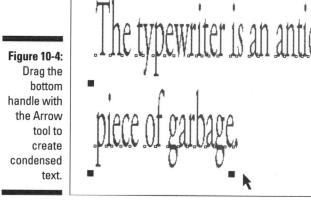

Figure 10-4:
Drag the
bottom
handle with
the Arrow
tool to
create
condensed
text.

The Paragraph Text tool

Here's how to use the Paragraph Text tool to create paragraph text:

1. **Select the Paragraph Text tool.**

   If the page icon is not available in the toolbox, select the tool from the flyout menu. If that's too much effort — which it *is* — press Shift+F8.

2. **Drag in the drawing area to specify the size of the text block.**

   You create a marquee (a dotted rectangle), as shown in Figure 10-5.

3. **Bang those keys.**

   As you work out your aggression, text fills up the text block. Unlike artistic text, paragraph text wraps to the next line when it exceeds the right-hand boundary of the text block, as demonstrated in the lower example of Figure 10-5.

4. **When you finish, select the Arrow tool.**

   Eight square handles surround the text block, just as they do when you create artistic text.

Some of the stuff I said about artistic text applies to paragraph text as well. For example, you can add more characters to a block of paragraph text by clicking inside the text block with either the Paragraph Text tool or the Artistic Text tool and then typing away. You can move a selected block of paragraph text to a new location by dragging it with the Arrow tool or by pressing one or two arrow keys.

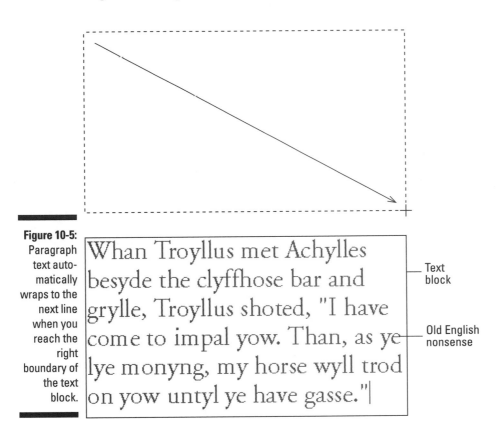

Figure 10-5:
Paragraph
text auto-
matically
wraps to the
next line
when you
reach the
right
boundary of
the text
block.

Text
block

Old English
nonsense

But a few operations work very differently:

- Dragging a corner handle of a block of paragraph text scales the text block, but the text inside remains the same size. CorelDraw reflows the text to fit it inside the new text block borders, as demonstrated in Figure 10-6.

- Click on the text block twice with the Arrow tool to display the rotate and skew handles. When you rotate a block of paragraph text, the characters inside the text block rotate, just as they do when you rotate a block of artistic text. But when you skew a block of paragraph text, CorelDraw slants only the text block, as shown in Figure 10-7. The characters remain upright and reflow to fill the borders of the text block.

You can put no more than 4,000 characters into a single paragraph — which is roughly the equivalent of two pages in this book with no figures. You're also limited to 860 paragraphs per .CDR file. Okay, so maybe George Bernard Shaw would have had problems with this limitation. He and William Faulkner could have moaned about it endlessly in 10,000-character postcards to each other. But I don't think you'll have any problems. (If you do find yourself creating anything close to 860 paragraphs in CorelDraw, see a professional doctor and look up the definition of "word processor.")

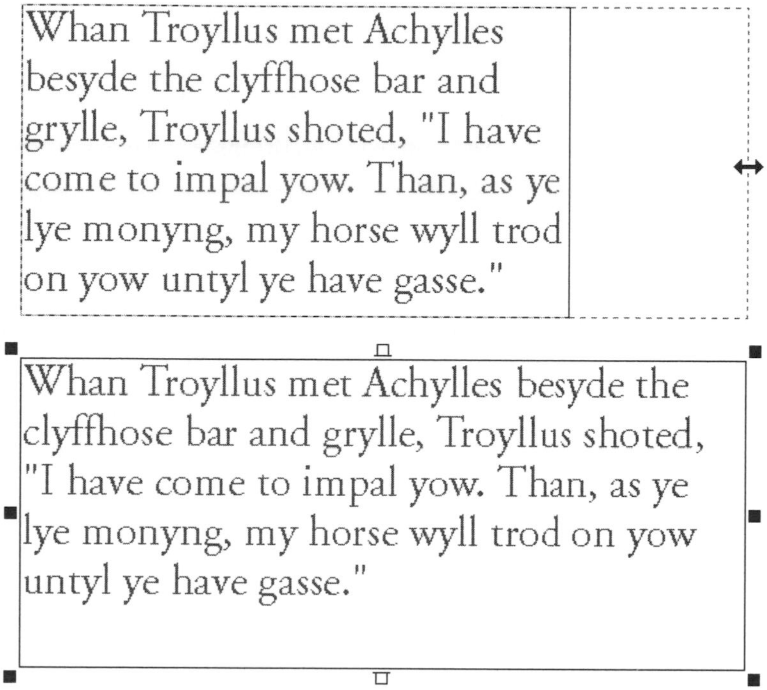

Whan Troyllus met Achylles besyde the clyffhose bar and grylle, Troyllus shoted, "I have come to impal yow. Than, as ye lye monyng, my horse wyll trod on yow untyl ye have gasse."

Figure 10-6: Draw resizes the text block and reflows the characters to fit the new boundaries.

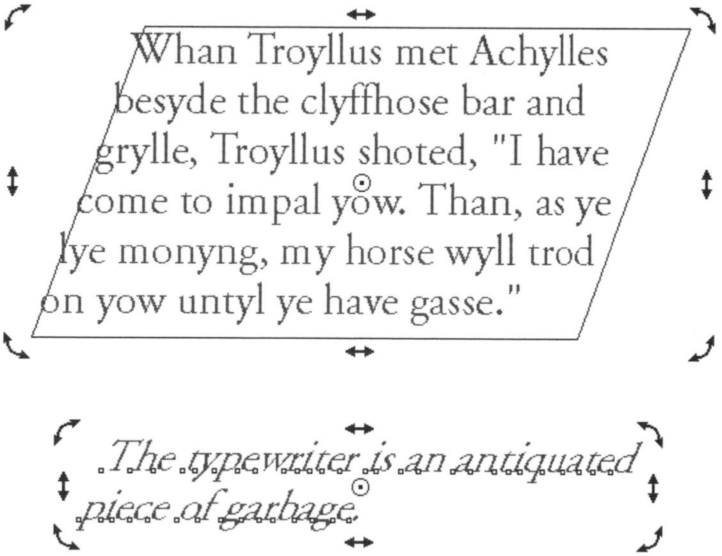

Whan Troyllus met Achylles besyde the clyffhose bar and grylle, Troyllus shoted, "I have come to impal yow. Than, as ye lye monyng, my horse wyll trod on yow untyl ye have gasse."

Whan Troyllus met Achylles besyde the clyffhose bar and grylle, Troyllus shoted, "I have come to impal yow. Than, as ye lye monyng, my horse wyll trod on yow untyl ye have gasse."

Figure 10-7: Skewed paragraph text (top) compared with skewed artistic text (bottom).

The typewriter is an antiquated piece of garbage.

Navigating among the letters

Whether you're working with artistic or paragraph text, you can specify the location of the insertion marker inside the text by clicking in the text block with either of the Text tools. After you position the insertion marker, you can move it around by using any of the following techniques:

- ✔ When the Text tool is active, the arrow keys move the insertion marker inside a text block. Press the left- or right-arrow key to move the insertion marker in one-character increments. Press the up- or down-arrow key to move from one line of type to the next.

- ✔ To move in whole-word increments, press Ctrl plus the left- or right-arrow key.

- ✔ Press Ctrl and the up-arrow key to move to the beginning of the current paragraph. Press Ctrl and the down-arrow key to move to the end of the paragraph.

- ✔ Press the Home key to move the insertion marker to the beginning of the current line. Press End to move to the end of the current line.

- ✔ Ctrl+Home moves the insertion marker to the beginning of the text block currently being viewed. Ctrl+End moves you to the end of the text block being viewed.

Flowing Text Between Multiple Blocks

When you're entering long passages of paragraph text, the text may exceed the boundaries of the text block. Every character that you entered still exists; you just can't see it. To view the hidden text, you can do the following:

- ✔ Reduce the size of the characters so that they fit better, as described later in this chapter.

- ✔ Enlarge the text block by dragging one of the handles.

- ✔ Pour the text into a new text block.

That's right, you can *pour* excess text from one text block into another as if it were liquid. It's like splitting a bottle of Dom Perignon with a date. At the end of the bottle, you pour yourself a heaping glass and then exclaim, "What, no champagne left? How outrageous! I am so sorry. Here, let me pour you some from my own glass." Not spilling a drop, you evenly transfer half the contents of your glass to your date's glass. How extremely valiant.

Pouring text is similar to pouring champagne, except that it doesn't cost any money and it won't impress your date. Here's how it works:

1. **Drag with the Paragraph Text tool to create a text block.**

2. **Enter far too much text.**

   Type every page of *Beowulf.* This is your chance to bone up on classical literature.

3. **Select the Arrow tool.**

   Much of the text you entered should not be visible on-screen.

4. **Click on the top or bottom handle of the text block.**

   These hollow handles are called *tabs.* Click on the top tab to pour the first lines of text into a new text block. Click on the bottom tab to pour the hidden lines of text. After you click on a tab, your cursor changes to a page icon (see Figure 10-8).

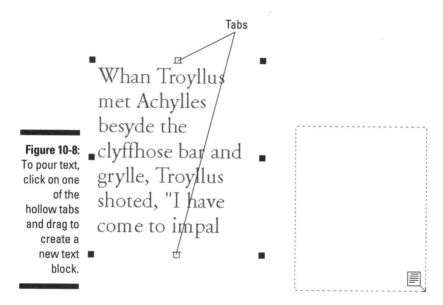

Tabs

Whan Troyllus met Achylles besyde the clyffhose bar and grylle, Troyllus shoted, "I have come to impal

Figure 10-8: To pour text, click on one of the hollow tabs and drag to create a new text block.

5. **Drag to create a second text block.**

   Figure 10-8 illustrates this process. CorelDraw then automatically takes the lines of text you originally entered into the first text block and pours them into the next text block, as shown in Figure 10-9.

   Notice that plus signs appear inside the bottom tab on the first text block and the top tab on the second. The signs show that a *link* exists between the two text blocks.

   To experiment with the link, keep stepping:

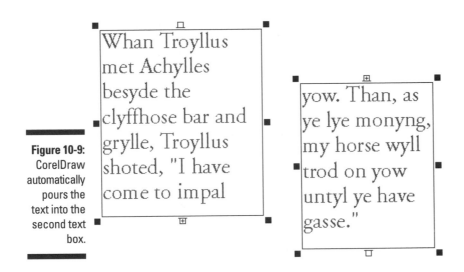

Figure 10-9:
CorelDraw
automatically
pours the
text into the
second text
box.

> Whan Troyllus met Achylles besyde the clyffhose bar and grylle, Troyllus shoted, "I have come to impal

> yow. Than, as ye lye monyng, my horse wyll trod on yow untyl ye have gasse."

6. **Drag the bottom tab of the first text block upward.**

   You now have less room in the first text block for text. The overflow text automatically pours into the second text block.

7. **Press the Delete key.**

   Assuming that the first text block is still selected, Draw deletes the text block. But it does not delete the text inside the text block. Instead, it pours the text into the second text block.

   Pretty keen, huh? As long as at least one text block in the link remains in your drawing, the text remains intact. Now, if you go and delete the second text block, CorelDraw indeed deletes the text because there is no longer any place for the text to go.

CorelDraw 5 lets you pour text between as many text blocks as you like. (Okay, I bet there's some maximum, like 32 or 256 or something, but who cares? You'd be a nut to *want* to pour text between that many text blocks!) You can even pour your text across multiple pages; I discuss multipage documents in Chapter 12.

Before You Can Format, You Must Select

To change the appearance of characters in a text block, you assign *formatting attributes* such as typeface, style, size, and a few others that I'll get to later. But before you can assign formatting attributes, you have to select the text.

You can select text in two ways in CorelDraw. You can either click on the text block with the Arrow tool, in which case any formatting changes affect all characters inside the text block. Or you can highlight individual characters and words with the Artistic Text tool or the Paragraph Text tool. Your formatting changes then affect only those selected characters.

You know what? I'm really sick of saying "either the Artistic Text tool or the Paragraph Text tool" and I bet you're just as sick of reading it. From here on out, it doesn't matter which tool you use, so I'm just going to say "a Text tool," which means either of them, or "the Text tools," which means both of them, or "the elbow wrench," which means neither of them.

Selecting with a Text tool

Using the Text tools is the preferred method for selecting text because it enables you to make selective changes. For example, you can make a single word **bold** or *italicize a passage of text.* The following items explain how to use a Text tool to select type in any kind of text block:

- Drag with a Text tool over the characters that you want to select. To show that the characters are selected, CorelDraw *highlights* them — that is, sets them against a gray (or other colored) background. Generally, you use this technique to select type within a single text block. However, you can drag across type in linked text blocks, as illustrated in Figure 10-10.

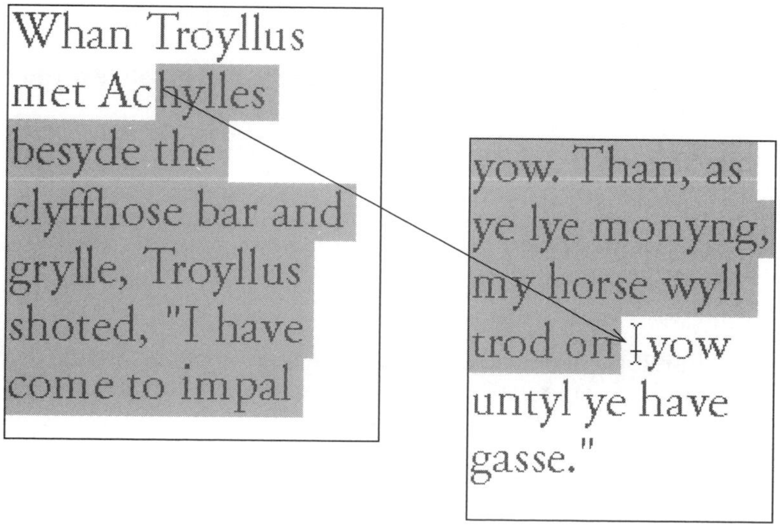

Figure 10-10: Drag with a Text tool to select type in linked text blocks.

Whan Troyllus met Achylles besyde the clyffhose bar and grylle, Troyllus shoted, "I have come to impal

yow. Than, as ye lye monyng, my horse wyll trod on yow untyl ye have gasse."

- ✔ Double-click on a word to select the word.

- ✔ Ctrl+click on a word to select the entire sentence.

- ✔ Click to set the insertion marker at one end of the text you want to select. Then Shift+click at the other end of the desired selection. Draw selects all text between your click and Shift+click. For example, to select the highlighted text in Figure 10-10, you would click between the *c* and *h* in *Achylles* and then Shift+click between the words *on* and *yow* in the second text block.

- ✔ Press the Shift key in tandem with the left- or right-arrow key to select one character at a time. Press Shift plus the up- or down-arrow key to select whole lines.

Converting from artistic to paragraph text and vice versa

Want to put your newfound selection capabilities to work? Here are a few techniques that *require* that you select with a Text tool rather than the Arrow tool.

Here's the scenario: You created a block of artistic or paragraph text, but now it occurs to you that you made the wrong choice. No problem. You can easily convert one variety of text to the other by selecting the text with a Text tool and transferring it to a new text block via the Clipboard.

To convert paragraph text to artistic text, follow these steps:

1. **With the Paragraph Text tool, select the paragraph text you want to convert.**

2. **Press Ctrl+C or Ctrl+Insert.**

   This action copies the text to the Clipboard.

3. **Select the Artistic Text tool and click the cursor somewhere in the document.**

4. **Press Ctrl+V or Shift+Insert.**

   CorelDraw automatically pastes the text into a new artistic text block. Now you can perform all those amazing special effects that are only applicable to artistic text (see Chapter 11).

You say you don't want artistic text? You want to be able to create long passages that flow between multiple linked text blocks? Well then, to convert artistic text to paragraph text, do this:

1. **With the Artistic Text tool, select the artistic text you want to convert.**

   Don't select the text with the Arrow tool; it won't do for this purpose.

2. **Press Ctrl+C or Ctrl+Insert.**

   Again, the text hightails it to the Clipboard.

3. **Select the Paragraph Text tool.**

4. **Drag to create a new text block.**

   Or click inside an existing text block to set the location of the insertion marker.

5. **Press Ctrl+V or Shift+Insert.**

   CorelDraw pastes the heretofore artistic text into the block of paragraph text.

Okay, Now You Can Format

Yes, indeed, after you select some text to play around with, you're ready to assign formatting attributes. Now, a lot of folks use the Character Attributes dialog box (Text⇨Character) to change the typeface and other stuff, but I'm going to ignore it because there's a better way. The Text roll-up, which appears in Figure 10-11, provides access to all essential formatting functions without a lot of flopping about or monkeying around, two activities which are beneath such a rarefied life form as you.

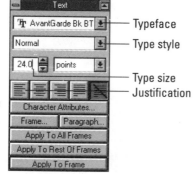

Figure 10-11:
The Text
roll-up.

To display the Text roll-up, choose Text⇨Text Roll-Up or press Ctrl+F2.

The primary formatting attributes that you can change with the Text roll-up are typeface, type style, type size, and justification, each of which is described in the following sections.

Selecting a typeface

Changing the typeface is your number-one method for controlling the appearance of your text. Just in case you're wondering what I'm talking about, a *typeface* is a uniquely stylized alphabet. The idea is that the *a* in one typeface looks different from the *a* in another typeface.

Some folks refer to typefaces as *fonts.* Back in the old days — until as recently as 20 years ago — each letter was printed using a separate chunk of metal, and all the pieces of metal for one typeface were stored in a container called a *font.* (This use of the word, incidentally, is based on the French word *fonte,* which means a casting, as in typecasting. It has nothing to do with the baptismal font — you know, one of those basins that holds holy water — which is based on the Latin word *fontis,* which means spring. Dang, this stuff is interesting!)

CorelDraw includes about 50 quintillion fonts (typefaces) on CD-ROM that you can install in Windows. You also can use any PostScript or TrueType font that you've installed in Windows. If you don't know what PostScript and TrueType are, read the Technical Stuff sidebar — or, better yet, don't worry about it.

You must select the text first before you can apply changes to it.

If you want to preview what a font looks like, do this:

1. **Click on the typeface option.**

   The typeface drop-down list appears. CorelDraw also displays a preview box to the left side of the roll-up (see Figure 10-12).

2. **Use the down- and up-arrow keys to scroll through the list.**

   Draw updates the preview box to show the selected typeface.

Typeface preview box

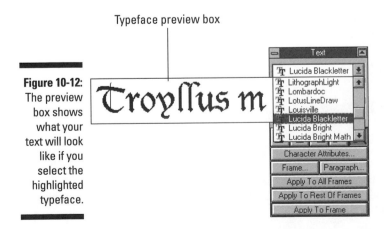

Figure 10-12: The preview box shows what your text will look like if you select the highlighted typeface.

Changing the type style

Most typefaces offer four *type styles*: plain, *italic,* **bold,** and ***bold italic.*** You can choose one of these styles by selecting it from the type style drop-down list and then clicking on the Apply button. The type style menu is the second drop-down list in the Text roll-up (see Figure 10-11).

As you can with typefaces, you can preview type styles by clicking on the type style option and pressing the down- and up-arrow keys.

Enlarging or reducing the type size

Remember the discussion of line widths back in Chapter 7? I said that line widths are measured in *points* and that one point equals ½ of an inch. Well, type is also measured in points. After all, type is generally pretty little. Even monster-big headlines in supermarket tabloids — you know, like "England Frets as Princess Di Wears Unbecoming Swimsuits" or "Aliens Ate My Sweetheart and Then Complained about the Taste" — don't get much bigger than an inch tall. For this reason, points are an ideal and time-honored unit of measure among typographers, layout artists, and others who do their best to try to attract your attention to the written word.

The typeface rivalry that isn't worth knowing about

You may not associate something as fundamental as a technology with a brand name, but the truth is, *everything* has a brand name. Billy Joel is a registered trademark, for crying out loud. So if your last name is Joel, don't even *think* about naming your kid Billy.

Anyway, the two big brands in the world of digital typography are PostScript and TrueType. Developed by Adobe Systems — the folks who create rival drawing program Adobe Illustrator — the *PostScript font format* is the professional printing standard. Hewlett-Packard and several other printer manufacturers offer support for PostScript. Adobe also sells a Windows font manager called ATM (Adobe Type Manager) that lets you print PostScript fonts to non-PostScript printers.

Microsoft and Apple were sick of Adobe, a relatively small company, having this monopoly of the font market. So they got together and codeveloped the *TrueType font format,* a collaboration that seemed as likely as the United States and Russia joining forces to organize a worldwide polo tournament right after the Bay of Pigs.

They pulled it off, though, and Microsoft amassed its 17th fortune by selling TrueType fonts to eager consumers. Windows offers built-in support for TrueType and can print TrueType fonts to nearly any printer model. It's been such a success, in fact, that CorelDraw converted its entire 50 quintillion-font library to TrueType format.

Type is measured from the bottommost point on a lowercase *g* to the tippy-topmost peak of a lowercase *b*. (Lowercase letters such as *b, d, k,* and others are generally taller than capital letters.) If you're familiar with typewriter terminology, *elite type* is 10 points tall — roughly the size of the type you're currently reading — while *pica type* is 12 points tall.

To change the type size of your text in Draw, enter any value between 0.7 and 2160.0 points (30 inches!) in the type size option box (labeled in Figure 10-11). Then click on the Apply button.

If you are missing some text in the paragraph box after applying a typesize change, resize the box or flow the extra hidden text to a new paragraph box.

Mucking about with justification

The buttons in the middle of the Text roll-up control the alignment of the lines of type in a text block, which is known as *justification* — as in, "We need no justification to call this what we please." Reading from left to right, the justification buttons work as follows:

- ✔ The *left justification* button aligns the left sides of all lines of text in a text block. The text in this book, for example, is left justified.

- ✔ The *center justification* button centers all lines of type within the text block.

- ✔ The *right justification* button aligns the right sides of all lines of text.

- ✔ The *full justification* button aligns both the left and right sides of the text. As you can see in the last example of Figure 10-13, CorelDraw has to increase the horizontal space between characters and words to make this happen. This option is applicable to paragraph text only.

- ✔ The *no justification* button — the one on the far right of the row of justification buttons — doesn't work. I know, that's a terrible thing to say, but it's true. Usually, the no justification button produces the same effect as the left justification button. But when you get into the more complicated techniques described in the next chapter, it can wreak havoc on your text. The technical support guy I talked to claimed that he never in his career received a call about this option. So not only does it not work, nobody cares about it.

Figure 10-13 shows the results of applying the left, center, right, and full justification options. The gray areas behind the text represent the text blocks.

When applied to artistic text, the justification options actually change the location of the text block on the page. If you select the right justification button, for example, the right side of the text block scoots over to where the left side of the text block used to be.

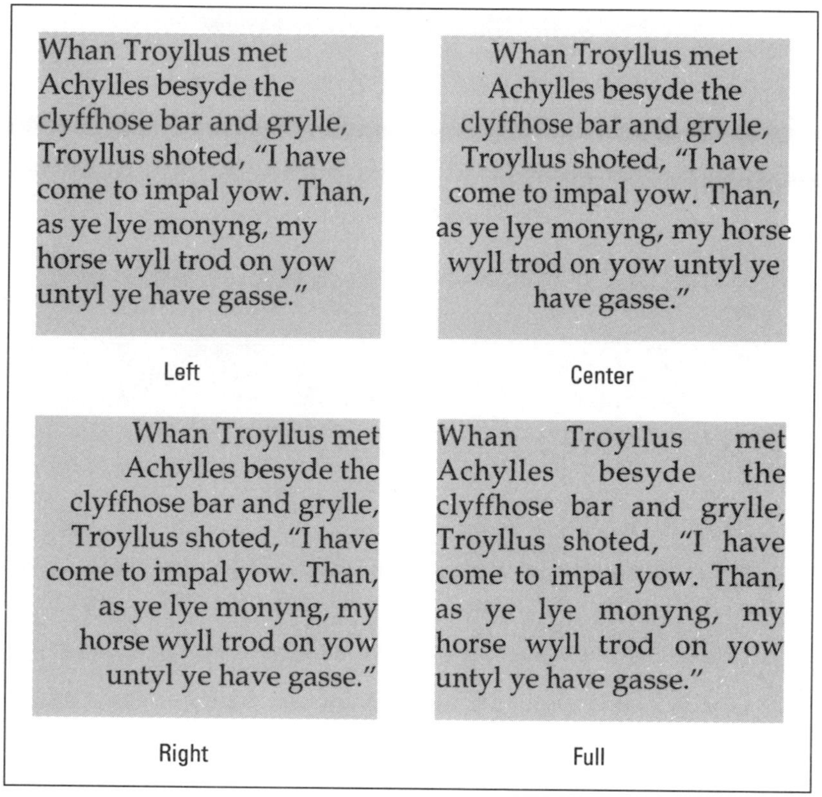

Whan Troyllus met Achylles besyde the clyffhose bar and grylle, Troyllus shoted, "I have come to impal yow. Than, as ye lye monyng, my horse wyll trod on yow untyl ye have gasse."

Left

Whan Troyllus met Achylles besyde the clyffhose bar and grylle, Troyllus shoted, "I have come to impal yow. Than, as ye lye monyng, my horse wyll trod on yow untyl ye have gasse."

Center

Whan Troyllus met Achylles besyde the clyffhose bar and grylle, Troyllus shoted, "I have come to impal yow. Than, as ye lye monyng, my horse wyll trod on yow untyl ye have gasse."

Right

Whan Troyllus met Achylles besyde the clyffhose bar and grylle, Troyllus shoted, "I have come to impal yow. Than, as ye lye monyng, my horse wyll trod on yow untyl ye have gasse."

Full

Figure 10-13: The primary justification options offered by CorelDraw.

Checking Your Spelling

Granted, CorelDraw isn't a word processor. But that doesn't mean that you want to look stupid because you can't spell *leptodactylous* (that word, by the way, means that you have slender toes). For this reason, Draw can check and help you correct your spelling. Okay, so it doesn't know how to spell *leptodactylous* any better than you do. But it does know several thousand common words, and you can teach it to spell *leptodactylous* if you so desire.

Correcting your work

Here's how to check the spelling of words in your document:

1. **Select artistic text or the paragraph text box that you want to check.**
2. **Choose Text⇨Spell Checker.**

   The Spell Check dialog box shown in Figure 10-14 appears.

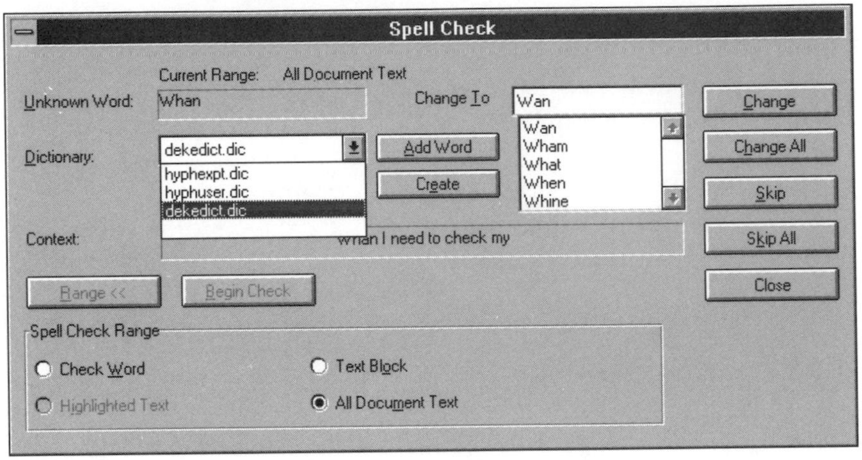

Figure 10-14: Draw finds many spelling problems in my historically authentic Old English text.

3. **Click on the Range button.**

   In the Spell Check Range portion of the dialog box, choose a radio button to tell Draw which part of the document you want to spell-check. You can tell it to check a word that you enter into the Unknown Word text box; all highlighted text; a selected text block; or all the document text.

4. **Click on Begin Check and wait for CorelDraw to find a unknown word.**

   When it does, it displays the word in the upper-left corner of the dialog box.

5. **Select an alternative from the scrolling list.**

   In Figure 10-14, CorelDraw suggests such humorless replacements as *whine, wan,* and *when.*

6. **Click on the Change button.**

   Draw replaces your misspelled word with the alternative you selected from the scrolling list. Then the program automatically sets about searching for the next misspelling.

7. **Repeat Steps 4 through 6.**

8. **When you see the** Spelling Check Finished **box, click on Close.**

Correcting CorelDraw

That's how you use the dialog box if your word is indeed misspelled. But what if your word is correct and CorelDraw is the one with a spelling problem? Take my Old English text, for example. It's 100 percent historically authentic, guaranteed by Lloyd's of London. Yet CorelDraw questions nearly every word. Just goes to show you how much things have changed since the 15th century.

Sometimes, you have to teach CorelDraw how to spell. If your word is spelled correctly, you can create your own custom dictionary and add your word to it as follows:

1. **Click on the Create button in the Spell Check dialog box.**

2. **Enter an eight-character name in the Create Personal Dictionary dialog box that appears on-screen.**

    (You only have to perform this step the very first time you teach Draw. From then on, you can keep adding words to this dictionary.)

3. **Click on OK.**

4. **Click on the Add Word button.**

    CorelDraw adds the word to your new dictionary and then sets about hunting down the next misspelling.

Formatting options you have my permission to ignore

CorelDraw offers a mess of other formatting options that you may find interesting depending on, well, your level of interest. You can access these options in Draw by clicking on the Character Attributes, Frame, and Paragraph buttons at the bottom of the Text roll-up. In very general terms, these options work as follows:

🗸 Select a few characters of text and click on the Character Attributes button to access options that affect selected characters of text. You can change the amount of horizontal space between neighboring letters, whether you care to squish letters together or spread them apart. You can create superscript or subscript type.

🗸 Click on the Frame button to divide the text in the active text block into multiple columns.

🗸 Click on the Paragraph button to be completely overwhelmed by the options in the Paragraph dialog box. Along the top of the dialog box are four Tab icons. When you first enter the dialog box, the left tab, Spacing, is selected. In the Spacing tab, you can change the justification, the amount of horizontal space between words, and the amount of vertical space between lines and paragraphs of type. But the best option in this section of the dialog box is the Automatic Hyphenation checkbox. When you select this option, CorelDraw automatically hyphenates long words so that they better fill the width of a text block.

🗸 Select the Tabs tab to position tab stops as you would on a typewriter. You need to use these options only if you're creating price lists or other tables. Select the Indents tab to indent text inside a text block. Select the Bullet tab to add a symbol to the beginning of a paragraph.

🗸 After you make your changes, click on the OK button. CorelDraw returns you to the roll-up menu. Click on the Apply to Frame button to apply your changes to that particular text block. Click on Apply to Rest of Frames to apply the changes to that text block and others that follow it on subsequent pages. Click on Apply to All Frames to—you guessed it — apply changes to all paragraph text blocks in the file.

Using the other spelling options

You now know how to use most of the options in the Spell Check dialog box. But I did miss a few, so here's how they work:

- ✔ If you don't want to correct a word and you don't want to add it to the dictionary — you just want CorelDraw to get on with it — click on the Skip button.

- ✔ To make CorelDraw ignore all occurrences of a word throughout the current spelling session, click on the Skip All button.

- ✔ If you're the type who misspells consistently, click on the Change All button to replace all occurrences of a particular misspelling with the selected correction.

- ✔ Click on the Close button to stop looking for misspellings and close the dialog box.

Type Assist: DWIM is here?

When Captain Picard says "Tea, Earl Gray, hot" to his computer, the computer knows that Picard wants a cup full of steaming hot tea. If the computer actually did what Picard said to do (also known as DWIS, or Do What I Say), it would toss a dry, hot tea bag his way. But the computer does what he *means* (DWIM, or Do What I Mean) and not what he *says*.

Though most PCs could use a DWIM button, it looks like CorelDraw is already building one. Type Assist (Text➪Type Assist) automatically fixes the most common capitalization errors and other spelling mistakes. You can also tell it to convert your shorthand into words; for example, you can have the letters *acct.* automatically converted to the word *account* as you type (see Figure 10-15). Type Assist kicks in when you select any of the features in the Type Assist dialog box and then click on OK. If you want to turn off Type Assist, just open the dialog box (Alt+T, E) and deselect all the features.

Finding a Word in the Thesaurus

In the event that you have problems thinking of a word — like, what's that word, you know, that one that means you have skinny toes? — you can tap into CorelDraw's Thesaurus. You use it like this:

1. Select the word for which you want a synonym.

I think I want to replace that word *trod* in my block of Old English prose.

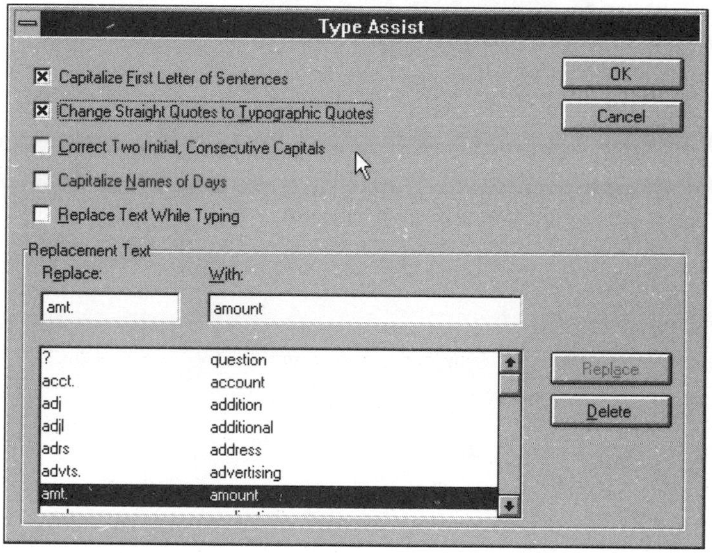

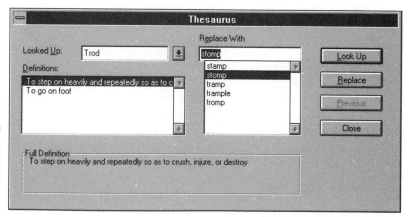

Figure 10-15:
The Type
Assist
feature
helps the
computer to
do what you
mean rather
than do
what you
say.

2. **Choose Text⇨Thesaurus.**

   The Thesaurus dialog box heaves into view, as shown in Figure 10-16.

3. **If the word has multiple meanings, select your meaning from the Definitions list.**

   I'm thinking of the crush-and-destroy meaning.

4. **Select the desired substitute from the Replace With list.**

   Ah, yes, *stomp,* that's much classier.

5. **Click on the Replace button.**

   CorelDraw closes the dialog box and replaces the selected word.

Figure 10-16:
The classy
Draw
Thesaurus.

A Different Kind of Alphabet

I haven't yet described one kind of text: symbols.

To display the Symbols roll-up shown in Figure 10-17, select Special⇔Symbols Roll-Up or just press Ctrl+F11. The roll-up offers access to a variety of simple pictures that you can use to accent or enhance a drawing. You can even combine symbols to create drawings in and of themselves.

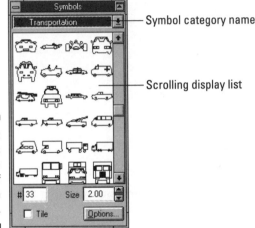

Symbol category name

Scrolling display list

Figure 10-17:
Symbols
are like
alphabets of
modern
hieroglyphs.

"Little pictures?" you're probably thinking. "Wait a minute. Pictures don't constitute text. What's going on here?" Hey, take it easy. Your problem is that you're used to a Western-style alphabet, in which abstract letters stand for sounds, the same way that a dollar bill stands for a piece of gold approximately the size of a single-cell microorganism. Letters are merely metaphors for real communication.

Try thinking Eastern. Think hieroglyphics. Think kanji. In these bazillion-character alphabets, each character represents a word or phrase. Similarly, CorelDraw's symbol library is a big alphabet. If you want to say "chair," for example, show a chair.

To select a symbol, take the following steps:

1. **Press Ctrl+F11.**

2. **Select a symbol category name from the drop-down list at the top of the Symbols roll-up.**

3. Enter the size of the symbol into the Size option box.

The size is measured in the same unit displayed in the rulers, which most likely is inches.

4. Select a symbol from the scrolling display list.

Use the up and down arrows in the lower-right portion of the roll-up to scroll from one panel of symbols to the next.

5. Drag the symbol into the drawing area with your mouse.

To view more symbols at a time, drag out on one of the corners of the roll-up.

You can edit symbols in the same way you edit free-form paths, described in Chapter 5. You also can fill and outline symbols as described in Chapter 7; duplicate symbols as described in Chapter 8; and transform symbols as discussed in Chapter 9. Come to think of it, symbols may be drawings after all.

Chapter 11

Mr. Typographer's Wild Ride

. . . .

In This Chapter

▶ Why CorelDraw is better than Disneyland

▶ Dragging characters to new locations

▶ Kerning special character combinations

▶ Changing the amount of space between characters and lines

▶ Fitting text to a path

▶ Changing character orientation and vertical and horizontal alignment

▶ Wrapping text around a circle

▶ Converting character outlines to editable paths

. . . .

*I*magine that you're a character of text. An *H,* for example. Or a *P.* It's not important. Be a *S* if you want to. So far, you've been riding through CorelDraw's functions on an even keel. Sometimes you wrap to the next line of type; other times you get poured into a different text block. But ultimately, life is about as exciting as a traffic jam. There are characters above and below you; you even have a few riding your rear end. It's no fun being a character in a standard text block.

But then one day, you rub shoulders with a streetwise character who really gets around — like an *E* or an *S* — and it tells you about a whole world of possibilities you haven't yet explored. You can play bumper cars, ride loop-de-loop roller coasters, or even stretch yourself into completely different shapes and forms. It's one big amusement park for text!

This chapter is your golden admission ticket. Have a blast.

Rules of the Park

Before I stamp your hand and let you into the park, a word of caution is in order. Just as too many rides on the Tilt-O-Whirl can make you hurl, too many wild effects can leave a block of text looking a little bent out of shape. The trick is to apply text effects conservatively and creatively.

If you're not sure how an effect will go over, show it to a few friends. Ask them to read your text. If they read it easily and hand the page back to you, you know that you hit the mark. If they say, "How did you *make* this?" the effect may be a little overly dramatic, but it's probably still acceptable. If they have trouble reading the text or they say, "How did you make *this*?" — in the same way they might say, "What did I just *step* in?" — your effect very likely overwhelms the page and is therefore unacceptable.

Then again, I don't want to dampen your spirit of enthusiasm and exploration. Use moderation in all things, including moderation, right? So what if you make yourself sick on the Tilt-O-Whirl. It's part of growing up. So what if your first few pages look like run-amuck advertisements for furniture warehouses? It's part of learning the craft.

And if some blue-blood designer looks at your work and exclaims, "Gad, this page! Oh, how it frightens me! Tell me who let you near the computer, and I'll go slap that person briskly!" you can retort, "Well, at least my text has more fun than yours." That's one way to get fired, anyway.

Playing Bumper Cars

You know that you can drag points and handles with the Shape tool. Well, this basic functionality of the Shape tool permeates all facets of CorelDraw, including text. If you select the Shape tool and click on a text block, you see three new varieties of nodes and handles, as shown in Figure 11-1. These nodes and handles appear when you click on a block of artistic text or paragraph text. They enable you to change the location of individual characters and to increase or decrease the amount of space between characters and lines of text.

Selecting and dragging text nodes

Text nodes enable you to change the locations of individual characters in a text block. You can nudge the characters slightly to adjust the amount of horizontal spacing, or you can drag a character several inches away from its text block just to show it who's boss.

Text nodes

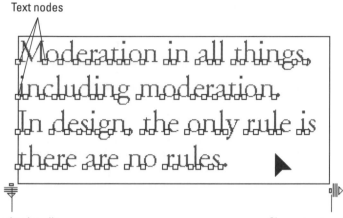

Figure 11-1:
Click on a
text block
with the
Shape tool
to display
these nodes
and
handles.

Line spacing handle　　　　　　　　　　　　Character spacing handle

✔ Each *text node* is associated with the character directly to its right. Click on a node to select it and its character. Black nodes are selected; white nodes are not.

✔ Marquee (click+drag with the Arrow tool) around multiple text nodes to select them all at once. You also can Shift+click on a text node to add it to the selection.

✔ If you select a few too many nodes when you're marqueeing, Shift+click on the ones you want to deselect.

✔ Drag a selected text node to reposition all selected characters. In Figure 11-2, for example, I selected every other letter in the word *Moderation* and dragged the selected node associated with the *n*.

Figure 11-2:
Drag
selected
characters
with the
Shape tool
to create a
line of
uneven text.

✔ Ctrl+drag nodes to constrain the drag to an existing line of type. In other words, you can Ctrl+drag horizontally along the current line of type or Ctrl+drag vertically to move along different lines of type.

✔ Use the arrow keys to nudge selected characters. You specify the nudge distance in the General tab of the Preferences dialog box (Ctrl+J).

✔ To undo all changes you made by dragging text nodes, choose Text➪Straighten Text.

Kern, kern, the baffling term

You can drag entire lines, drag whole words, or just create crazy text blocks by dragging individual characters six ways to Sunday, whatever that means. But the most practical reason for dragging nodes is to adjust the amount of horizontal space between individual characters, a process known as *kerning*.

In *Webster's Second Edition* — the sacred volume that editors swear by — *kern* is defined as the portion of a letter such as *f* that sticks out from the stem. Those nutty lexicographers say that it's based on the French word *carne,* which means a projecting angle.

Now, I don't know about you, but where I come from: 1) we don't go around assigning words to projecting angles; and 2) *kern* means to smush two letters closer together so they look as snug as kernels of corn on the cob. Of course, I don't have any Ivy League degree and I don't wear any fancy hat with a tassel hanging off it, but I'm pretty sure them Webster fellers are full of beans.

Not like *you* care. You're still trying to figure out what I'm talking about. So here goes: Consider the character combination *AV.* It comes up in conversation about as often as the French word *carne,* but it demonstrates a point. The right side of the letter *A* and the left side of the character *V* both slope in the same direction. So when the two letters appear next to each other, a perceptible gap may form, as shown in Figure 11-3. Although the *A* and the *V* in *AVERY* aren't any farther away from each other than the *V* and the *E,* the *E* and the *R,* and so on, they appear more spread out because of their similar slopes.

To tighten the spacing, I selected the *V*s as well as all letters to the right of the *V*s. Then I pressed the left-arrow key a few times. (Selecting the letters to the right of the *V*s ensures that I don't widen the spacing between any *V* and the letter that follows it.) Figure 11-4 shows the result of kerning the *A*s and *V*s. I also kerned a few other letters for good measure. (The nodes of these letters are selected in Figure 11-4.)

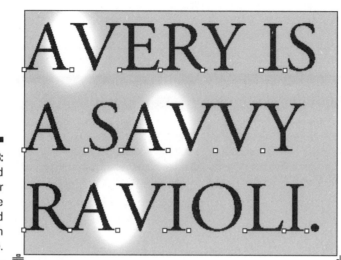

Figure 11-3:
I wish I had
a dime for
every time
we taunted
Avery with
this one.

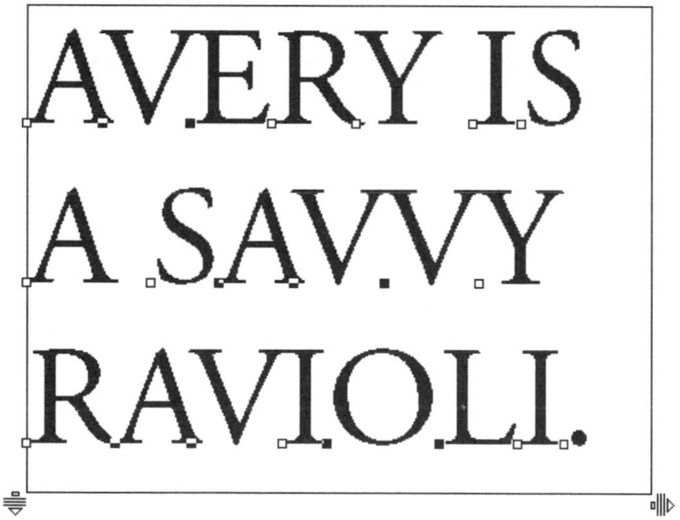

Figure 11-4:
Avery feels
vindicated
now that
those who
would
malign him
have kerned
their ways.

Kerning with CorelKern

In addition to manually kerning letters in CorelDraw, you have another option for changing spacing between letter pairs: Use CorelKern. With CorelKern, you can generate and modify kerning pairs for a font so that you don't have to edit them manually. Unfortunately, CorelKern doesn't work with TrueType fonts; it works only with Adobe Type1 fonts.

To use Adobe Type1 fonts in Windows (and CorelDraw), you must also have installed Adobe Type Manager. The good folks at Corel have given you Adobe Type Manager; it's installed when you install the Adobe Acrobat Reader to access Corel's on-line electronic manual. And the quadrillion TrueType fonts that Corel gives you are also available in a Type1 format on the Corel CD.

A PFM (Printer Font Metric) file containing information about kerning pairs is attached to each Adobe font. Using CorelKern, you can get into this file and change the kern pairs, as shown in the following figure. You drag the slider bar along the bottom of the window to adjust the kerning between characters.

If you find yourself kerning the same pairs over and over again in a particular font, you may want to give CorelKern a spin. Otherwise, you probably won't want to bother.

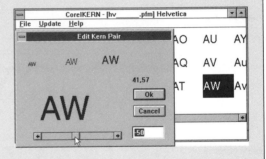

Changing overall spacing

To recap, dragging text nodes changes the space between selected characters only. If you want to evenly adjust the spacing between *all* characters in a text block, you need to drag one of the two spacing handles, labeled back in Figure 11-1.

- ✔ Drag the *character spacing handle* (located on the right side of the text block) to change the amount of horizontal space between all characters in the text block, as in the first example of Figure 11-5.

- ✔ Ctrl+drag the character spacing handle to change the size of the spaces between all words in the text block, as in the second example of Figure 11-5.

- ✔ Drag the *line spacing handle* (located on the left side of the text block) to adjust the amount of vertical space between all lines of type except those that are separated by a carriage return. In other words, lines in the same paragraph are affected, but neighboring lines in different paragraphs are not, as the first example in Figure 11-6 shows.

- ✔ Ctrl+drag the line spacing handle to change the amount of vertical space between paragraphs, as in the second example of Figure 11-6.

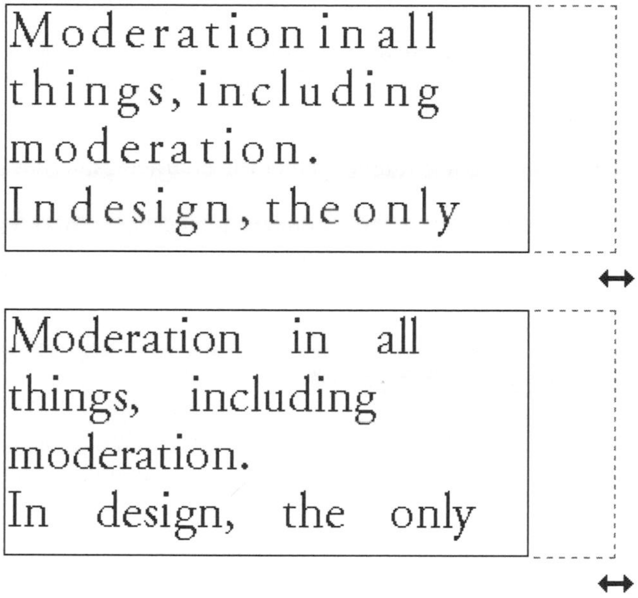

Moderation in all
things, including
moderation.
In design, the only

Moderation in all
things, including
moderation.
In design, the only

Figure 11-5:
The results
of dragging
(top) and
Ctrl+dragging
(bottom) the
character
spacing
handle.

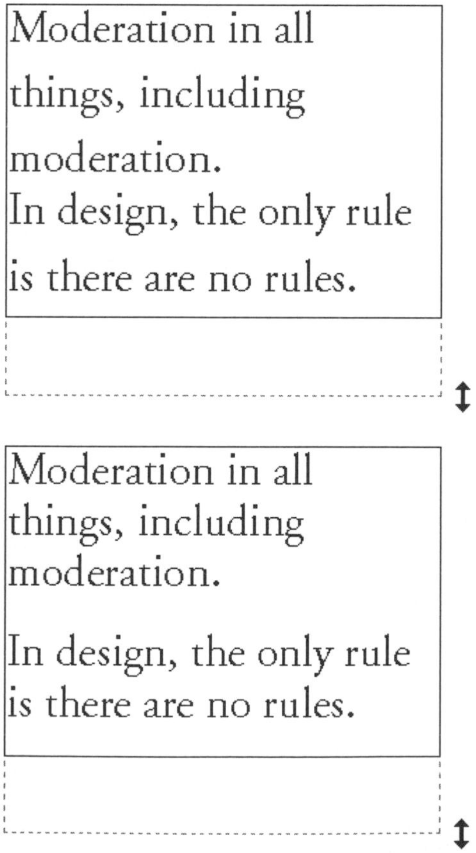

Moderation in all
things, including
moderation.
In design, the only rule
is there are no rules.

Moderation in all
things, including
moderation.

In design, the only rule
is there are no rules.

Figure 11-6:
Here's what
happens
when you
drag (top)
and
Ctrl+drag
(bottom) the
line spacing
handle.

Notice that dragging a spacing handle has no effect on the size of a block of paragraph text. The block itself remains the same size, and the newly spaced characters reflow to fit inside it.

Also, changes you make to a text block affect the characters in that text block only. If the text block is linked to another text block, some reformatted characters may flow into the linked text block. But the characters that originally occupied the linked text block remain unchanged.

Riding the Roller Coaster

CorelDraw calls the feature I'm about to discuss *fitting text to a path*. But I call it giving your text a ride on the roller coaster. After all, when your text is fit to a path, it appears to be having the time of its life, as Figure 11-7 clearly illustrates.

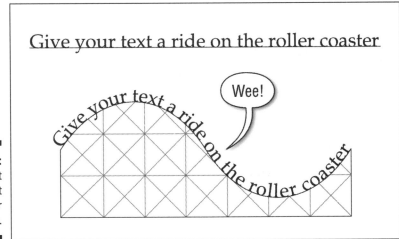

Figure 11-7:
For text, it doesn't get any better than this.

Text normally sits on an imaginary flat line, as shown in the top example of Figure 11-7. This line is called the *baseline.* Anyway, you can substitute an oval or free-form path for the baseline like so:

1. **Select a block of artistic text with the Arrow tool.**

   This feature is applicable only to artistic text. You cannot fit paragraph text to a path.

2. **Shift+click on a path.**

   CorelDraw adds the path to the selection. Circles, ovals, and gradually curving paths work best, but any path is acceptable.

3. Choose Text⇨Fit Text to Path.

Or just press Ctrl+F. The Fit Text To Path roll-up appears. If the selected path is a free-form path, the roll-up looks like the left example in Figure 11-8. If the selected path is an oval or rectangle, the roll-up looks like the right example in Figure 11-8.

Text
orientation

Vertical
alignment

Horizontal
alignment

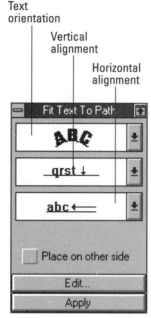

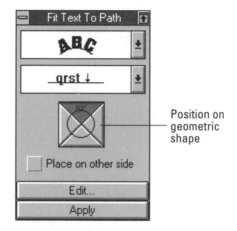

Position on
geometric
shape

Figure 11-8:
Two
variations
on the Fit
Text To Path
roll-up.

4. Select the desired options.

I describe all this stuff momentarily. For now, you don't need to select anything. You can just accept the default settings and go on.

5. Click on the Apply button.

Watch the baseline adhere to that path. Those little characters are probably losing their lunches (in a good way, of course).

6. If the text doesn't attach to the path the way you anticipated, select the Place on Other Side checkbox and click on the Apply button.

The text switches to the opposite side of the path and flows in the opposite direction.

The Fit Text To Path roll-up offers either three drop-down lists or two drop-down lists and a group of buttons, depending on the kind of shape to which you adhere your type. These options determine the orientation of characters on a path, the vertical alignment of the text, and the horizontal alignment. The following sections explain how they work.

Text orientation

The first drop-down list lets you rotate characters along the path, skew them horizontally or vertically, or none of the above. Figure 11-9 shows the effects of each of the options on the text from Figure 11-7. The options are illustrated in the same order that they appear in the drop-down list.

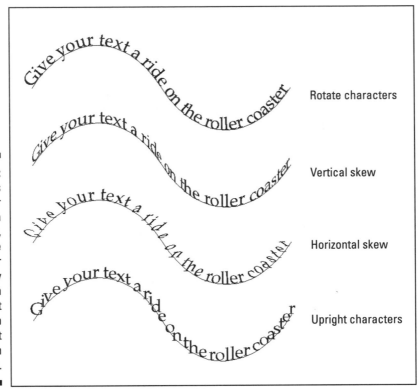

Figure 11-9: The effects of the four orientation options, shown in the same order that they appear in the first drop-down list of the Fit Text To Path roll-up.

Want my *real* opinion? All right. Here goes:

- ✔ The rotate characters option is the most useful of the four, which is probably why it's the default setting. When in doubt, stick with this option.

- ✔ The vertical skew option is also very useful, as long as your path doesn't have any super-steep vertical inclines. Along the left and right sides of a circle, for example, characters skew into nothingness.

- ✔ The horizontal skew option is set up backwards, so letters skew against the path instead of with it. The *G* at the beginning of the text in Figure 11-9, for example, should skew to the right, into the path, and not to the left, away from it. Use this option only if you want to illicit comments like, "Gee, this is weird," or, "Maybe we should go back to typewriters."

✔ The upright characters option is so ugly, it makes the horizontal skew option look like a good idea.

Vertical alignment

The vertical alignment drop-down list lets you change the vertical positioning of characters with respect to the path. Here's how the options work:

✔ The first option on the menu adheres the baseline of the text to the path.

✔ The next option aligns the tops of the tallest characters, called ascenders (*b, d, k*), to the path. The text hangs from the path like a monkey hangs from a tree limb, except that the text doesn't swing back and forth and scratch for ticks.

✔ The third option aligns the bottom of the hanging-down characters, called *descenders* (*g, j, p*), to the path so that the letters balance like little tight-rope walkers.

✔ The fourth option causes the path to run smack dab through the middle of the text like a gold chain threaded through beaded pearls.

Don't you just love these clever little analogies?

✔ The last option lets you drag the text anywhere you want with respect to the path. After selecting the option, drag the text with the Arrow tool. When you release, CorelDraw redraws the text at the new location.

Generally, you should stick with the default setting, which adheres text by its baseline. The one time to change this option is when you create text on a circle, as I describe in the section after next. (First, I have to describe the horizontal alignment options, or the section after next won't make sense.)

Horizontal alignment

When you're attaching text to a free-form path, the Fit Text To Path roll-up offers a third drop-down list. Options on this list enable you to change the horizontal alignment of text as follows:

✔ The first option aligns the first character of text with the first point in the path. This option works like the left justification option in a normal text block.

✔ The second option centers the text on the path, just as the center justification option centers text in a normal text block.

Starting to get the idea?

✔ The last option aligns the last character of text with the last point in the path. It works like — you guessed it — the right justification option in a normal text block.

When you attach text to a geometric object — an oval, circle, rectangle, or square — CorelDraw replaces the third drop-down list box with a square that has four inset triangular buttons (see Figure 11-8). The buttons work like radio buttons; that is, you can only select one button at a time. You can either center the text along the top of the object, along the left or right side, or along the bottom.

Creating text on a circle

Want to see the vertical and horizontal alignment options put into use? Well, too bad, because I'm going to show you anyway.

I don't know why, but when folks want to fit text to a path, nine times out of ten the path they have in mind is a circle. Ironically, however, placing text on a circle is the least intuitive kind of roller-coaster text you can create. If you simply attach a single text block around the entire circle, half of the text is upside down. So you have to attach two text blocks to a single circle — one along the top of the circle and another along the bottom. Here's how it works:

1. **Draw a circle.**

   If you need help, go to Chapter 4.

2. **Create two blocks of artistic text.**

   Create one for the top of the circle and one for the bottom. And keep them short.

3. **Select the circle and the first block of text.**

   Using the Arrow tool, click on one and Shift+click on the other.

4. **Press Ctrl+F to bring up the Fit Text To Path roll-up.**

   If the roll-up is already displayed, skip this step.

5. **Click on the Apply button.**

   The default settings are fine for now. The text adheres to the top of the circle, as in Figure 11-10.

6. **Click with the Arrow tool in an empty portion of the drawing area.**

   This step deselects everything. You have to do this so you can select the circle independently in the next step.

7. **Select the circle and the second block of text.**

   Click somewhere along the bottom of the circle to make sure that you select the circle only. (If you click along the top of the circle, you might select the text as well.) Then Shift+click on the second block of text.

8. **Click on the bottom triangular button in the Fit Text To Path roll-up.**

   See the location of the arrow cursor in Figure 11-11.

Figure 11-10:
The result of fitting the first text block to the circle.

Figure 11-11:
The result of fitting the second text block to the bottom of the circle.

9. Click on the Apply button.

The second block of text wraps around the bottom of the circle, as shown in Figure 11-11. Unfortunately, the text is upside-down. To remedy this . . .

10. Select the Place on Other Side checkbox.

11. Click on the Apply button.

The text now appears as shown in Figure 11-12 — right-side up, but scrunched. To loosen the text up a bit, perform Step 12.

12. Select the second option from the vertical alignment drop-down list.

Figure 11-13 shows me selecting this option, which, as you may remember, aligns the ascenders of the characters to the circle so that the text hangs down.

13. Click on the Apply button.

Your text looks something like the text shown in Figure 11-13.

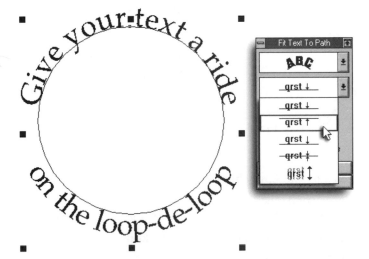

14. Click with the Arrow tool in an empty portion of the drawing area.

Notice that the top row of type doesn't look like it's quite aligned with the bottom row. To fix this discrepancy, you need to select the top text block independently of the other. But first, to prepare for this step, you must deselect everything.

15. Ctrl+click twice on a character in the top text block.

Normally, you only have to Ctrl+click once to select the text on a path. But because this path contains two blocks of text, you have to Ctrl+click twice. When you see the text nodes, you know that you selected the top text block independently of both the second text block and the circle.

16. Select the third option from the vertical alignment pop-up menu.

In Figure 11-14, I select this option, which aligns the descenders of the characters to the circle, causing the text to walk the tightrope.

17. For the billionth time, click on the Apply button.

The top text block now aligns correctly with the bottom text block. Figure 11-14 shows text on a circle as it was meant to be.

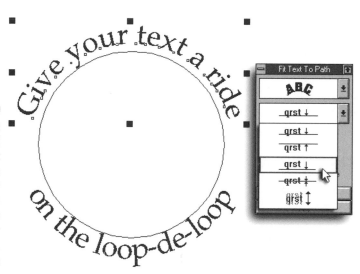

Figure 11-14: Upper and lower text blocks align perfectly after I apply the descender option.

Editing text on a path

After you fit a block of artistic text to a path, you may notice that CorelDraw no longer allows you to edit the characters or apply different formatting attributes. At least, it doesn't when you select the text/path combination normally. You need to select the text independently of the path. I mentioned this technique in passing in Step 15 of the preceding section, but it bears repeating.

✔ Ctrl+click with the Arrow tool on the text — *not* on the path — to select the text independently of the path. You know that the text is selected because you see the little text nodes.

✔ To edit the content of the text, choose <u>T</u>ext➪Edit Te<u>x</u>t, or bypass the command by pressing Ctrl+Shift+T. Draw displays a dialog box that enables you to edit characters or words. You can even change the typeface, style, and size.

- ✔ To apply new formatting, use the options in the Text roll-up as you do when formatting normal text (I discussed the Text roll-up in Chapter 10).

- ✔ Click inside the color palette to apply color to the text.

- ✔ Kern the text by selecting text nodes with the Shape tool and dragging them. Draw automatically constrains the movement of the text to the contour of the path.

Editing the path

You can change the fill and outline of the path to which you attach your text. Just select the object and use the fill and pen options described back in Chapter 7. It's very straightforward — no special tricks required.

In many cases, you'll want to hide the path. To do so, select the object and right-click on the X button in the lower-left corner of the color palette. By right-clicking, you delete the color from the outline.

You also can use the Shape tool to edit the shape of free-form paths. Just be sure that you click on the path and not on the text.

Breaking it up

To detach text from a path and return it to the straight and narrow, do the following:

1. **Click on the text to select it.**

   Don't go clicking on the path.

2. **Choose Arrange⇨Separate.**

   CorelDraw separates the text from the path. However, the text remains all twisty-curly.

3. **Click on an empty portion of the drawing area.**

4. **Then click on the text you want to straighten.**

5. **Choose Text⇨Straighten Text.**

Better yet, just press Alt,A,S and then press Alt,T,S. The text returns to its plain old self.

Meddling with Type

If you're interested in creating logos or other special text, you should know about one more command before I close this chapter down. This technique is only applicable to artistic text.

If you select a block of artistic text with the Arrow tool or one of the Text tools and choose Arrange⇨Convert To Curves (Ctrl+Q), CorelDraw converts the outlines of every single character in the text block to free-form paths. An *A,* for example, ceases to be a letter of text and becomes a triangular path with a bar across it.

After you convert the characters to paths, you can edit the paths by using the Arrow and Shape tools (described in Chapter 5) exactly as if you drew the characters with the Pencil tool. The top example in Figure 11-15 shows a block of standard, everyday, mild-mannered text. The second example is the same block of text after I convert it to paths and edit the holy heck out of it.

Try this process out a few times and you soon find that converted characters are as easy to integrate and edit as symbols and other pieces of clip art. Converted text serves as a great jumping-off point for creating custom logos and other exciting effects.

Figure 11-15:
A line of
artistic text
as it
appears
before and
after
converting it
to paths and
editing the
paths with
the Shape
tool.

TIP

Make a copy before you start

Before you convert text to curves for node editing, make a duplicate of it (press Ctrl+D). When you do so, you

✔ Save an original text version in case you really mess up the nodes.

✔ Keep the original handy for comparison during node edit.

✔ Gain an extra object because it's so easy to press Ctrl+D.

✔ Retain an extra original text copy in case the boss wants you to change the wording of the text.

The 5th Wave   By Rich Tennant

OK-don't use the Spell Checker! We'll just issue a whole line of cards that wish people a "Happy Hollidog", "Seasons Creepings", and "Bon Voyeur". and "Joy To The Whirled".

Bob's Card Co.

Chapter 12

The Corner of Page and Publish

· ·

In This Chapter

▶ The biting sarcasm of trees

▶ Creating a multipage document

▶ Turning pages

▶ Deleting excess pages

▶ Pouring overflow text from one page to another

▶ Repeating objects by using the master layer

▶ Hiding master layer objects selectively

▶ Changing page size

· ·

Desktop publishing has revolutionized the way folks churn up and spit out bits of Oregon forestry, thereby remedying the grossly inefficient way we churned up the forests back in the 1970s. Happily, we now have more open space in which to park our cars so that people can stick computer-created fliers that we don't want under our windshield wipers. Now you can be a part of this ever expanding field.

Okay, that bit of sarcasm is overstated. Certainly, computers will lessen our reliance on paper in the long run. But for now, the printed page remains the medium of choice. Furthermore, although I'd love to get on my high horse and warn you about the evils of it all, I'm obviously in no position to lecture, having myself wasted more paper than most people use in a lifetime. Don't get me wrong; I'm a dedicated recycler. Ecocycle loves me. I only use the cheapest bond available, and I only print when I absolutely have to. I don't even own a photocopier. Hey, you want to get off my case or what?

Now that I've insulted folks on both sides of the spotted owl debate, I'll get down to business. The next two chapters are devoted to output. This chapter explains how to set up pages; Chapter 13 explains how to print them. After you finish reading these chapters, you'll be able to create fliers to stick under windshield wipers with the best of them.

Remember, always use bright pink or dull yellow paper. That way, folks can spot your fliers nine miles away and mentally prepare themselves to snatch them up and wad them into balls at their earliest convenience.

Pages upon Pages

Unless you've read outside sources or scoped out the Layout menu, you may assume that CorelDraw is only good for creating single-page documents. The perfect program for creating a nice, letter-sized drawing suitable for framing, but that's about it.

The truth is that with Draw 5, you can add as many pages as you want. (As usual, I'm sure there's a maximum, but I'll be darned if I care what it is. I mean, if you're trying to lay out an issue of *National Geographic,* you're going to have a tough time doing it in this program. If you have in mind a newsletter, a report, or maybe a short catalog, however, Draw will suffice.)

Adding new pages to work on

When you create a new drawing (by using File⇨New, naturally), it begins life as a one-page document. To make it a multipage document, you have to add pages manually, like so:

1. **Choose Layout⇨Insert Page.**

   Or simply press the PgUp or PgDn key, which brings up the dialog box shown in Figure 12-1.

2. **Enter the number of pages you want to add in the Insert option box.**

   For example, if you want to create a four-page newsletter, press 3. (You already have one page.)

3. **Press Enter.**

   Draw adds the specified number of pages to your document.

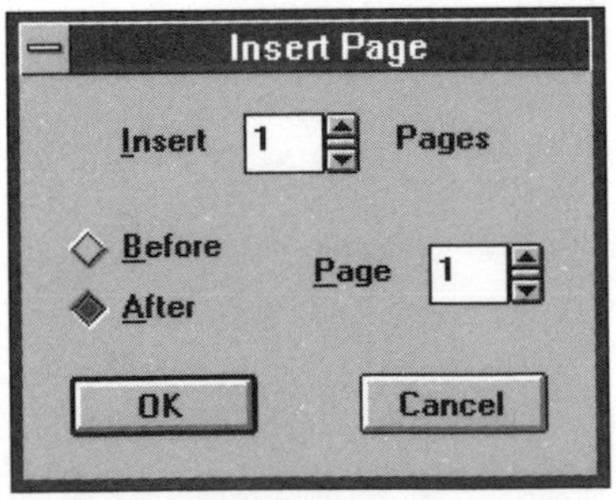

Figure 12-1:
The Insert Page dialog box lets you add pages to a drawing.

Insert Page

Insert [1] Pages

◇ Before   Page [1]
◆ After

[OK]   [Cancel]

✔ PgUp and PgDn access the Insert Page dialog box immediately when you have a one-page document.

✔ If you have a multipage document, you must be on the first or last page of the document (get there by pressing the PgUp or PgDn key the necessary number of times). Then you can press the respective PgUp or PgDn key in order to access the Insert Page dialog box.

Adding pages bit by bit

The rest of the options in the Insert Page dialog box are useful when you find yourself adding pages sporadically rather than in one fell swoop. Suppose that you set up a four-page document and then later discover that you need six pages to hold all your wonderful drawings and ideas. By using the Before and After radio buttons together with the Page option in the Insert Page dialog box, you can tell CorelDraw exactly where to insert the pages. If you want to insert them between pages three and four, for example, you can do either of the following:

✔ Enter 3 in the Page option box and select the After radio button. Then click OK.

✔ Enter 4 in the Page option box and select the Before radio button. Then click OK.

Rocket science it ain't. If the pages you want to insert aren't sequential, you have to use the Layout⇨Insert Page command more than once. For example, to insert one page between pages two and three and two others between pages three and four, you have to choose the Insert Page command twice, once for each sequence.

Thumbing through your pages

After you add pages to your previously single-page drawing, Draw displays three page controls in the lower-left corner of the interface, as shown in Figure 12-2. Here's how they work:

✔ Click on the left-pointing Page Back button to back up one page — from page two to page one, for example.

✔ Click on the right-pointing Page Forward button to advance one page.

✔ You can also change pages by pressing the PgUp and PgDn keys. The PgDn key backs up one page, and the PgUp key advances one page.

✔ Ctrl+click on the Page Back button to return to the first page of the document. Ctrl+click on the Page Forward button to advance to the last page.

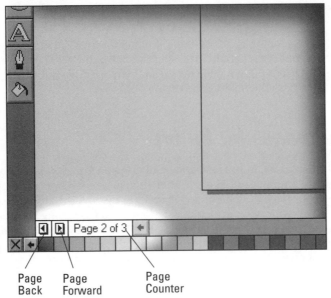

Figure 12-2:
Page
controls
appear only
when the
open
document
contains
more than
one page.

Page
Back
Page
Forward
Page
Counter

✔ When you're working on the first page of your document, the Page Back button displays a plus sign. The same sign appears on the Page Forward button when you're on the last page. Click on the plus sign to display the Insert Page dialog box, which is set up to add pages automatically before the first page or after the last page in your document.

✔ Click in the Page Counter area (see Figure 12-2) to display the Go To Page dialog box, which allows you to turn to any page in the document. Just type the page number, press Enter, and off you go. (You can also access this dialog box by choosing Layout⇨Go To Page.)

Removing the excess

If you add too many pages, you can always go back and delete a few by choosing Layout⇨Delete Page. A dialog box asks you which pages you want to delete. You can either delete a single page or a sequence of pages. You cannot, however, delete all pages in the document.

If you delete a page that you didn't mean to delete, choose Edit⇨Undo Delete Page or press Ctrl+Z.

Flowing text from one page to another

In Chapter 10, I mentioned that you can pour text across multiple pages. You daring types probably went ahead and tried it right that second. But a few of you — all right, most of you — are still wondering how that little feature works. Give the following a try and you'll see:

1. **Drag with the Paragraph Text tool to create a block of text.**

2. **Type more text than the text block can hold.**

3. **Select the Arrow tool and click on the bottom tab of the text block.**

    You get the page cursor.

4. **Press PgUp and then Enter.**

    This action adds one page after the current page. (It's the same as choosing Layout⇨Insert Page and accepting the default settings.)

5. **Drag with the page cursor on your new page.**

    The overflow text appears in the new text block.

Isn't that a trip? Despite the fact that the two text blocks are on separate pages, they're linked. If you drag the tab in the text block on page one, excess text flows into the text block on page two. Incidentally, linked text blocks don't have to be on sequential pages; they can be several pages apart. You can start a story on page 5 and continue it on page 44. You can even make a separate text block that tells readers, "Continued on page 44." These here are professional page-layout capabilities.

Your Logo on Every Page

Here's yet another feature to make you glad that you use CorelDraw 5. It's called a *master layer*. No, I'm not talking about a person who really knows the ins and outs of bricks and mortar. This feature enables you to repeat special text and graphic objects on every page of your document. For example, when you're creating a company newsletter, you may want to repeat the name of the newsletter at the bottom of each page and the company logo in every upper-right corner.

Establishing a master layer

The following steps explain how to establish a master layer and put stuff on it:

1. Choose Layout⊃Layers Roll-Up.

Or press Ctrl+F3 to access the Layers roll-up shown in Figure 12-3.

Figure 12-3:
The Draw 5
Layers
roll-up.

2. Choose the New command from the roll-up submenu.

Click on the right-pointing arrow to display the submenu and then click on the New command. The New Layer dialog box appears, as shown in Figure 12-4.

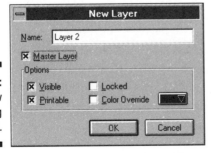

Figure 12-4:
The New
Layer dialog
box.

3. Name the layer (optional).

Type a name in the top option box. By default, the layer is named Layer 2 (assuming that you haven't assigned any other layers to this drawing). Notice that the options in this dialog box match up with those pretty little icons in the Layers roll-up (Figure 12-3): Monitor means visible, printer means printable, and lock means locked.

4. Select the Master Layer checkbox.

5. Press the Enter key.

CorelDraw closes the dialog box and returns you to your drawing. Notice that Layer 2 is now highlighted in the Layers roll-up.

6. Add text and graphics to taste.

Create those logos, add those newsletter names, and draw those boxes. Everything that you want to put on every page should appear on this layer. (Incidentally, it doesn't matter what page you're on. A master layer applies to every page of the document.)

7. Click on Layer 1 in the Layers roll-up.

This action returns you to your original layer.

8. Draw something simple.

An oval, for example. You're just drawing this object for the sake of comparison.

9. Turn to a different page.

Press PgDn to go forward a page or PgUp to go back. It doesn't matter. When you turn to the other page, you see all the objects that you added to the master layer in Step 6. But you don't see the oval you drew on the standard layer in Step 8.

10. Choose MultiLayer from the Layers roll-up submenu.

Click again on the right-pointing arrow to display the submenu and then click on the MultiLayer command. This step turns the command off so that you can manipulate objects only on the current layer, thus protecting the master layer objects.

Hiding master layer objects on page one

As a general rule of thumb, you don't display master layer objects on the first page of a multipage document. For example, what's the point of listing the name of the newsletter at the bottom of the first page? The name is already listed at the top of that page in big, bold type. Very likely, the company logo is part of the newsletter title, so there's no reason to repeat it either.

Special info about the Layers roll-up

Layers are useful for segregating objects in extremely complex drawings. People who go around drawing human anatomies and blow-outs of car engines — we're talking about folks with the patience of saints — use layers. However, most intermediate and novice users have little reason to so much as touch layers, and they're all the merrier for it. I almost never use layers and I'm an *expert.* At least that's what my wife tells me every time I take the trash out to the curb. And she's not just saying it either; I can sense that she really means it.

To hide master layer objects on a single page, do the following:

1. **Turn to the first page.**

   If you want to remove the master layer objects from some other page, turn to that page.

2. **Double-click on the name of the master layer in the Layers roll-up.**

   If you didn't change the name of the layer, it's called Layer 2. The Layer Options dialog box appears.

3. **Deselect the Set Options for <u>A</u>ll Pages option.**

   This action allows you to change the settings only for the current page.

4. **Deselect the <u>V</u>isible checkbox.**

   This step hides the master layer objects.

5. **Press Enter.**

   Draw closes the dialog box and returns you to the drawing area. All master layer objects now disappear from view.

Telling Your Drawing How Big to Be

In the United States, most folks use letter-sized paper. That's 8½ inches wide × 11 inches tall, in case you've never worked in a stationery store or set foot in an office-supply warehouse. In other countries, page sizes vary. But no matter what — at least, I don't know of any exceptions — CorelDraw is set up for the most likely scenario. If you're using the most common page size in your neck of the woods, don't worry about the command I'm about to describe.

But what if you're doing something slightly different? Maybe you're printing to legal-sized paper, a longer page size designed for lawyers to scribble their many §s on. Or maybe you're printing to letter-sized paper but you want to flip the page on its side. In these and other cases, you need to choose <u>L</u>ayout⇨<u>P</u>age Setup to display the Page Setup dialog box shown in Figure 12-5.

 Come to think of it, you can forget those commands for getting to the Page Setup dialog box. Draw lets you double-click on the edge of the paper in your current drawing for immediate access to the Page Setup dialog box. It's easiest just to click where there's a shadow.

Here's how to use the options in the dialog box:

 ✔ To change the size of the pages in the document, click on the Size tab. Then select a predefined page size option from the first drop-down list box.

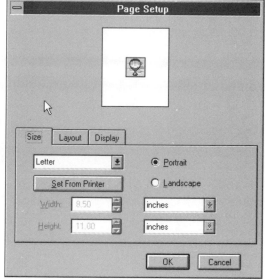

Figure 12-5:
The Page
Setup dialog
box lets you
change the
size of the
pages in
your
document.

✔ If you don't know how large a predefined page size is, just select it. CorelDraw automatically displays the dimensions of the selected page size in the dimmed Width and Height option boxes.

✔ If you just want to set the page size to match the size of the paper loaded in your printer, click on the Set From Printer button.

✔ If none of these page sizes strikes your fancy, select the Custom option and then enter your own dimensions in the Width and Height option boxes.

✔ Select the Landscape radio button to lay the page on its side. Select Portrait to stand it up again. DTP experts call this the *orientation* of the page.

✔ Don't even bother with the Layout tab options. Unless you're creating three-fold fliers on bright pink paper with ugly borders around each page, they're a complete waste of time.

✔ Click on the Display tab and then select the Facing Pages checkbox to display two facing pages in the drawing area at once. For example, when you open a four-page newsletter, pages two and three face each other. The even-numbered page (page two) is on the left and the odd-numbered page (page three) is on the right. If you want to see these pages as your reader sees them, select the Facing Pages option. If you want to quickly make a rectangle that's the size of the page, simply click on the Add Page Frame.

Chapter 13

Those Poor, Helpless Trees

- -

In This Chapter

▶ Preparing a drawing to be printed

▶ Orienting a drawing on the printed page

▶ Selecting paper size

▶ Printing every page of a document

▶ Printing multiple copies

▶ Printing a specific range of pages

▶ Scaling a drawing

▶ Tiling poster-sized artwork onto several pages

▶ Using the Page Preview options

▶ Creating color separations

- -

*A*dvising a perfect stranger like you how to use your printer is like trying to diagnose a car problem without ever having seen the car, without knowing the make and model, and without having driven more than ten different models in my entire life. Printers come in so many different types and present so many different potential printing hazards that I can't possibly give information designed specifically for your machine.

In other words, I'm completely in the dark. I'm the blind leading the blind. Sure, I can tell you how to print from CorelDraw — in fact, that's exactly what I'm going to do in this chapter — but every word I write assumes that:

✔ Your printer is plugged in.

✔ Your printer is turned on and in working order.

✔ Your printer is properly connected to your computer.

✔ Windows is aware of your printer's existence.

✔ Your printer is stocked with ribbon, ink, toner, paper, film, and whatever else it requires in the way of raw materials.

One other thing: Make sure that you *have* a printer. I've known people who have tried to print when there's no printer in the building.

If you barely know the location of the printer, let alone anything else about the blasted thing, assume for now that everything is A-OK and follow along with the text in this chapter. If you run into a snag, something is probably awry with your printer or its connection to your computer. As a friend of mine likes to say, "When in trouble or in doubt, run in circles, scream and shout." (I'm sure that he's quoting someone, but I'll be darned if I know whom.) If you shout loudly enough, a computer guru may come to your rescue and fix your problem.

The Printing Process

The overall printing process includes these steps:

1. **Turn on your printer.**

   If you're working in an office and the printer is far from your desk, shout down the hall or across the vast expanse of cubicles to find out whether it's turned on. I suggest, "Is the printer on, you bonehead?" If the person near the printer responds with anything but, "Aye-aye," speak to your supervisor immediately.

2. **Choose File⇨Print Setup.**

   This command allows you to make sure that you're printing to the correct printer and that the page doesn't print on its side. (More info about this option in later sections.)

3. **Choose File⇨Save.**

   Although only a precaution, it's always a good idea to save your document immediately before you print it because the print process is one of those ideal opportunities for your computer to crash. Your computer gleans a unique kind of satisfaction from delivering pristine pages to the printer and then locking up at the last minute, all the while knowing that the document on disk is several hours behind schedule. If you weren't the object of the joke, you'd probably think it amusing, too.

4. **Press Ctrl+P.**

   Or choose File⇨Print. A dialog box appears in which you can specify the pages you want to print, request multiple copies, scale the size of the printed drawing, and mess around with a horde of other options.

5. **Press the OK key.**

   And they're off! The pages start spewing out of your printer faster than you can recite the first 17 pages of *Beowulf*.

It's magic, really. With the modern miracle of computing, you've taken what is for all practical purposes a completely imaginary drawing — a dream known only to you and your machine — and converted it into a tangible sheet of hard copy. Don't be surprised when you show your work to fellow amateurs and they kick you out of their club for good. That's the price of progress.

Making Sure That Everything's Ready to Go

Choosing File➪Print Setup is the equivalent of checking for your car keys as you exit your house. It's by no means essential; just as you probably have your keys, everything is probably already in order to print. But it's a good idea that may help you avoid some grief later on.

When you choose File➪Print Setup, Draw displays the Print Setup dialog box, as shown in Figure 13-1. This dialog box indicates the printer out of which your pages will spew. Select your printer from the Name drop-down list box.

Figure 13-1: These dialog boxes let you make sure that everything's in order.

When you click on the Setup button in the Print Setup dialog box, you are offered three more areas of interest, as shown in the lower dialog box of Figure 13-1.

 ✔ Select a radio button from the Orientation area to ensure that your drawing lines up correctly on the printed page. If your drawing is taller than it is wide, select Portrait. If not, select Landscape.

 ✔ Select the correct paper size from the Paper Size drop-down list box. Ideally, the paper size should match the page size you select in the Page Setup dialog box (described in the preceding chapter). Unless you have loaded some special kind of paper, you probably want letter-sized paper.

> ✔ Specify where the paper is coming from by selecting an option from the Paper Source drop-down list box. Some office printers have more than one paper tray. If you want to print on letterhead or some other special kind of paper, select Manual Feed. Then shout to the person next to the printer, "Shove a sheet of letterhead into the manual feed slot, would you?"

This process may sound like a lot of work, but in all likelihood you can entirely ignore the two options in the Paper area. The size and paper tray are already set up correctly in 90 percent of the world's printing scenarios. So if you're in a hurry, just check that the Printer and Orientation settings are correct and press Enter.

Printing Those Pages

When you press Ctrl+P, CorelDraw responds by displaying a Print dialog box very much like the one shown in Figure 13-2. The dialog box is riddled with options that are either repetitive or fall outside the range of everyday use.

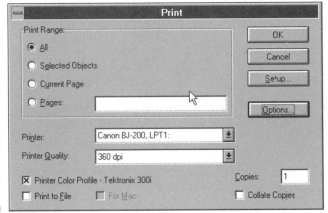

Figure 13-2: The Print dialog box.

Figure 13-2 shows the options that appear when you print to a PostScript printer, the Rolls Royce of printing technology. Depending on the printer you use, many of these options may not appear in your Print or Print Options dialog box. If I were you, I wouldn't mourn their absence. You pay for technology so that it can automate and simplify your life, not introduce whole new worlds of confusion and anxiety. As far as the entirely acceptable and admirable I-want-to-go-home-and-be-with-my-family quotient is concerned, you're better off without these missing options.

For the moment, I'll assume that you're more interested in getting the job done than in learning about Draw's printing options on an item-by-item basis. To this end, the following sections outline some common printing scenarios. Later, I describe each of the most important printing options individually.

Printing the entire document

To print your entire document — whether it's a single-page drawing or a multipage document — do the following:

1. **Shout at the person next to the printer to make sure that everything's ready to go.**

   Or just check for yourself that your printer is on.

2. **Choose File⇨Print.**

   The Print dialog box appears.

3. **Click on the OK button.**

   This action initiates the printing process.

As CorelDraw works on printing your drawing, it displays a message like the one shown in Figure 13-3. A progress bar indicates how close the printer is to completing the process. If you think of something you missed — like, "Aaugh, I forgot to draw the toenails!" — and you're interested in saving a bit of tree and a bit of time, click on Cancel or press Esc. Draw closes the message box and returns you to your drawing.

Figure 13-3:
Just so you don't think that the program is goofing off, Draw tells you what it's doing.

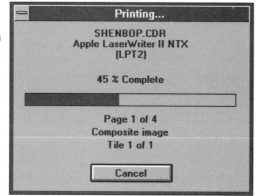

After you've printed every page of a document about 17 times, you can't be so methodical about it. Just press Ctrl+P, Enter.

Be sure to wait for the dialog box to appear between pressing Ctrl+P and Enter. If you press Enter before the dialog box comes up, CorelDraw ignores you (talk about uppity programs).

Printing multiple copies

Generally, the tried-and-true methods for producing multiple copies of a drawing, newsletter, or other document are to print a single copy and then photocopy it or to trundle it off to a commercial printer. The latter offers the benefit of a wide variety of paper stocks and the satisfaction of truly solid inks, as opposed to the malaise of toner and weak ribbon inks supplied by computer printers. Even a fly-by-night, cut-rate commercial printer delivers better results than a photocopier.

However, if you don't have time for a commercial printer and the office photo-copier is out of whack as usual, you can print multiple copies directly from CorelDraw. Do the following:

1. **Make sure that the printer is on and stocked with paper.**

   A full paper tray is a happy paper tray.

2. **Choose File⇨Print.**

   There's that Print dialog box again.

3. **Enter the number of pages you want to print in the Copies option box.**

   You can go as high as 999 (maybe higher . . . but do you want to test it?), a sufficient number of copies to send most printers to the repair shop.

4. **Click on OK.**

If you plan to go somewhere for some coffee and a croissant while your 126 copies print, you may want to warn your office mates that the printer will be tied up for a while, not so much for their benefit as for your own. I used to work at a service bureau, so I know what coworkers do when you leave a long print job running. They walk over to your machine and click on the Cancel button. When you return an hour later, confident that the pages are finished, you find three copies waiting on your desk with a sticky note that reads, "Quit hogging the printer!"

In an office environment, every long print job requires a sentinel. At least have someone keep an eye on your machine while you're gone.

If you're looking for the lazy person's way to print multiple copies, press Ctrl+P, Alt+C,*X,* Enter, where *X* is the number of copies you want to print.

Printing selected pages only

When working on a multipage document in Draw, you won't always want to print every page. One time you might want to see only page two. The next you may want to reprint page six after fixing a typo. Still another time, you'll have to print a new copy of page three after the first one jams in the printer. To print only certain pages, follow these steps:

1. **Is the printer on?**

   Check and see.

2. **Is your head screwed on straight?**

   Always good to check.

3. **Press Ctrl+P.**

   You've been through this process enough times to use the keyboard equivalent.

4. **Click on the Pages radio button to turn it on.**

5. **In the text box to the right of the Pages radio button, enter the page numbers of the pages you want to print.**

   If you want to print pages 1 through 3, for example, you can either type **1,2,3** or **1-3.** If you want to print pages 1, 3, 8, 9, and 10, type **1,3, 8-10** or **1,3,8,9,10.**

6. **Click on OK.**

Or to heck with all that. Just press Ctrl+P, Alt+P, and Tab and then type the numbers of the pages you want to print.

- Enter the number of copies of each page you want to print in the Copies option box.

- In the Print Range area, select the All checkbox to print all pages of a multipage document.

- When the Selected Objects option is checked, Draw prints only the selected objects in the drawing. (This option isn't visible unless one or more objects in the drawing area are selected.)

Individual Printing Options

If your only printing interest is getting the pages out, you've read everything that you need to know. But if you want to store away some extra printing knowledge for a rainy day, read the following descriptions of the most useful options found in the Print and Print Options dialog boxes. To access the Print Options dialog box, shown in Figure 13-4, click on the Options button in the Print dialog box.

Page preview area

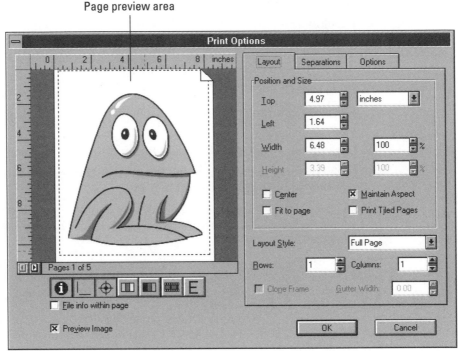

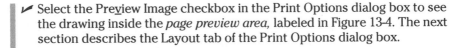

Figure 13-4:
The Print
Options
dialog box.

✔ Select the Preview Image checkbox in the Print Options dialog box to see the drawing inside the *page preview area,* labeled in Figure 13-4. The next section describes the Layout tab of the Print Options dialog box.

✔ Select the Fit To Page checkbox to reduce or enlarge the size of the drawing so that it just fits onto a sheet of paper. This option is especially useful when printing poster-sized drawings to printers that only handle letter-sized paper.

✔ To center the drawing on the printed page, select the Center checkbox.

✔ When you want to print a large drawing to small paper without reducing the drawing, you can cut it up into paper-sized chunks by selecting the Print Tiled Pages checkbox. For example, when printing an 11 × 17-inch drawing to a standard laser printer, the Print Tiled Pages option divides the drawing into four pieces and prints each piece on a separate page. The separate pages can be assembled after printing to produce your 11 × 17 drawing.

TIP

✔ Man, is this stuff dry or what? Reading about printing options is like having sand in your mouth. Makes you want to spit. Ptwu, ptwu.

Go get a drink of water. Some liquid refreshment may cut down on that sandy taste. But before you do, deselect the Fit to Page option in the Print Options dialog box. The option has to be deselected in order for the options described in the following three paragraphs to work.

✔ Enter values in the Left and Top option boxes to specify the location of the drawing as measured from the upper-left corner of the printed page.

✔ Enter values in the Width and Height option boxes to change the width and height of the drawing. You can also enter values in the % option boxes to enlarge or reduce the size of the printed drawing. These options have no effect on the actual size of the objects in the drawing area; they affect output only.

✔ If you check the Maintain Aspect radio button, all changes in size will be proportional. In other words, if you modify the height of your drawing, CorelDraw will automatically recalculate the width to ensure that the drawing won't be stretched or squeezed.

Using the page preview area

Back in Figure 13-4, I labeled the page preview area included in CorelDraw's Print dialog box. Figure 13-5 shows an isolated view of the page preview area and its various parts.

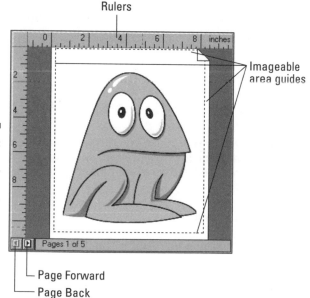

Rulers

Imageable area guides

Figure 13-5:
The page preview area found in the Print Options dialog box.

Page Forward

Page Back

Here's how the parts work:

- The four *imageable area guides* outline the area in which your printer can print objects. Except for typesetters and other fabulously expensive high-end printers, all printers have a dead zone around the outside of the page on which they cannot print.

- When you select the Print Tiled Pages option, the size of the preview increases to the size of several — usually four — printable pages placed end on end. (Too bad the preview doesn't display the page breaks so that you know what in tarnation is going on.)

- The rulers are entirely decorative; they don't even offer tracking lines like rulers in the drawing area do (discussed in Chapter 6).

- Click on the Page Back arrow to preview the preceding page. Click on the Page Forward icon to preview the following page. These icons apply to multipage documents only.

Printing full-color artwork

So far, I've covered and ignored roughly equal halves of CorelDraw's printing options. For reasons that I've already discussed, I intend to leave it that way. But you should know about one other option, the Print Separations checkbox (found in the Separations tab in the Print Options dialog box), especially if you intend to print color drawings.

Before I go any further, some background information is in order. There are two ways to print a color drawing. You can either print your drawing to a color printer or you can separate the colors in a drawing onto individual pages. Each method has benefits and drawbacks:

- Printing to a color printer is easy. And you get what you expect. The colors on the printed page more or less match the colors on-screen. Unfortunately, a commercial printer can't reproduce from a color printout. Sure, you can make color photocopies, but professional printing presses can print only one color at a time.

- If you want to commercially reproduce your artwork, you have to tell Draw to print *color separations,* one for each primary color: cyan, magenta, yellow, and black (introduced in the section "Making a new color from old favorites" in Chapter 7).

To print color separations in CorelDraw, do the following:

1. **Click on the Options button in the Print dialog box.**

   The Print Options dialog box appears.

2. **Click on the Separations tab.**

3. **Click on the Print Separations checkbox.**

4. **Click on OK to close the Print Options dialog box.**

5. **Click on OK in the Print dialog box to initiate the print process.**

Draw automatically prints a separate page for each of the four primaries.

Each page looks like a standard black-and-white printout, but don't worry. When you take the pages to a commercial printer, a technician photographically transfers your printouts to sheets of metal called *plates*. Each plate is inked with cyan, magenta, yellow, or black ink. The technician prints all the pages with the cyan plate first and then runs the pages by the magenta plate, the yellow plate, and finally the black plate. The inks mix together to form a rainbow of greens, violets, oranges, and other colors. For example, the four separations shown in Figure 13-6 combine to create a green Shenbop sitting on a royal purple lily pad. (Use your imagination — this is a black-and-white book.)

When you select the Print Separations option in the Separations tab of the Print Options dialog box, Draw automatically selects several other checkboxes. *Don't deselect any of them;* they enable the commercial printer to line up the separations and keep them in order. Better yet, call the printer and ask what's needed as far as negatives, emulsion up/down, densitometer, and so on are concerned.

Cyan

Magenta

Figure 13-6:
The color separations required to print a full-color Shenbop.

Yellow

Black

Part IV
Corel's Other
Amazing Programs

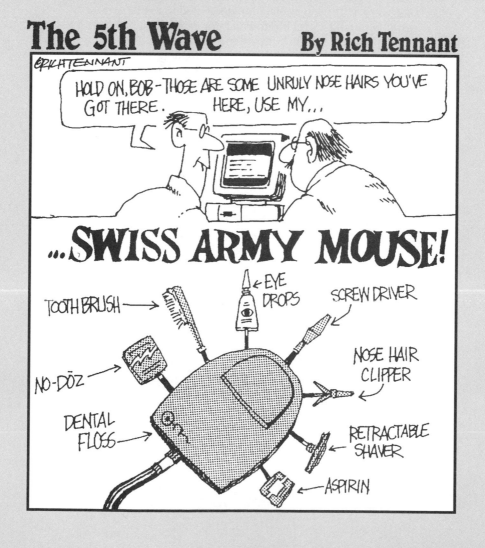

The 5th Wave   By Rich Tennant

In this part...

CorelDraw is first and foremost a drawing and publishing program. But by night, it doubles as a community of software, with each application dedicated to a different artistic pursuit. Corel Photo-Paint, for example, lets you edit digital photographs and create free-form images. CorelChart lets you chart numerical data using bars, lines, and pies. CorelShow lets you assemble on-screen slides shows, CorelMove lets you create your own animated masterpieces, and CorelVentura lets you put together long documents such as research papers and best-selling novels.

Frankly, none of these program rivals CorelDraw in terms of its range of capabilities or its overall utility. Although some people have argued that CorelDraw is the best drawing software for Windows, none of the other programs qualify as the best in their respective classes. But taken as a whole, they make up a full-fledged graphics studio, something that you can't say about any of CorelDraw's competitors. The combined features of these programs pack the kind of punch that no other graphics software can hope to match, particularly if you're just beginning to learn your way around the immense world of computer art.

Chapter 14

Programs in the Night, Exchanging Data

● ●

In This Chapter

▶ A variety of OLE that has nothing to do with matadors

▶ South-of-the-border birthday celebrations

▶ Embedding objects step-by-step

▶ A first look at Photo-Paint

▶ What to do when embedding doesn't work

▶ Linking objects to disk files

▶ When all else fails, import

● ●

*T*echnology and progress bring with them an element of terror. Machines help you work more productively and reduce physical effort, but an unmistakable promise lurks in the background: You're barely keeping up. The next bit of technology is going to leave you in the dust.

At least it seems that way sometimes. And believe me, I'm every bit as suscep-tible to the technology trap as you are. Every time I turn around, some new piece of software or hardware is bound and determined to make me feel like I've been covering the computer industry for five minutes.

So when I tell you that the stuff in this chapter is a piece of cake, you can believe me. Unlike other wacko technological breakthroughs, this one isn't going to give you any problems. I promise.

OLE's Not That Bad

Well, all right, *object linking and embedding* — *OLE* for short — does have a certain eerie ring to it. But such phrases exist just to amuse the computer zealots who aren't happy unless they know at least a dozen 15-syllable phrases that are guaranteed to shock their like-minded friends into frenzied states of information-age envy.

For everyone else, OLE should be known as a *birthday party*. Program A gives Program B a gift of text, graphics, or other digital stuff. Program B remembers who gave it what so that Program B can call on Program A to make any necessary changes or alterations. Okay, it's an idealized birthday party — if your Uncle Elmer gave you a jacket that didn't fit, he probably would give you the receipt rather than return it himself. Let's just say that computer programs have better manners than that. When a program gives a gift, it guarantees the gift for life.

I'm telling you about OLE because it links all of Corel's diverse and independent programs and enables them to work together like . . . well, I think you've had enough analogies for one day. When Corel Photo-Paint gives an object to CorelDraw, you can revisit Corel Photo-Paint and edit the object by double-clicking on the object in CorelDraw. It's like one big, happy family. Oops, that's an analogy, isn't it?

Taking OLE by the Horns

You need to remember that there's no command, file, option, or anything else called OLE. It's an invisible function built into Microsoft Windows 3.1 that paves the way for a variety of commands and options that I'll describe shortly, the same way that natural selection paves the way for fish to walk on their fins and protozoa to attain higher education. (These analogies are going downhill, aren't they?)

Now, you and I could explore every nook and cranny of OLE — and eventually, I'll explore a few of them — but the best way to really understand how OLE works is to try it out.

The following steps explain how to create something in Corel Photo-Paint, *embed* it in a CorelDraw drawing, make changes to the embedded object within Photo-Paint, and have those changes incorporated automatically in Draw:

1. **Open any old drawing in CorelDraw.**

   For the purposes of this exercise, it doesn't matter which one. I opened the Shenbop file (gosh, what a surprise).

2. Press Ctrl+Esc.

Or choose S<u>w</u>itch To from the Control menu in the upper-left corner of the interface. Windows — not CorelDraw — displays the Task List dialog box shown in Figure 14-1.

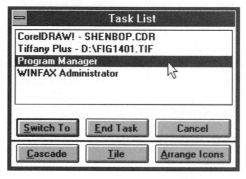

Figure 14-1:
The Task
List dialog
box lets you
switch
between
running
programs.

3. Double-click on the name Program Manager in the scrolling list.

Windows switches from CorelDraw to the familiar Program Manager (shown ages ago in Figure 2-1).

4. Double-click on the Corel Photo-Paint icon.

You'll find it inside a window called Corel. If you can't find the window, choose <u>W</u>indow⇨Corel. After you double-click on the icon, Photo-Paint starts.

5. Inside Photo-Paint, open an image.

As in CorelDraw, you open a file on disk by choosing <u>F</u>ile⇨<u>O</u>pen or by pressing Ctrl+O and selecting a file from the ensuing dialog box. In Figure 14-2, I opened the APPLE.PCX file, which is included in the COREL50\PHOTOPNT\SAMPLES directory.

6. Select the Lasso tool.

Press and hold down the Arrow tool in the toolbox and then choose the Lasso tool from the flyout menu, as demonstrated in Figure 14-2.

7. Select the image.

Click+drag around the image with the Lasso tool to encircle it. As if it were using a real lasso, Photo-Paint tightens the selection outline around the image.

8. Press Ctrl+C.

Or choose <u>E</u>dit⇨<u>C</u>opy. This command copies the image to the Clipboard.

Paintbrush tool
Arrow tool flyout menu   Lasso tool

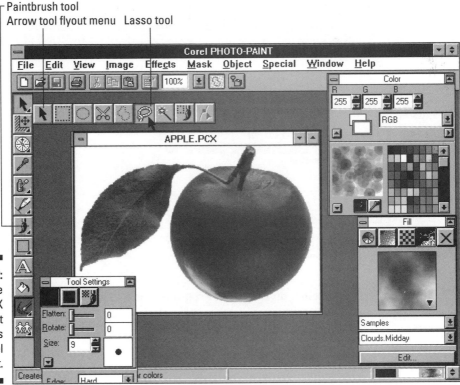

Figure 14-2:
The
APPLE.PCX
image as it
appears
inside Corel
Photo-Paint.

9. Switch to CorelDraw.

To do so, press Ctrl+Esc to display the Task List dialog box and then double-click on the name CorelDraw (followed by the name of the open file) in the scrolling list.

10. Press Ctrl+V.

Or choose Edit⇨Paste to retrieve the image from the Clipboard and paste it in the drawing area. Figure 14-3 shows the result of pasting the apple image in the Shenbop drawing. Notice that the status line recognizes the apple as a Photo-Paint object, which shows that the image is an *embedded object,* or a birthday gift from Photo-Paint to Draw.

11. Switch back to Corel Photo-Paint.

Press Ctrl+Esc and double-click on the name Corel Photo-Paint in the scrolling list.

12. Press Alt+F4.

You don't need Photo-Paint anymore, so choose File⇨Exit to quit the Photo-Paint program. If a message appears asking you whether you want to save the image, click on the No button. Windows automatically returns you to CorelDraw.

Figure 14-3:
Your drawing may not react as enthusiastically to embedding as mine does.

13. Save your drawing.

Then close it. Do whatever you want. You can even exit CorelDraw, exit Windows, turn off your computer, and wait several weeks before performing the next step. It doesn't matter. When you're ready to go on, restart Draw and open the drawing that contains the embedded object.

14. Suppose that you want to edit the image.

I don't know whether *supposing* actually qualifies as an active step, but it's essential to this exercise. In my case, I want to draw a horrified face on the apple to demonstrate its natural fear of being digested by a cartoon frog.

15. Double-click on the image.

Or choose Edit⇨Edit PHOTOPAINT Object. CorelDraw sends a message to Windows requesting that it locate and run Photo-Paint. Windows, being a good-natured soul, obliges. In a few moments, the Photo-Paint interface appears on-screen, complete with the open image, as shown back in Figure 14-2.

Isn't this awesome? You have to admire the way these programs communicate with each other. Pretty soon, they'll eliminate the need for users entirely, and we humans can go lie in hammocks sipping mint juleps for the rest of our days.

If you use an underpowered computer, Windows may not be able to carry out your request because your computer doesn't have enough memory to run Photo-Paint and Draw at the same time. If you get an error message that mentions memory or RAM in any way, you can't take advantage of embedding. However, you can try out embedding's cousin, *linking,* described later in this chapter.

16. **Edit the image as desired.**

If you're interested, I describe how to use Photo-Paint's painting tools in Chapter 15. For now, just select the Paintbrush tool (seventh tool down) and doodle away. I added big eyes and sweat droplets to make my apple appear frightened.

17. **Press Alt+F4.**

Or choose File⇨Exit & Return to FILENAME.CDR, where FILENAME.CDR is the name of your drawing. A message appears asking you whether you want to update *not* the Photo-Paint image but the drawing inside CorelDraw. Click on the Yes button. Windows then returns you to Draw, where you find the image updated according to your edits in Photo-Paint, as demonstrated in Figure 14-4.

Figure 14-4: Adding a look of abject terror to the apple in Photo-Paint improves my Draw scene considerably.

You now know how to take an object created in one of Corel's satellite programs — Photo-Paint, Chart, and so on — and embed it in CorelDraw. You also know how to edit an embedded object. If you got the preceding exercise to work, you don't have to read another page in this chapter. Just repeat the exercise every time you want to trade information between a satellite program and Draw. However, if you encountered an out-of-memory error or are simply feeling adventurous and want to find out more about OLE, read on.

More Ways for CorelDraw to Receive Gifts

Altogether, you can introduce objects into CorelDraw in three ways:

✔ You can copy an object from any Corel program and paste it in CorelDraw to embed the object, as demonstrated in the exercise you just finished. This technique is called *embedding* because Windows implants additional information about the object, such as which program created it and how to call up the program when it's time to edit the object.

✔ *Linking* — the second half of OLE — isn't so smart. You link an object by loading it from disk into CorelDraw, much as if you were opening a drawing. Draw maintains a link between the object and the disk file. If you later change the disk file, the object updates automatically. (Incidentally, this kind of linking has nothing to do with the linked text blocks discussed in Chapter 10.)

✔ *Importing* an object is like giving a gift anonymously. CorelDraw has no idea where the object came from, nor can it call another program to edit the image. As with linking, you load the file from disk into Draw. But that's it. No automatic updates, no quick editing techniques, no nothing. If you change the object later by using a different program, you have to import it from scratch in order to update the object in Draw.

✔ The beauty of importing is that it has nothing to do with OLE, so it works even when embedding and linking give you fits.

Linking, the semismart technique

There are two ways to link objects for use in CorelDraw. You can copy an object in Photo-Paint or some other program and then choose Edit⇨Paste Special in CorelDraw to establish a link. This technique has the advantage of working with Versions 3, 4, and 5. But unfortunately, it provides less flexibility than choosing the standard Paste command — which embeds the object, remember? At the same time, it requires you to run two programs simultaneously, thereby inviting the same old memory errors. To sum it up in layperson's terms, it's a dopey technique.

The second and much smarter way to link an object is to load it directly from disk by using the Edit⇨Insert Object command. The following is a typical CorelDraw linking scenario:

1. **Create an image in Corel Photo-Paint.**

   When you're finished, save it to disk.

2. **Quit Photo-Paint by pressing Alt+F4.**

3. **Start CorelDraw.**

   This way, you don't run two programs at once and clog up the works.

4. **Choose Edit⇨Insert Object.**

   The dialog box shown in Figure 14-5 appears on-screen.

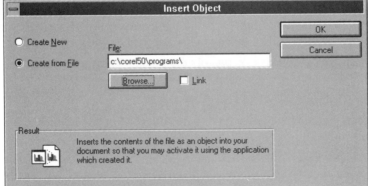

Figure 14-5:
The Insert
Object
dialog box.

5. **Select the Create from File radio button.**

   You'll find it on the left side of the dialog box.

6. **Click on the Browse button and locate the file you created in Photo-Paint.**

   The Browse button brings up a standard open-up-a-file dialog box (just like the Open Drawing dialog box described in Chapter 3). When you locate the Photo-Paint file, double-click on it to return to the Insert Object dialog box.

7. **Check the Link check box.**

   If you don't select Link, CorelDraw embeds the file. Then you have the same old problems you had when editing an embedded object earlier in this chapter.

8. **Click on the OK button.**

   Or press Tab and then Enter. Draw works away for a few moments, after which the image appears in the drawing area.

9. **Save the drawing.**

10. **Quit CorelDraw by pressing Alt+F4.**

11. **Start Corel Photo-Paint.**

12. **Open the image you just linked and edit it.**

    Go nuts.

13. **Press Alt+F4 to exit Photo-Paint.**

14. **Start CorelDraw again.**

    Hoo boy, these steps sure are exciting.

15. **Open the drawing you saved in Step 9.**

    CorelDraw displays the message shown in Figure 14-6 to demonstrate that it is indeed updating all linked objects in the drawing. When the drawing appears on-screen, the linked objects appear with all edits intact.

16. **Save the drawing.**

    Just to make it official.

Figure 14-6:
Draw
opening a
drawing that
contains
linked
objects.

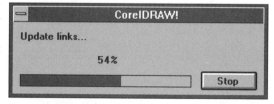

Importing, the last-ditch effort

If nothing else works and you don't want to tear out your hair (or the hair of the computer expert in your office), you can import an object created in any Corel program into CorelDraw. Here's how:

1. **Create an image in Corel Photo-Paint or some other program.**

   Don't forget to save it to disk.

2. **Quit the program by pressing Alt+F4.**

3. **Start CorelDraw.**

4. **Choose File⇨Import.**

   Draw responds by displaying the Import dialog box shown in Figure 14-7.

5. **Select the kind of file from the List Files of Type drop-down list box.**

   This drop-down list box appears in the lower-left corner of the dialog box. To import a Photo-Paint image, for example, you would select the TIFF Bitmap (*.tif, *.sep, *.cpt) option for Version 5. For the older Photo-Paint and the clip art on the CD-ROM, select Paintbrush (*.pcx), as in Figure 14-7.

6. **Locate the file that you want to import.**

   The scrolling lists and drop-down list boxes work just like those in the Open Drawing dialog box explained in Chapter 3.

7. **Click on the OK button.**

   Or double-click on the file you want to import. CorelDraw displays the imported object in the drawing area.

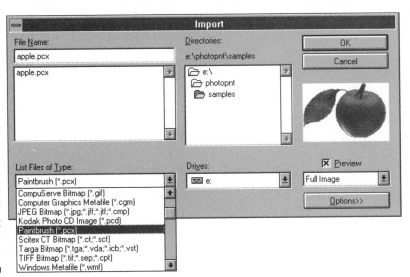

Figure 14-7:
The Import dialog box requires you to specify the type of file you want to introduce into Draw.

Chapter 15

Twisting Reality Around Your Little Finger

In the world of print-media advertising, nearly everything you see is a distortion of reality. Food products are slathered with hair spray, the performance of major appliances is simulated, and prefab clothing is custom tailored to fit the actors. As your mom warned you, "Believe only half of what you see in person and none of what you see in ads."

But what goes on in front of the camera is nothing compared to what happens after the film enters the mind of the computer. Rumor has it, for example, that every major movie poster is a veritable collage of body parts and other elements. The body you see rarely belongs to the actor whose head is pasted on top of it. In most cases, there's nothing *wrong* with the actor's body; it's simply more convenient to have an extra strike some poster pose and later slap one of the hundred or so head shots of the actor onto the body.

Corel Photo-Paint is the same sort of program. Although it's not by any means on par with the million-dollar image-editing systems used by professionals, Photo-Paint performs more than adequately for the price. You can open an image stored on disk and edit it on your computer. Draw a mustache on Aunt Patty, put Grandma Ida's eyebrows on Grandpa Neil's face, or distort little baby Melvin until he looks like Mighty Joe Young. The possibilities are just about endless.

Photo-Paint Blasts Off

You start Photo-Paint by double-clicking on the Corel Photo-Paint program icon in the Corel window in the Windows Program Manager. (For a quick refresher on starting programs in Windows, read the first few pages of Chapter 2.)

After Photo-Paint starts up, you see the Photo-Paint interface, which looks something like the one shown in Figure 15-1. If you see only a large gray area with a menu bar at the top, do the following:

1. **Press Ctrl+O.**

   Or choose File⇨Open to display the Load a Picture from Disk dialog box.

2. **Double-click on an image file to open it.**

   Corel includes a few sample images in the \SAMPLES directory, which resides in the \PHOTOPNT directory. (Try APPLE. PCX again.)

3. **Press F2, F3, F6, and F8.**

   These commands display all the roll-ups. You can also select View and choose the various roll-ups one at a time.

4. **Press Ctrl+T to display or hide the toolbox.**

   If the toolbox is hidden and you want to see it, press Ctrl+T. If it gets in your way and you want to put it away, press Ctrl+T again.

Don't worry if your interface doesn't look *exactly* like mine. Beyond the fact that Corel doesn't provide a dolphin image, your roll-ups may appear in different locations, and some that are rolled up in Figure 15-1 may be unrolled on your screen and vice versa. Don't freak out or anything.

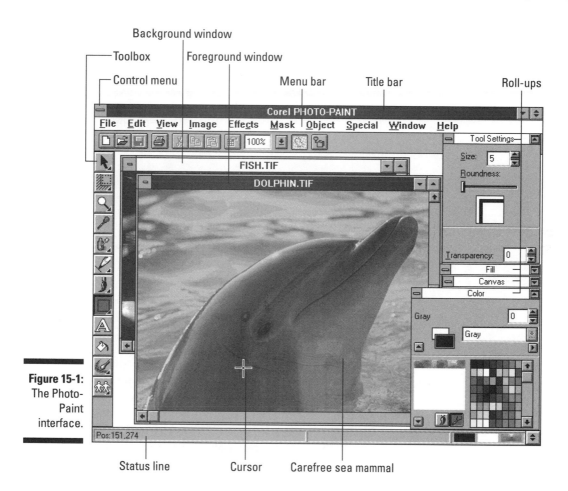

Figure 15-1: The Photo-Paint interface.

Background window

Toolbox

Foreground window

Control menu

Menu bar

Title bar

Roll-ups

Status line

Cursor

Carefree sea mammal

Paint in Yer Face

Hopefully, you'll recognize a few old friends from CorelDraw in Figure 15-1. Photo-Paint offers a title bar, a menu bar, and a status line, all of which perform like their counterparts in Draw.

But a sharp eye should notice a major difference. You can open more than one image at a time in Photo-Paint. Isn't this concept novel? You'd think Corel would have introduced this feature into Draw at about the same time "Bewitched" changed Darrens. As in other multidocument programs, each open image in Photo-Paint appears in its own independent window, which you can move, resize, scroll, and otherwise make a mess of in a variety of ways.

Most of Photo-Paint's core functions parallel those in CorelDraw. But to make sure that you don't lose anything in the translation — or perhaps more aptly, to ensure that the translation doesn't lose you — the following list lays it on the line:

- ✔ To open an image, press Ctrl+O or choose File➪Open. Photo-Paint displays the Load a Picture from Disk dialog box. Photo-Paint can open images saved in any of the most popular image formats, including .TIF, .PCX, and .JPEG. For the lowdown on file formats, see Chapter 22.

- ✔ Click on the Preview checkbox in the Load a Picture from Disk dialog box to preview the image that you select from the scrolling list.

- ✔ To open an image you've opened recently, choose its name from the bottom portion of the File menu.

- ✔ To save an image, press Ctrl+S or choose File➪Save. Remember, if you save early and often, the brain you save could be your own.

- ✔ Press Ctrl+P or choose File➪Print to display the Print dialog box. You can scale the image as you would in CorelDraw's Print dialog box and even fit the image to the page size. Click on the OK button or press Enter to accept your settings and initiate printing.

- ✔ To close the image in the foreground window, press Ctrl+F4, choose File➪Close, or double-click on the control menu in the upper-left corner of the image window. If you haven't saved your most recent round of changes, Photo-Paint asks you whether you'd like to save the changes or chalk them up as a waste of time.

- ✔ Press Alt+F4 or choose File➪Exit to get out of Dodge. If you have changed any open image since you last saved it, Photo-Paint asks whether you'd like to save the image to disk. When you've answered this question for every altered image (and I suggest that you do save your changes), you exit the Photo-Paint program and return to the Windows Program Manager.

Forging Ahead into the Void

If you'd rather not work from an existing image — which you do every time you press Ctrl+O — you can create an empty canvas and paint a new image from scratch. If you're still with me after that last daunting sentence, I can only assume that you're willing to forge ahead into the barren wasteland of the blank page utterly on your own. You're a pioneer — maybe a little short on common sense, but full of confidence and bravery.

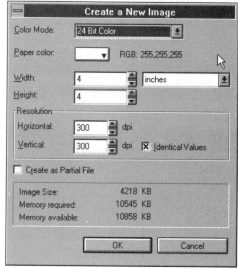

Figure 15-2:
The Create
a New
Image
dialog box.

To create a new image, press Ctrl+N or choose File➪New. Photo-Paint displays
the dialog box shown in Figure 15-2, which asks you three things:

How large an image do you want to create?

Which resolution do you want?

How many colors do you want to play with?

You don't need any help with image size; that specification is entirely up to you.
But resolution and color open up whole new cans of worms, as I explain shortly.
(Don't say that I didn't try to warn you.)

Dots per inch

Remember Chapter 1? I know you read it a long time ago, but you may want to
take a moment and quickly reread the Corel Photo-Paint section. It explains
acquiring images and covers a few other items that you may have found
yourself wondering about, such as how images work.

Here's a quick recap of this information. Unlike drawings in CorelDraw, which
defines drawings with complex mathematical equations, Photo-Paint images are
made of tiny colored dots called *pixels*. The number of dots in an inch is called
the *resolution*. So if you create an image that measures 4 × 5 inches with a
resolution of 72 dots per inch (the resolution value is always measured in dots
per inch), Photo-Paint creates an image that is (4 × 72 =) 288 pixels wide ×
(5 × 72 =) 360 pixels tall.

Though Photo-Paint can build an image that has different horizontal and vertical resolutions, you will rarely need to use this feature. If you use different resolutions, your pixels look like skinny rectangles instead of squares, which can make your image look unnatural. So unless you're trying to create some unusual effect, select the Identical Values option to ensure that your pixels are square.

Selecting your crayons

When you're creating a new image, Photo-Paint requires you to specify the number of colors you want to display on-screen at one time. It's as if your mom required you to select a box of crayons before you sat down to color. Photo-Paint's Color Mode drop-down list box lets you select one of six boxes of crayons:

- The first, Black and White, contains only two crayons, a black one and a white one. That's all you get.

- The next option is Gray Scale, which offers 256 shades of gray ranging from white to black. Unlike the 256 Color option (coming up), you can't alter any of the grays.

- The third option is 16 Color, which I call the econo-color mode. It uses a limited number of crayons and mixes them to produce the effect of more colors. Kinda like mixing red and blue to get purple even though your mom didn't get you a purple crayon.

- The next one, 256 Color, contains 256 crayons. But with this box you can swap crayons after you begin working on your image. If you don't like a certain shade of blue — cornflower, for example — you can change it to one of 16 million other possible color variations at any time. Any pixels in your image that are colored cornflower blue then update to the new color.

- 24 Bit Color (RGB) gives you access to all 16 million colors at once. This option provides the most versatility, but it comes at a price. A 16 million-color image takes up to three times as much room on disk as the same image created in 256 colors.

- The last option is 32 Bit Color (CMYK), which gives you access to all 16 million colors as well.

This option is for the true professionals who have color-matching posters on their walls. The 32-bit model is intended for print separations — a separated bitmap (as well as a CorelDraw file) separates into CMYK sheets. When you separate a 24-bit image, PhotoPaint does magical internal conversions to create the CMY sheets and then consults Merlin's Magical Spellbook to conjure up the missing black (K) sheet. When you separate a 32-bit image, no calculations are required. For control freaks only, a 32-bit image is four times as large as a 256-color image.

Growing and growing

The lower-right portion of the Create a New Image dialog box tells you how much memory your image consumes. The Memory Required value can't exceed the Memory Available value. If it does, Photo-Paint displays a message telling you that you don't have enough memory to create the picture.

Keep this restriction in mind when creating a new image because every option — Width, Height, Resolution, and Color Mode — contributes to the size of the image in memory. If you run into a memory limitation problem, try lowering the Resolution value. If that trick doesn't work, change the Color Mode option from 24 Bit Color to Gray Scale or 256 Color. And if the problem persists, lower the Width and Height values.

Too Many Tools for Its Own Good

Tools are central to any painting program. But before I go any further, let me make one thing clear: I'm no more going to explain every one of Photo-Paint's tools than I explained every one of Draw's capabilities in previous chapters. I just don't have the patience, and neither do you. Version 5 offers 51 tools. Are they all useful? Well, marginally. Are they all necessary? No way. Take the Locator tool, for example. It tells you where you are when you have two windows open for a single image. Sure, some very experienced users do that kind of thing when they have extra time to kill, but you and I never will. *Never.*

So bear with me while I concentrate on the tools that I think you'll find most useful. There are more than enough of those to keep you busy.

Toolbox tricks

Before I can discuss so much as a single tool, I need to tell you how the Photo-Paint toolbox works, because it's different from the Draw toolbox. Similar to Draw's toolbox, Photo-Paint's toolbox includes flyout menus. Photo-Paint distinguishes tools that offer access to flyout menus with small right-pointing arrowheads (see Figure 15-3).

You select an alternate tool from a flyout menu by clicking and holding on a tool in the toolbox and then dragging to the desired tool in the flyout menu. In Figure 15-3, for example, I dragged from the Arrow tool to the Polygon Selection tool Scissors, which makes the Polygon Selection tool the occupant of the first slot in the toolbox.

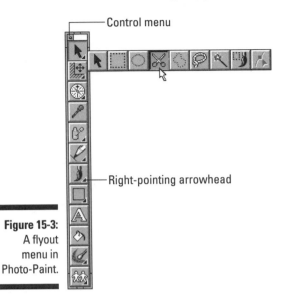

Control menu

Right-pointing arrowhead

Figure 15-3:
A flyout
menu in
Photo-Paint.

If you'd rather not have to deal with flyout menus, which I would best characterize as slow and unresponsive, you can reformat the toolbox to display all tools at once. Here's how:

1. Choose View⇨Toolbox⇨Floating.

Clicking on Floating disengages the toolbox from the left side of the editing window. Click on the control menu icon for the toolbox (labeled in Figure 15-3). Deselecting Grouped turns off the command and breaks up the tools so that every tool has its own slot in the toolbox, as shown in Figure 15-4.

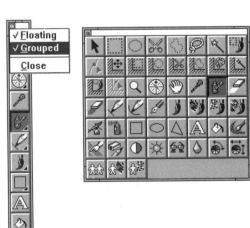

Figure 15-4:
Turning off
the Grouped
command
eliminates
the need for
flyout
menus.

2. **Choose a shape for your new toolbox.**

   After you ungroup the tools, Photo-Paint lists them in a big square blotch, which can be difficult to manage. You can pick up the sides of the box and reshape it to make it more vertical or more horizontal, as demonstrated in Figure 15-5.

Figure 15-5:
Reshape the toolbox to make it more vertical or horizontal and thus easier to deal with.

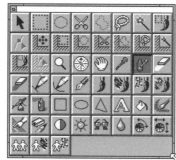 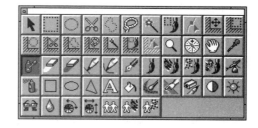

Moving the toolbox

Simply click and hold on the white bar above the tool icons. The bar changes color (stating that it's active), and you can drag it to a new position on-screen. To reanchor the toolbox, click on its control menu icon and deselect Floating. The toolbox folds itself back into its original configuration and glues itself back to the left side.

The Navigation Tools

Two navigation tools are worth worrying about. The *Zoom tool,* which looks like a magnifying glass (see Figure 15-6), allows you to magnify an image or back away from it. Click with the Zoom tool to magnify an image to twice its previous view size. Right-click to zoom out to half the preceding view size. Press Ctrl+1 or choose <u>V</u>iew⇨<u>1</u>00% (No Zoom) to return to the 100 percent view size. The title bar lists the current level of magnification.

If an image is so large that it exceeds the boundaries of its window, you can scroll the image by selecting the *Hand tool* and dragging inside the image window. Try it and you'll see that this method is about ten times more intuitive than messing around with scroll bars.

As I mentioned earlier, the *Locator tool* has no business consuming space in your brain. I labeled it in Figure 15-6 only because it's a notorious example of a good-for-nothing tool.

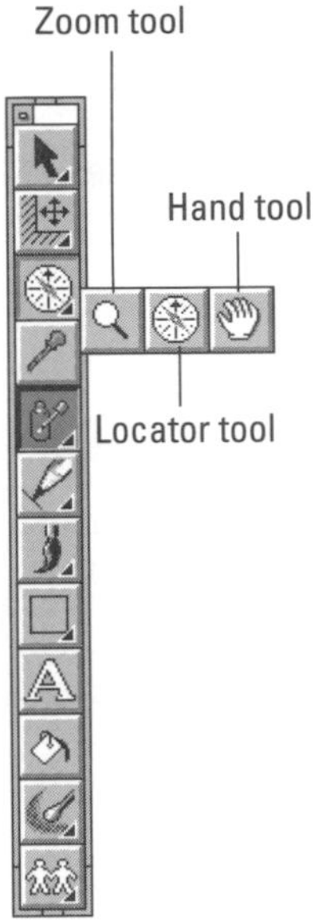

Zoom tool

Hand tool

Locator tool

Figure 15-6:
The three
navigation
tools in
Photo-Paint.

The Selection Tools

As in CorelDraw, you have to select portions of an image in Photo-Paint before
you can manipulate them. But instead of selecting discrete objects, you select
areas of the image much as if you were cutting patterns out of a bolt of fabric.
And Photo-Paint provides you with nine different types of scissors to cut with,
as shown in Figure 15-7 and described in the following list:

✔ I lied — the Pick tool isn't really a cutting tool. After you marquee an area
with one of the following tools, come back to this tool to move it or to
stretch, squeeze, rotate, or make julienne fries with it.

✔ Drag with the Rectangular Selection tool to marquee a rectangular portion
of the image.

✔ Drag with the Circular Selection tool to marquee a circular portion of the
image.

✔ Use the Scissors tool to create a free-form selection outline with straight
sides, such as a star or other polygon. Click to set the first point and
continue clicking to add corners to the polygon. Photo-Paint automatically
draws a straight line between each click. When you have finished drawing
your polygon, double-click to convert it to a selection.

✔ Drag with the Freehand Selection tool to marquee an irregular portion of
the image. When you drag with the left mouse button, it grabs everything,
and when you drag with the right mouse button, it ignores the background
(which is usually white).

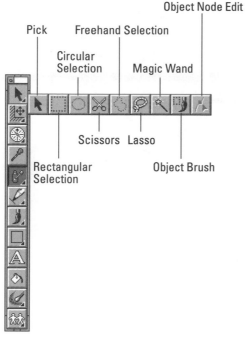

Figure 15-7:
The nine
Selection
tools in
Photo-Paint.

✔ Drag with the Lasso tool to select a free-form area of the image. After you finish dragging around the area you want to select, Photo-Paint tightens the selection outline around everything that isn't white, as if it were a real lasso. (You Easterners prob'ly don't get that lassoin' analogy, but out here in the West, we spend all our free time ropin' calves, payin' grazin' fees, and tryin' to stop our herds from stampedin', so it makes perfect sense t' us.)

✔ Click with the Magic Wand tool to select an area of continuous color. For example, I clicked at the location shown by the Magic Wand cursor in Figure 15-8 to select an area of ocean. The Magic Wand tool can take several minutes to work because it involves complex mathematical operations that tax Photo-Paint's tiny brain.

✔ Drag with the Object Brush tool to grab an area based on the shape of your brush. It's kinda like picking up fallen bus fare with large fuzzy mittens. Easterners may like this tool, but us Westerners tend to outlaw public transportation and snowflakes.

✔ You use the Object Node Edit tool (the last one) *after* you select an object with any of the preceding tools. After you create an area, go back to the Object Node Edit tool and click on it; nodes and control points, much like the ones you see when you play with the Envelope feature in CorelDraw, appear. Now you have more precision when attempting to select a region.

Figure 15-8:
The result of selecting an area of continuous color with the Magic Wand tool and changing its fill color.

Editing a Selection

After you select an area of your image, you can wreak havoc on the selection in a variety of ways:

✔ Drag the selection to move it to a different location in the image.

✔ Use the Cut, Copy, and Paste commands to duplicate the selected area. These commands are especially useful for creating image collages. For example, you can copy an area from one image and paste it into another (doing so can invoke a cool layering issue, which I'll get to soon).

✔ Drag a corner handle to enlarge or reduce the image.

✔ Click on a selected image to access the rotate and skew handles, which work just like those discussed in Chapter 9. Figure 15-9 shows the result of selecting the dolphin with the Scissors tool and then reducing and rotating the selection.

✔ Click on the image a third time to access the perspective mode, just like in Draw.

✔ Choose commands from the Image⇨Flip and Image⇨Rotate submenus to apply automated transformations.

✔ You can paint inside a selection with one of the painting tools that I describe later in this chapter. The selection acts as a stencil (or *mask*), preventing you from painting outside the lines. For example, after selecting

Figure 15-9:
You can transform a selection by dragging its handles.

the dolphin with the Scissors tool, I gave it the stripes shown in Figure 15-10 by painting inside the selection with the Freehand Brush tool. In order to create a mask, click on the second tool in the toolbox, and use the resulting set of flyout tools (shown in Figure 15-11). All these tools are identical to the tools found under the Pick tool (Rectangle, Circular, Node Edit, Magic Wand, and so forth) except that they create a *mask,* not a selection.

✔ To dramatically change the appearance of a selection, experiment with the commands in the Effects menu.

Figure 15-10:
In Photo-Paint, selections ensure that you paint inside the lines.

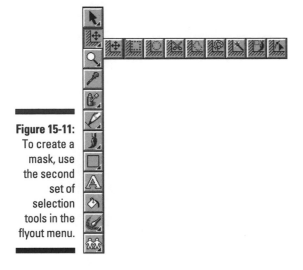

Figure 15-11:
To create a
mask, use
the second
set of
selection
tools in the
flyout menu.

Selecting Colors

Shown in Figure 15-12, the Eyedropper tool allows you to select colors from the image itself and then turn around and apply those colors with other tools. It's as if you were to draw color into your brush by dipping it into your painting. The benefit of the Eyedropper tool is that it allows you to match new colors to colors that already exist in the image.

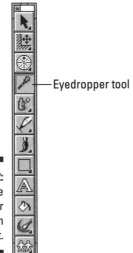

—Eyedropper tool

Figure 15-12:
The
Eyedropper
tool in
Photo-Paint.

✔ Click on a color in the image to replace the *outline color,* which is used by the Line and Brush tools. The outline color also affects the outlines of shapes drawn with the Geometric Shape tools.

✔ Right-click with the Eyedropper tool on a color to replace the *fill color,* which is used by the Text tool and Fill tools. The fill color also appears inside shapes drawn with Filled Geometric Shape tools.

✔ Ctrl+click the left mouse button with the Eyedropper tool on a color to replace the *background color,* which is used by the Eraser tool. When you select an area and press the Delete key, Photo-Paint fills the area with the background color.

✔ You can double-click on the Eyedropper tool to display or hide the Color Selection roll-up or press the F6 key to display or hide the Fill Selection roll-up, which keeps track of the colors you select with the Eyedropper.

The Painting Tools

The Painting tools come in three varieties: Standard Brush tools, which are extremely useful in a wide variety of situations; Goofball Brush tools, which are fun but generally useless gimmicks; and Line tools, which are functional but by no means the kinds of tools you'll use on a daily basis.

But you know the weirdest thing about these tools? There are three tools in each of the three categories. A coincidence, or divine intervention? I ask you.

The Standard Brushes

As shown in Figure 15-13, Photo-Paint provides three Standard Brush tools, which work as follows:

✔ Drag with the Freehand Brush tool to paint soft, free-form lines inside the image window. The lines you paint appear in the selected outline color.

✔ To change the way the brush paints, double-click on the Brush tool icon or press F8 to display the Tool Settings roll-up. Enter a value into the Width option box to specify the thickness of the line. Select one of the eight brush shapes to define the shape of the brush's tip.

✔ Drag with the Airbrush tool to create even softer lines than those drawn with the Freehand Brush tool.

✔ To access advanced brush options, select the Airbrush or Paintbrush tool and click on the down-pointing arrowhead in the Tool Settings roll-up. Here, you can change the appearance of the edges of your lines, make your lines transparent, or make them fade away as you drag as if you were lifting up on the brush.

✔ Use the Spraycan tool to paint a random pattern of pixels. For best results, use this tool in combination with a <u>W</u>idth value of 20 or greater.

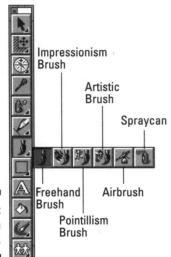

Figure 15-13:
The Brush tools.

Impressionism Brush

Artistic Brush

Spraycan

Freehand Brush

Pointillism Brush

Airbrush

The Goofball Brushes

One of the recent trends in professional-level painting and image-editing programs is *natural media,* which uses tools designed to emulate traditional, precomputer tools. In a program called Fractal Design Painter, for example, the Pencil tool draws as if it's actually made of graphite, and the Felt-Tip Marker tool lays down a translucent layer of what appears to be ink. You can even specify the distance between the individual bristles of a Japanese brush. Natural media is truly amazing.

Photo-Paint's answer to natural media is the set of Goofball Brushes shown in Figure 15-13, none of which even remotely resembles a traditional tool. But what the heck, maybe I'm too much of a curmudgeon for my own good. Maybe you'll think that these tools are the cat's meow. (Personally, I find *my* cat's meows irritating, which just goes to show you.) Anyway, here's how they work:

✔ The Impressionism Brush tool paints multiple lines in different colors. The lines weave back and forth, so I guess that you're supposed to think that Van Gogh may have used this tool. But come on, just because the guy cut off his ear doesn't mean that he was *totally* insane.

✔ If the Impressionism Brush captures the spirit of Van Gogh, then the Pointillism Brush tool embodies Georges Seurat. This brush lays down a bunch of differently colored dots. Wow, it's just the thing for painting a Hawaiian lei or a DNA molecule.

✔ The Artistic Brush tool is the stupidest of all. It just stretches one of eight oil splotches in a straight line between the point at which you begin your drag and the point at which you end it. It doesn't even follow the course of your drag. As Mr. T would say, "I pity the fool who would use this tool."

The Line tools

As their name implies, the Line tools draw hard-edged lines. Shown in Figure 15-14, these tools work like so:

✔ Drag with the Line tool to draw a straight line between two points.

✔ Drag with the Curve tool to draw a straight line with two round handles evenly spaced between the two end points. Drag the round handles to bend the line. When you are satisfied with the curvature of the line, click anywhere in the image window.

✔ Drag with the Pen tool to create a free-form line.

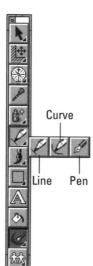

Figure 15-14: The Line tools.

The Erasers

If you make a mistake, you can use one of Photo-Paint's three Eraser tools (see Figure 15-15) to remedy the error:

Local Undo

Eraser

Color Replacer

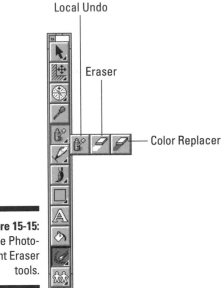

Figure 15-15:
The Photo-Paint Eraser tools.

✔ Drag with the Local Undo tool to undo the effects of the most recent operation. In other words, whereas choosing Edit⇨Undo undoes every effect of the preceding operation, the Local Undo tool undoes only those effects that lie in areas over which you drag. This tool is especially useful for erasing small portions of a line that you just finished drawing.

✔ The standard Eraser tool paints with the background color. Double-click on the Eraser tool icon or press the Delete key when nothing is selected to erase the entire image to the background color.

If you erase the entire image accidentally, choose Edit⇨Undo immediately!

✔ As you drag with the Color Replacer tool, it replaces all occurrences of the outline color with the fill color. For example, if you want to change a black line to white, change the outline color to black, make the fill color white, and then trace over the line with the Color Replacer tool.

The Color Replacer tool is great for creating candy cane lines. Try this trick: Draw a really fat line with the Pen tool. Then trace back and forth over it in a zigzag pattern with the Color Eraser. You have an instant candy cane.

My Take on the Other Tools

As I promised, I haven't discussed all of Photo-Paint's tools. The following list summarizes the remaining tools — and occasionally even offers insights into why I decided to breeze over them:

- ✔ Photo-Paint offers a bunch of Geometric Shape tools for drawing rect-angles, ovals, and the like. These tools are moderately interesting, but face it: Geometric shapes lend themselves to image editing about as well as vampire bats lend themselves to deep-sea diving. Harsh corners and jagged curves interrupt the naturalistic appearance of almost every image.

- ✔ Photo-Paint's Text tool — it looks like an *A* — is a tool that you shouldn't use. After you're finished with the text, it's no longer text; it's a bitmap. No spell-checker here. If your text is too small, enlarging it makes it very bumpy, and you have to remove it and retype the text with a larger font in mind. If you *really* want to add text to an image (such as a map to your house), embed the image in CorelDraw as described in the preceding chapter and then use Draw's much more capable Text tool.

- ✔ You access the Fill tools by pressing and holding down the Paint Bucket icon. As its name suggests, the Primary Fill tool lets you fill areas of continuous color with the current fill color. Other Fill tools let you fill areas with patterns, gradients, and textures. Unlike the Text tool, the Fill tools work beautifully. You probably won't use them as often as the Painting, Selection, and Navigation tools described in the previous sections, but they're great for making a picture of your grandma in front of an Amazon rain forest or a stellar nebula. Definitely keeps the neighbors guessing what your family roots are.

- ✔ The Retouching tools make precise changes to scanned photos. For example, the Water Droplet tool blurs an image as you drag inside the image window, and the Sharpener tool increases the focus. Other tools lighten the image, darken it, and change the amount of contrast between neighboring pixels. Arguably the most useful of the bunch is the Smear tool — the one that looks like a cotton swab — which smears colors into each other.

- ✔ The tool that looks like a couple of paper dolls is the Clone tool. Right-click with this tool to specify the portion of the image you want to clone and then drag to clone the area in a different portion of the image.

- ✔ In addition, Photo-Paint offers Impressionism and Pointillism Cloning tools that are as silly as their Goofball Brush counterparts.

Enough Layers to Make a Cake

The concept of layers is natural — shall I say intuitive? — in CorelDraw. It's easy to think of a chunk of text sitting on top of a circle and being able to move that text around without touching the circle beneath it.

The concept of layers is utterly alien to a painting program, however. Thou shalt work in Flatland. Thou shalt only put pixels in rows and columns. Thou shalt not pile the pixels on top of each other and expect to see the light underneath.

But Corel did it. In PhotoPaint, layering allows you to push around different images, rearrange their order, and have a lot of power that you thought you could only get out of something like CorelDraw. When you push one layered object out of the way, whatever was underneath becomes visible again.

This means that you can scan in a picture of the Golden Gate Bridge as one layer and a picture of the castle from Disneyland as the second. Then you can take the castle and float it on the water under the bridge! If you don't like that (or Mickey's lawyers threaten a lawsuit), you can pick up the castle and put it at the entrance to the bridge.

The possibilities are endless . . . almost. Layering adds a lot of overhead to the size of the file. If your bridge picture was 300K and the castle was another 300K, your image is now 600K, and it takes twice as much RAM to hold the image in memory as well. Power with a price.

Here's how to create and manipulate layers in Photo-Paint:

1. **Open a file.**

   Select File⇨New. This image will be your background or base image. I've picked an image of Stonehenge from the Sampler Photo-CD from Corel. Pick something that fits your lifestyle.

2. **Press F7 to access the Layers/Object roll-up.**

   Or choose Object⇨Layers/Object roll-up. Notice that the image appears on a little slide at the bottom of the roll-up, as shown in Figure 15-16.

3. **Import another file.**

   Select Edit⇨Paste from File to import the image. The image of the clown is called SAMPLE.CPT in your PHOTOPNT/SAMPLE subdirectory. After the second image comes in (shown in Figure 15-17), notice that another slide appears on the Layers/Object roll-up. The white around the man is part of the second image, like the white around an egg yolk. In order to remove it, I'll be doing some cooking from here on.

Figure 15-16:
The Layers/
Objects
Roll-up, with
one layer
displayed.

Figure 15-17:
The
imported
image
comprises a
second
layer.

4. Select the Lasso tool from the Pick tool flyout menu.

Select the Pick tool in the toolbox and then select the Lasso from the various tools presented to you. With the Lasso tool selected, click and drag the lasso around the clown. When you get close to where you started dragging, try to draw over the line, like rope over rope. Once Photo-Paint is done working, select Object⇨Create⇨Copy. Though nothing new appears on-screen, you've created another layer that contains just the man — no white stuff. The roll-up should confirm that you have a third layer. If you don't believe me, pick up the man and move him with the Pick tool, as shown in Figure 15-18.

Figure 15-18:
The copied image makes up a third layer.

5. Deselect the second layer.

Simply click on the second frame in the roll-up to deselect it. You should see something similar to that in Figure 15-19. You can now pick up and move the clown and place him anywhere in Stonehenge. Notice that wherever you place him, what is underneath is not destroyed. That's it — or is it? Check out what you can do to individual layers.

6. Click on the clown to rotate him.

(If you deselected the clown since the last move, you'll have to double-click.) As with CorelDraw objects, grab the rotate handle and pull (see Figure 15-20).

Figure 15-19:
When you deselect a layer in the roll-up, that layer disappears from view.

Figure 15-20:
Double-click on the layer/object to rotate and skew it, just as you do in CorelDraw.

7. Click on the clown a third time to create perspective.

Again, just like in Draw, pick up the nodes and pull (see Figure 15-21).

Figure 15-21:
Triple-click on the layer/object to create a perspective effect.

Little House of Horrors

Special effects are a lot of fun — not very practical, but a lot of fun. They're so much fun that I have to show you what you can do, if for nothing else than to impress your friends by scanning in a picture of them and giving them a severe pixel abuse treatment. These effects are called *plug-ins*. Plug-ins from your other favorite paint programs (such as Adobe Illustrator) can be used here, too.

Figures 15-22 through 15-28 show you some of the useless (but fun) effects that Corel Photo-Paint can do for you — or to you.

Figure 15-22:
The
Impressionist
effect
makes it
seem as if
you are
viewing the
object
through
glazed
glass.

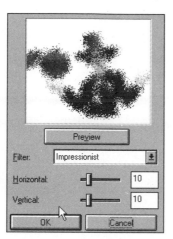

Figure 15-23:
The Map to
Sphere
effect.

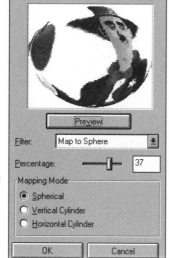

Figure 15-24:
The Pinch/
Punch
effect.

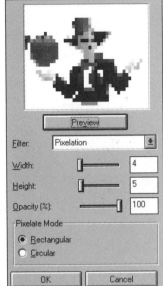

Figure 15-25:
The
Pixelation
effect.

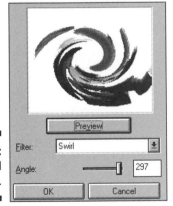

Figure 15-26:
The Swirl
effect.

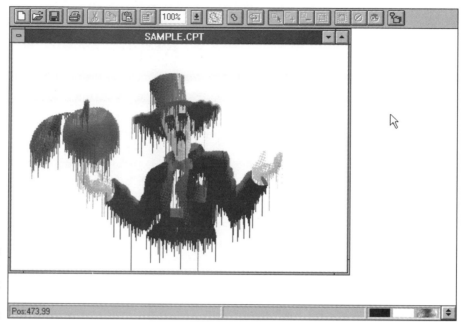

Figure 15-27:
The Wet
Paint effect.

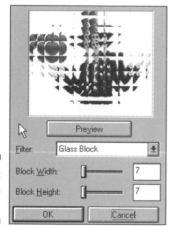

Figure 15-28:
The Glass
Block effect.

Chapter 16

Make Your Own On-Screen Snow Job

. . . .

In This Chapter

▶ Getting up and running with CorelChart

▶ Creating a new graph

▶ Learning how graphs work

▶ Using bar charts, line graphs, area graphs, and pie charts

▶ Adding depth to your charts

▶ Entering and organizing data

▶ Navigating in the Data Manager worksheet

▶ Inserting and deleting rows and columns in the worksheet

▶ Manipulating objects in Chart View

▶ Formatting titles, notes, and other labels

▶ Creating a screen show with CorelShow

. . . .

*I*f Ross Perot has done one thing for us salt-of-the-earth types, he's made us familiar with the power of graphs and charts (which are just different words for the same thing, by the way). Big bar charts show us the size of the ever-increasing deficit. Huge pie slices show us how much of our tax dollar goes toward paying interest on that monumental deficit. Large wiggly line graphs show us how exciting our lives would be if there were no deficit.

Whatever your impression of renegade politicians who have enough money to make a significant dent in the deficit if they would only stop yakking about it, you have to admit that graphs *are* impressive. I mean, you can recite statistics until you're blue in the face, but the moment you put some visuals behind those numbers is the moment that they start to make sense. Graphs don't tell; they show. They take your mountains of bewildering measurements, inventories, ledger values, and calculations and etch them into the unsuspecting brains of your audience. It's like a blast of math exploding through the optical nerves and embedding itself in the frontal lobe. Resistance is useless.

Well, that's the idea behind CorelChart, anyway. Chart is an artist's graphing program. Not only can you automatically convert numbers into graphical objects, but you can also edit those objects and make them look good.

Chart Sails onto the Screen

As with Draw and Photo-Paint, you start CorelChart by double-clicking on the CorelChart program icon in the Windows Program Manager. That's the easy part. After Chart starts up, it greets you with one of the most unfriendly sights offered by any Corel program — an empty window filled with dimmed tools and buttons and two menu options, as shown in Figure 16-1.

The File menu offers six commands. Mosaic Roll-Up, Color Manager, and Preferences relate to issues you deal with after you have a chart on-screen, so ignore them for now. The other three commands enable you to create a new graph, open an existing one, or leave the program. Presumably, you started this program for a reason, so that rules out the Exit command. If this visit is your first journey into CorelChart, you haven't created any graphs to open. That leaves you with the New command.

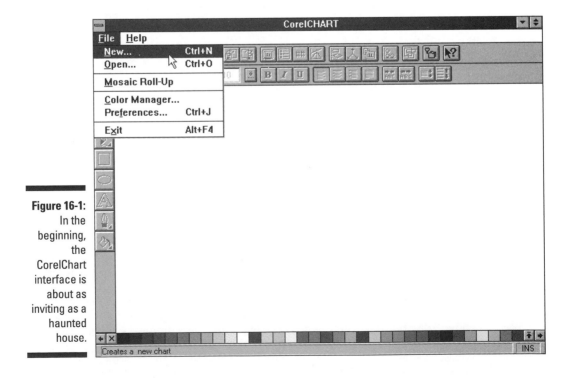

Figure 16-1: In the beginning, the CorelChart interface is about as inviting as a haunted house.

To create a new graph, do the following:

1. **Choose File⇨New.**

   Or press Ctrl+N. This command displays the New dialog box shown in Figure 16-2.

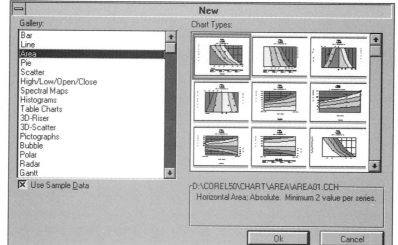

Figure 16-2:
Choose
File⇨New
and select
the type of
chart you
want to
create.

2. **Select the kind of graph you want to create from the Gallery scrolling list.**

   I describe most of these options in "The Many Makes and Models of Graphs" section later in this chapter. (A few options are so obscure that you don't want to know about them.)

3. **Select a design from the Chart Types list.**

   CorelChart briefly explains how the selected design works in the box below the Chart Types list.

4. **If it's not already selected, click on the Use Sample Data checkbox.**

   Corel's sample data helps you to organize your numerical data so that your graph comes out looking more or less the way you anticipate.

5. **Press Enter.**

   Or click on the OK button. Chart produces a sample graph that conforms to the category and design you selected in the New dialog box. Furthermore, the program now offers a tidy collection of menus, and the tools are no longer dimmed (see Figure 16-3).

6. **To edit the data, click on the Data Manager button.**

   Chart transfers you to the Data Manager, which lets you enter the numerical data that you want to include in your chart. As shown in Figure 16-4, the *worksheet* area contains Chart's sample data.

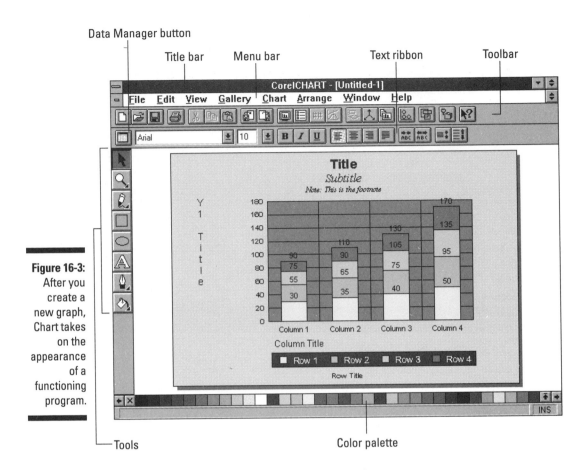

Data Manager button

Title bar   Menu bar   Text ribbon   Toolbar

CorelCHART - [Untitled-1]

File   Edit   View   Gallery   Chart   Arrange   Window   Help

Arial   10   B   I   U

Title

Subtitle

Note: This is the footnote

Column 1   Column 2   Column 3   Column 4

Column Title

Row 1   Row 2   Row 3   Row 4

Row Title

INS

Figure 16-3: After you create a new graph, Chart takes on the appearance of a functioning program.

Tools

Color palette

7. **Click on a cell and enter new text or numbers.**

   A *cell* is an individual block in the worksheet, sort of like a brick in a wall. Each cell contains a bit of text, such as the title of the graph or a number that you want to graph. After you enter a new value, press the Enter key.

8. **When you finish editing the data, press Ctrl+Tab.**

   Or click on the Chart View button. CorelChart returns you to the Chart View, which is the screen shown in Figure 16-3. Chart updates the Chart View to represent your new data.

9. **Press Ctrl+S.**

   Or choose File⇨Save to save both chart and data to disk. As always, you can't save frequently enough.

That's all there is to it. Pretty darn easy, right? Well, okay, there's the small issue of selecting one of the various kinds of graphs. All kinds of information about editing and formatting data may interest you. And of course, CorelChart offers many commands, tools, and buttons that I don't bother to mention. But you'll get the hang of it. Just keep playing around.

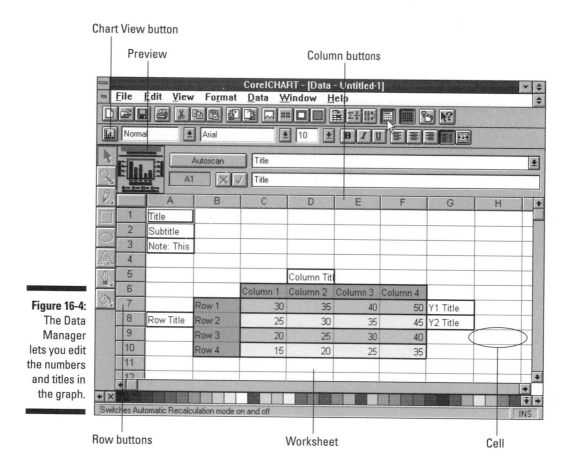

Chart View button

Preview

Column buttons

Figure 16-4:
The Data
Manager
lets you edit
the numbers
and titles in
the graph.

Row buttons   Worksheet   Cell

Getting to Know Graphs

Still want my help, huh? All right, then, let me start things off by explaining how graphs work. Suppose that you're the head of the baseball cap department for a clothing manufacturer. You want to show how well your department has done in comparison to other departments, specifically those that sell friendship bracelets and pajama bottoms (because you've thoroughly trounced both departments over the past year). Right away, you have three series of data:

- Baseball caps
- Friendship bracelets
- Pajama bottoms

In this case, you want to graph numerical data as a function of time. The data itself can be net profit margin, units sold, or any other measurement. The time may be weeks, months, years, millennia, or however long you've kept records of your data.

Figure 16-5 shows a typical data-over-time graph that contains the following elements:

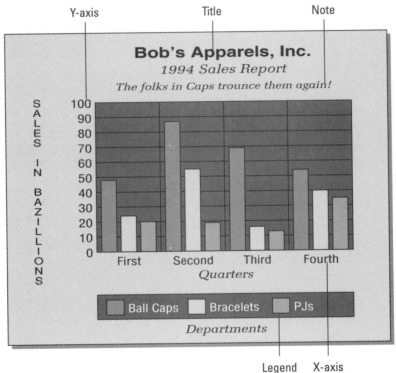

Figure 16-5: The anatomy of a graph.

- ✔ The numerical data — in this case measured in bazillions of dollars — is organized vertically on the *Y-axis*.
- ✔ Time, shown here in yearly quarters, puts in an appearance on the horizontal *X-axis*.
- ✔ The series to which a bar belongs determines its color in the graph. The tallest bars represent the largest numerical values.
- ✔ A *legend* beneath the graph explains which bar color corresponds to which series.
- ✔ Finally, titles, notes, and other labels explain the chart in plain English.

This data can appear in a bar graph, a line graph, an area graph, or one of several other kinds of graphs. The elements of a graph remain largely the same no matter what form your data takes.

The Many Makes and Models of Graphs

Although I endeavor to explain how different graphs affect your data, I have neither the time, space, nor inclination to show you examples of every kind of graph you can create in CorelChart. (Ah, isn't it refreshing to read such frank and honest text?) Don't get the wrong idea; I'll show you the stuff that's important for you to see. But you can view all the examples you want by choosing the New command from the File menu, selecting options from the Gallery and Chart Type lists, and pressing the Enter key. To test out variations on a graph you've already created, choose commands from the Gallery menu. These commands enable you to plot your data on a new kind of graph without starting over from scratch.

To view a *thumbnail version* (a small, rough sketch) of a graph before you apply it, press Alt,G to display the Gallery menu. Use the up- and down-arrow keys to highlight a graph variety. Then press the right-arrow key to display the submenu and press the down-arrow key to select a thumbnail, as shown in Figure 16-6. Once inside the submenu, use the up- and down-arrow keys to highlight different graphs and view the corresponding thumbnails. To exit a submenu, press the left-arrow key.

The following sections introduce the most useful varieties of graphs and explain how they work.

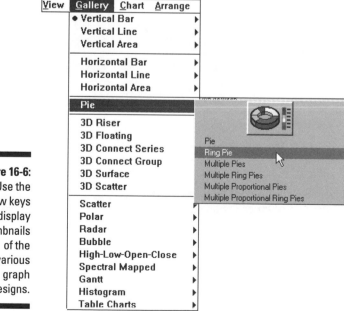

Figure 16-6:
Use the arrow keys to display thumbnails of the various graph designs.

Bar charts

Undoubtedly, the most popular form of graph is the *bar chart,* in which rectangles (or *bars*) represent data. Tall rectangles represent big values, and short rectangles represent small ones. Bar charts are ideal for graphing values as a function of time, as in the baseball cap scenario I mentioned earlier.

In vertical bar charts, also called *column charts,* the bars stand upright. In horizontal bar charts, the bars lie on their sides. Although vertical bars are more common, CorelChart only provides access to the horizontal variety from the New dialog box. When you want to create a chart with vertical bars, you have to choose one of the options from the Gallery⇨Vertical Bar submenu.

You can *cluster* matching bars from different series — for example, the bars representing baseball caps, friendship bracelets, and pajama bottoms for the second quarter — in one of four ways, as demonstrated in Figure 16-7.

Figure 16-7: The methods for clustering related bars from different series.

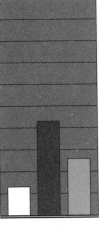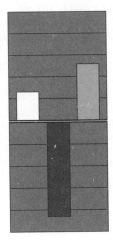

Side-by-side   Stacked   Paired (bipolar)   Percentage

- ✔ In a *side-by-side bar chart,* bars from different series rub shoulders.

- ✔ In a *stacked bar chart,* the bar from one series rests on top of the bar from another. This type of chart is useful when you want to show the sum of all series.

- ✔ *Paired bar charts* arrange bars from different series on opposite sides of the X-axis (or on opposite sides of the Y-axis in the case of horizontal bar charts). For some weird reason, CorelChart calls this graph *bipolar.* Use this kind of chart when you want to separate the bars and make them easier to read.

- ✔ A *percentage bar chart* is a variation on the stacked chart. Instead of simply adding up the values, CorelChart stretches or shrinks the bars so that each cluster adds up to 100 percent. This kind of chart is useful for demonstrating the relative performance of various series over time.

To create a three-dimensional bar chart, choose Gallery⇨3D Riser⇨Bars. Other variations include Gallery⇨3D Connect Series⇨Steps, Gallery⇨3D Connect Group⇨Steps, and the other options in the Gallery⇨3D Riser submenu. An example of the first method appears in Figure 16-8.

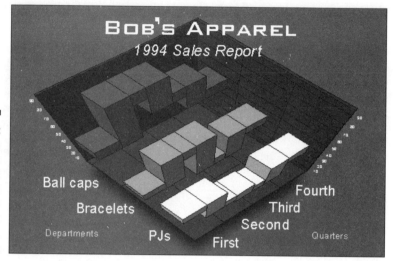

Figure 16-8: A variation on Figure 16-5 created by choosing Gallery⇨3D Connect Series⇨Steps.

Keep in mind that three-dimensional charts may look great but are more difficult to read than their two-dimensional counterparts. On one hand, the chart is more likely to attract viewer interest; on the other hand, the viewer is less likely to be able to determine what's going on. Therefore, as a rule of thumb, use 3-D charts only when you're more interested in wowing your audience than imparting concrete information. It's the ultimate snow-job function.

The chart design you can ignore

CorelChart offers yet another variety of bar chart, called *Dual Axis,* in the Gallery⇨Vertical Bar and the Gallery⇨Horizontal Bar submenus. A dual-axis chart provides two Y-axes, one along the left side of the chart and one along the right side. Different series conform to the different axes, which are themselves scaled differently. For example, if you wanted to bolster the pajama bottoms series, you could measure it against the right Y-axis. Then you could scale the right axis so that 50 is equal to 100 on the left axis, making every bar in the PJ series twice as tall as normal.

If you think that dual-axis charts sound confusing, just imagine how confusing they are for the folks trying to interpret your chart. Add that to the fact that CorelChart implements this feature very awkwardly, and you have the ingredients for a feature to ignore.

Line graphs

In terms of appearance, *line graphs* are very different from bar charts. Rather than using rectangles, line graphs plot data values as points measured along the X- and Y-axes. A straight segment connects each point to the next point in the same series. The result is several jagged lines that slope, spike, and occasionally cross.

Functionally, however, line graphs and bar charts are cousins. Like bar charts, line graphs are useful for mapping data over time, making them applicable to many of the same kinds of data. But at the same time, line graphs impart a sense of action and continuity that bar charts lack. The inclination of each segment demonstrates the performance of a series from one moment to the next. Because large changes result in steep inclinations, the most interesting line graphs show dramatic fluctuations. Furthermore, because each series is a connected, continuous element, line graphs best demonstrate the performance of a series that includes six or more data values.

Although line graph data may fluctuate dramatically, you don't want neighboring series to cross each other more than once or twice in the course of the graph. When segments cross too often, you create a *spaghetti graph,* which is difficult to read, not very pleasant to look at, and generally ineffective.

You can organize the series in a line graph in several different ways (see Figure 16-9):

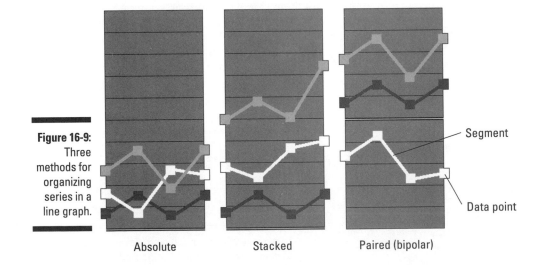

Figure 16-9: Three methods for organizing series in a line graph.

Absolute   Stacked   Paired (bipolar)

Segment

Data point

✔ In an *absolute line graph,* CorelChart graphs data values normally along the X- and Y-axes. Different series are allowed to overlap, as demonstrated in the first example of Figure 16-9.

✔ A *stacked line graph* adds the data values from one series to those from the preceding series and separates the lines as shown in the second example of Figure 16-9. In addition to displaying the sums of all series, stacking eliminates spaghetti graphs.

✔ *Paired line graphs* — again, CorelChart calls them *bipolar* — show different series on opposite sides of the X-axis (see the last example of Figure 16-9).

✔ A *percent line graph* is like a stacked graph except that it scales all values to add up to 100 percent.

For three-dimensional variations, choose Gallery⇨3D Connect Series⇨Ribbons or Gallery⇨3D Connect Group⇨Ribbons. Figure 16-10 shows an example of the former. Dramatic fluctuations in data values are very important in creating 3-D line graphs; minor fluctuations get lost in the special effects.

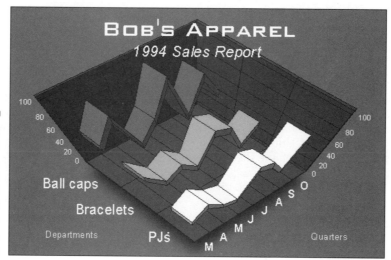

Figure 16-10: For this 3-D line graph, choose Gallery⇨3D Connect Series⇨ Ribbons.

Area graphs

Area graphs are just like line graphs except that each series is filled in and the data points don't appear as squares. You find the same options in the Gallery⇨Vertical Area and Gallery⇨Horizontal Area submenus that you find in the Gallery⇨Vertical Line and Gallery⇨Horizontal Line submenus. To demonstrate how these work, Figure 16-11 shows the charts from Figure 16-9 presented as area graphs. You can access 3-D area charts by choosing Gallery⇨3D Connect Series⇨Area or Gallery⇨3D Connect Group⇨Area.

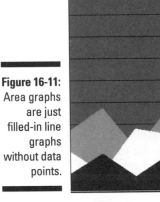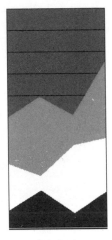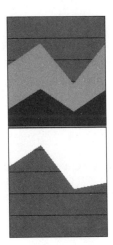

Figure 16-11:
Area graphs
are just
filled-in line
graphs
without data
points.

Absolute   Stacked   Paired (bipolar)

Pie charts

Unlike bar charts, line graphs, and area graphs, *pie charts* show one set of
values at a time. If you want to display more than one set of values, you have to
use multiple pies. The advantage of this system is that a pie always displays
data values in relation to the total, rather like a percentage chart. The pie is a
full circle, and each pie slice represents a data value as a percentage of that circle.

The options in the Gallery⇨Pie submenu work as follows:

✔ The Pie option creates a single 3-D pie for the first set of values in each
  series. For example, if I apply this option to my baseball cap data, the pie
  represents the data values for the first yearly quarter only and ignores the
  other quarters.

✔ The Ring Pie option cuts a hole in the center of the pie, making it look like
  a doughnut. Functionally, it's no different from a standard pie, but it looks
  cool, I guess.

✔ The Multiple Pies and Multiple Ring Pies options represent all sets of data
  values by assigning one pie to each set. In the baseball cap scenario, for
  example, four pies would show each of the four yearly quarters. All pies
  are the same size.

✔ If you want to scale the pies according to your data, choose the Multiple
  Proportional Pies or the Multiple Proportional Ring Pies option. This way,
  the yearly quarter with the heaviest sales gets the largest pie.

By default, all pies appear in 3-D. To remove the 3-D effect and make the pies
look like flat circles, choose Chart⇨Pie Thickness⇨No Thickness, followed by
Chart⇨Pie Tilt⇨No Tilt.

Making the Most of the Data Manager

After you find a variety of graph that you're more or less happy with — you can always go back and choose a different type later — you have to create the data that you want to graph in the Data Manager. You enter the Data Manager by clicking on the Data Manager button (refer to Figure 16-3).

The *worksheet* (shown in Figure 16-12) is the area in which you enter data in CorelChart. To do so, click on the cell in the worksheet that you want to change, type the data that you want to appear in that cell, and press Enter or the Tab key. The Enter key confirms your entry and selects the next cell down; the Tab key confirms your entry and selects the cell to the right.

The following list explains how to get around and use the controls in the worksheet area. All italicized terms are labeled in Figure 16-12.

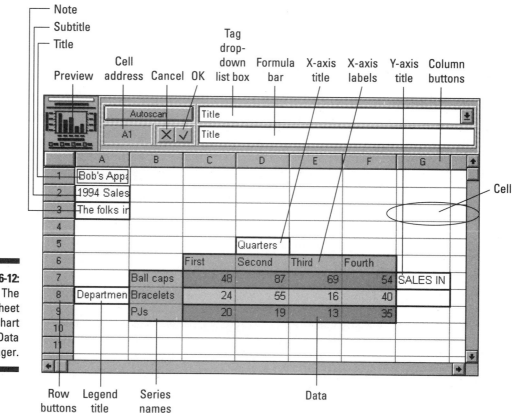

Figure 16-12: The worksheet in the Chart Data Manager.

✔ When you enter characters from the keyboard, they appear in the *formula bar*. You can select and edit individual characters by dragging over them in the formula bar. To select a whole word, double-click on it. To position the insertion marker, click inside the formula bar.

✔ If you make a mistake and want to restore the original contents of the formula bar, click on the *Cancel button* (the one that looks like an X) or press the Esc key.

✔ Clicking on the *OK button* (the one that looks like a check mark) is the same as pressing the Enter key, so why do it?

✔ To restore the contents of a cell after you press the Enter or Tab key, choose Edit⇨Undo.

✔ The *cell address* area — to the left of the Cancel button — lists the address of the selected cell as determined by its column and row location. Columns are lettered; rows are numbered. So cell E6 is five cells over and six cells down.

✔ Click on one of the *row buttons* to select an entire row of cells. Likewise, click on a *column button* to select an entire column of cells.

Setting up the data

CorelChart expects to find certain kinds of data in certain places. As I explain shortly, you can change how the data is organized, but here's how it starts out:

✔ Enter the title of the chart in the cell labeled *Title* (cell A1) in Figure 16-12. The same goes for *Subtitle* and *Note* (A2 and A3, respectively).

✔ Don't worry if you can't see all of your text in the cell after you press the Enter or Tab key. CorelChart only displays as much text as fits in the tiny cell space. For example, in Figure 16-12, cell G7 reads *SALES IN,* but the cell actually contains the text *SALES IN BAZILLIONS.* The word *BAZILLIONS* doesn't fit in the cell display, but it's still there and shows up just fine in Chart View.

✔ If you decide that you don't want an element in your chart, click on the appropriate cell in the worksheet, press the Backspace key, and select the None option from the *Tag drop-down list box.* For example, if you want to eliminate a note, click on cell A3, press Backspace, and select the None option. Then click on a different cell to confirm your change.

✔ Make sure to press Backspace and not Delete. When you press the Delete key, you display the Cut and Clear Options dialog box, which offers a little more than you need.

✔ Enter the names of the series in the area labeled *series names* in Figure 16-12. (Normally, the series names go in cells B7 through B10. My figure shows cells B7 through B9 because I changed things a bit.) Enter the title of the legend that explains the series in cell A8.

✔ Enter the X-axis labels — which commonly represent time — in the area labeled *X-axis labels* (cells C6 through F6). Enter the X-axis title in cell D5.

✔ When you opt for a horizontal graph instead of a vertical one, cells C6 through F6 and D5 adorn the Y-axis. Don't worry; it happens automatically and correctly.

✔ In a vertical chart, CorelChart automatically labels the Y-axis with numerical values scaled to fit your data. However, you should enter a title for the axis in cell G7.

✔ Again, CorelChart swaps this information to the X-axis when creating a horizontal graph.

✔ Unless you're creating a dual-axis chart, delete the contents of cell G8, which is the second axis label.

✔ Enter your numerical data in cells C7 through F10.

✔ The *preview* contains a little chart that shows you which labels you're currently entering. For example, when you click on cell A1, the title bar of the preview chart turns red. When you click on cell A2, the subtitle bar turns red. Pretty nifty feature, huh?

✔ If any of this process doesn't quite work the way I describe — for example, if the series names adorn the X-axis, and the X-axis labels appear in the legend — someone has changed the default settings on your copy of CorelChart. Choose Data⇨Data Orientation and make sure that the options are set as shown in Figure 16-13.

Figure 16-13:
The options
in the Data
Orientation
dialog box
should be
set so that
rows
indicate
series.

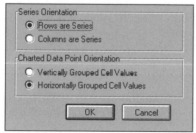

Changing the data to fit your needs

By default, the worksheet is set up to accommodate four series names and four data values per series. This default scenario is as good as any, but what if you want to change things? What if you want only three series and five values per series? Here's how to make these changes:

1. Click on the Row 10 button.

This action selects all of row 10, which represents the last series (the one you want to delete).

2. Choose Edit⇨Delete.

This command deletes the data from the entire row. Or press Delete to bring up the Cut and Clear Options dialog box and then press the Enter key.

3. Click on any cell.

It doesn't matter which one. The important thing is to deselect the row. Notice that the empty cells in row 10 are still formatted as they were when you entered the Data Manager. If you return to the Chart View, CorelChart still tries to chart this series and even dedicates space to the series in the legend.

4. Click on the Autoscan button.

This action forces CorelChart to reevaluate your data. Upon seeing the empty row of cells, the program eliminates any evidence of this series.

5. Click on the Column G button.

Doing so selects column G, the point at which you want to enter a new column of values for your three series.

6. Choose Edit⇨Insert.

Chart adds an empty column and scoots the previous column G — which contains the Y-axis labels — over to column H. Now you have a new column in which you can enter your data.

7. Press the Enter key five times.

Doing so moves the selection down to cell G6, the cell in which you want to enter the new X-axis label.

8. Type in the fifth X-axis label.

9. Press Enter and then type in some data.

This data is the last bit of information you have to enter for the first series.

10. Repeat Step 9 for the second and third series.

If you don't have any real values, enter dummy values for now so that you get the formatting squared away.

11. Click on a cell.

Again, you need to deselect the column.

12. Click on the Autoscan button.

CorelChart reformats the data again to include the fifth set of data values.

The key to adapting these steps to your particular needs is to know when to delete and insert rows and columns and when to click on the Autoscan button. Delete a row when you want to delete a series; insert a row when you want to add a series. Delete a column when you want to subtract data from existing series; insert a column when you want to add data. When you finish deleting and inserting, select a single cell and click on Autoscan.

Editing Any Old Element in Chart View

To see what CorelChart does with your new data, click on the Chart View button (refer to Figure 16-4) or press Ctrl+Tab. (If you have more than one chart open, stick with the Chart View button. Ctrl+Tab may switch you to the wrong open window.)

Assuming that you followed my instructions in the previous sections, all key elements should now be in place. But you're not going to like everything that Chart has done with them. Not to worry, though. As I mentioned earlier, CorelChart is an artist's graphing program. You can edit everything in Chart View to better meet your aesthetic demands. It's the perfect excuse to unleash that inner prima donna.

Scaling and coloring objects

You probably want to edit two varieties of elements: objects — which include the legend, the graph grid, series elements inside the graph, and even the background (see Figure 16-14) — and text. I cover editing objects in this section and editing text in the next section.

Editing objects in CorelChart is nearly identical to editing objects in CorelDraw. You'd probably pick up on it without my help if you sat down and played with it for an hour or so. But I'm supposed to help you eliminate all that experimentation, right? So without further ado, here's how it works:

 ✔ Click on the Arrow tool icon at the top of the toolbox to select it. This tool is the primary editing tool in CorelChart. Unless I state otherwise, you perform all of the following operations with the Arrow tool.

 ✔ To change the color of a series, select the little box — called a *series marker* — in the legend that corresponds to that series and then click on a color in the color palette at the bottom of the interface. You can also apply a new color to a series by selecting a bar, line, or pie slice associated with the series in the graph.

 ✔ You can change the colors of the graph grid, the legend box, and the background as well. Simply click on the object and then click on a color in the palette.

Arrow tool   Series element   Gridline   Graph grid   Background

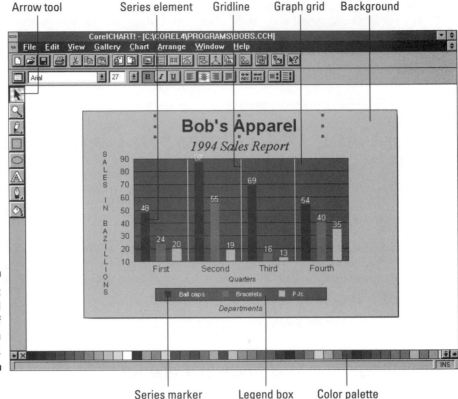

Figure 16-14:
Objects and
tools of
interest in
Chart View.

Series marker   Legend box   Color palette

🎯 ✔ To change the color of the gridlines inside the graph, click on the gridline and right-click on a color in the color palette. When you select a horizontal gridline, you change the color of all other horizontal gridlines as well, but the vertical gridlines remain unaltered. Select a vertical gridline and right-click on a color to change the color of all vertical gridlines.

✔ To select multiple objects, click on one and then Shift+click on another. Shift+click on an object that is already selected to deselect it.

✔ To move an object, click on it to select it and then drag it to a new location. You can move the legend and graph as much as you want, but you can't move series elements inside the graph or move the background.

✔ To move an object exclusively horizontally or vertically, Ctrl+drag it.

✔ To scale the legend or graph, select the object and then drag one of the eight handles that surround it. You can't scale the series elements or background.

✔ Click the right mouse button to apply special changes to series elements. When you select an object and then click the right mouse button, Chart displays a drop-down list box of editing options.

For example, when you click on a bar in a bar chart and click again with the right mouse button, you display the Bar Riser drop-down list box. Click on the Bar Thickness option to adjust the width of the bars in the graph (see Figure 16-15).

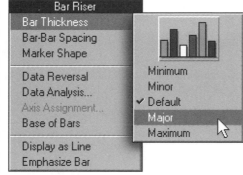

Figure 16-15:
Click on a bar with the right mouse button to display the Bar Riser drop-down list box.

 ✔ To adjust the thickness of a line in a line graph, click on the line and then select a line width option from the Pen tool flyout menu, just as you would in CorelDraw (refer to Chapter 7).

✔ To change the appearance of the points in a line graph, right-click on a line to display the Data Line drop-down list box. Then click on the Marker Shape option to display a list of possible point shapes. This option also changes the appearance of the series marker in the legend.

✔ And because I don't want to leave anybody out, you can right-click on a slice in a pie chart to display the Pie Slice drop-down list box. Click on Detach Slice to display a list of options that let you float the pie slice at various distances from the rest of the pie.

Editing those pesky labels

For the most part, you edit text like any other object by selecting the text block with the Arrow tool and then applying options. For example, to move a text block, select it with the Arrow tool and drag it. You can move the title, subtitle, notes, X- and Y-axes titles, and legend title. You cannot move X- and Y-axes labels, numerical values in the graph, or series names in the legend.

To change the formatting, select the text block and apply options from the *text ribbon,* which appears all decked out in Figure 16-16.

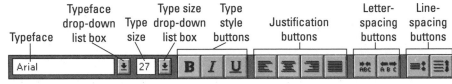

Figure 16-16:
The
annotated
text ribbon.

- Change the typeface by selecting an option from the far left drop-down list box.

- Change the type size by changing the value in the Type size option box or by selecting an option from the drop-down list box.

- Stylize the text by clicking on the **B** (bold), *I* (italic), and U̲ (underline) buttons.

- Change the alignment of lines of text by clicking on a justification button.

- Decrease or increase the horizontal space between characters (called *kerning*) by clicking on the left and right letter-spacing buttons, respectively.

- Click on the left or right line-spacing buttons to decrease or increase the amount of vertical space between lines of type (known as *leading*). The overwhelming majority of text blocks in CorelChart contain only one line of type, so this issue rarely arises.

Integrating Your Charts into CorelShow

As I explained in Chapter 1, CorelShow lets you merge graphs that you create in CorelChart to create an on-screen presentation. One chart comes up on-screen for a moment, then another chart takes its place, then another, and so on. Although I'm not going to go into all the possible stuff you can do with CorelShow — that would take several more chapters — the following step-by-step exercise offers a brief introduction to this unusual program. Consider it a bonus. A little something thrown in for free. Because let's face it, you wouldn't want to be caught dead *paying* for this information.

In order to complete this exercise, you must have CorelChart and CorelShow installed, and you must be able to run both programs at the same time. If an out-of-memory message appears on-screen at any point during the exercise, the great computer gods have deemed that CorelShow is not for you.

Here's how you merge a Chart image into Show:

1. **Start CorelChart.**

2. **Open a chart that you want to include in your amazing on-screen presentation.**

3. **Choose Edit⇨Copy Chart.**

This command copies the entire chart to the Windows Clipboard. Be prepared to wait a minute or so for Chart to pull this one off.

4. **Press Alt+Esc to access the Program Manager.**

5. **Start CorelShow.**

Double-click on the CorelShow icon. If you're going to run out of memory, it should happen here. If no error message appears, you're home free. After CorelShow is up and running, you see the New Presentation dialog box (see Figure 16-17).

6. **Select File⇨New or press Ctrl+N to start a new presentation.**

7. **Enter the number of charts you want to include in your presentation in the Start with option box.**

To keep things simple, press 3.

8. **Press the Enter key.**

CorelShow creates your new three-page presentation.

9. **Choose Edit⇨Paste Special.**

The Paste Special dialog box appears.

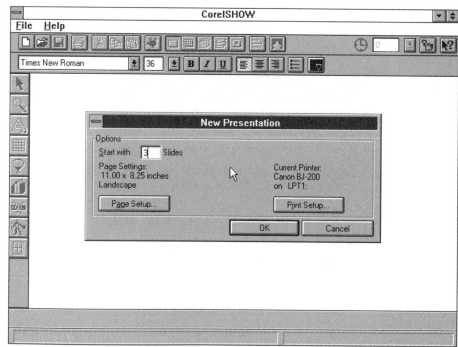

Figure 16-17:
You see this dialog box when you start CorelShow.

10. Select the Paste Link radio button.

This creates an OLE link (see Chapter 14) between the original chart and the one that you're about to paste into CorelShow. Show reflects any changes you made to the original chart.

11. Press Enter.

Show pastes a tiny version of the chart on the screen.

12. Scale the chart so that it fits in the page.

Drag the corner handles and the top and bottom handles. It works just like scaling an object in CorelDraw.

13. Press Ctrl+Esc to bring up the Task List.

Time to switch back to CorelChart and get some more charts.

14. Double-click on CorelChart in the list of running programs.

In a few seconds, Windows returns you to CorelChart.

15. Open the chart that you want to place on the second page of your presentation and choose Edit⇨Copy Chart.

16. Press Alt+Tab.

This combination switches you back to the last program you were using, CorelShow.

17. Click on the Page Two button in the lower-left corner of the interface.

The Page buttons appear highlighted in Figure 16-18. This action takes you to the second page of the presentation, which is naturally empty.

18. Repeat Steps 9 through 12.

Those are the ones in which you choose Edit⇨Paste Special, select the Paste Link radio button, press the Enter key, and scale the pasted chart so that it fits the page.

19. Press Alt+Tab.

Welcome back to CorelChart. You need to copy and paste one more graph and you're done with this nonsense.

20. Repeat Steps 15 through 18.

That's where you open a chart, choose Edit⇨Copy Chart, press Alt+Tab, click on the Page Three button in the lower-left corner of the CorelShow interface, watch an episode of "Green Acres," choose Edit⇨Paste Special, select the Paste Link radio button, press the Enter key, and scale the pasted chart so that it fits the page. Ta da!

21. **Before you do another thing, save this presentation to disk!**

22. **Click on the Run Screen Show button.**

    The Run Screen Show button is the projector just below the Arrange menu. A few moments after you click, a message appears and asks whether you want to start the screen show. Click on OK to answer in the affirmative. Then sit back and watch. CorelShow automatically pages through the three graphs, filling the screen with each one.

If CorelShow balks at running the screen show by suggesting that it can't allocate enough temporary space on disk, choose File⇨Preferences (Ctrl+J). Once inside the Preferences dialog box, deselect the Generate Slide Show in Advance checkbox and press Enter. Again click on the Run Screen Show button. It takes a few moments to display, but the show should run without any problems now.

Run Screen Show button

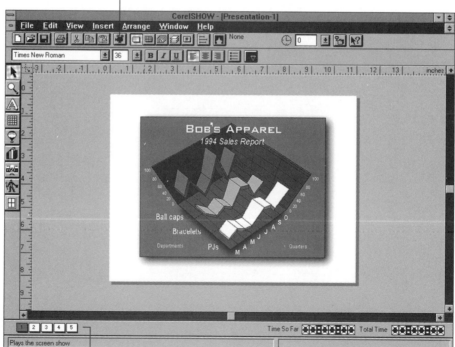

Figure 16-18: Some noteworthy controls in CorelShow.

Page buttons

Chapter 17
What Mary Shelley Never Dreamed

In This Chapter

▶ Understanding actors, props, and sounds

▶ Introducing cels

▶ Placing objects from libraries

▶ Playing an animated sequence

▶ Navigating from one frame to another

▶ Manipulating images in the Paint Editor

▶ Transforming all cels in an actor

▶ Tracing cels

▶ Moving actors along a path

I have two personal goals in life. I want to paint Georgia O'Keeffe's skull — you know, with some flowers artistically arranged around it — and dig up and reanimate Mary Wollstonecraft Shelley, the author of *Frankenstein*. Some say — most notably, my therapist — "Deke, you sick but idealistic dreamer, these things just can't be done." Nevertheless, I remain optimistic. I can easily paint Georgia O'Keeffe in Corel Photo-Paint, and now, with CorelDraw 5, I can reanimate Mary Shelley in CorelMove.

Move is an animation program. It lets you energize your still images and bring dead drawings back to life in ways that make Dr. Frankenstein look like an unimaginative fuddy-duddy as well as something of a rank amateur. For starters, you can animate anything you want. There's no need to hire the local tradesman to dig up the body of a six-foot guy wearing platform shoes. Equally important, you never have to worry about computer animation running amok and exciting the townsfolk. People and computer animation can live together in peace and harmony. And finally, an animated image will never ask you to build it a bride. Records show that cartoon questions don't get much more complicated than, "What's up, Doc?"

CorelMove is based on a product called ProMotion from Motion Works. Actually, Motion Works spells it PROmotion, which is probably what attracted Corel to the program in the first place, what with that company's penchant for strange capitalization — not to mention misplaced punctuation — as witnessed in *CorelDRAW!* I guess all this abuse of common words and sentence structure is supposed to bolster our faith in the product. At least, that's what it does for me.

Shocking CorelMove into Action

After you start CorelMove by double-clicking on the program icon in the Program Manager, you're greeted by a blank screen with a menu bar across the top of it, nearly as ominous as the welcome message offered by CorelChart. To create a new animated sequence, press Ctrl+N or choose File➪New. CorelMove asks you to name the sequence before it creates a new window. Don't think, however, that the program automatically saves your sequence for you; it does not. You still have to press Ctrl+S periodically just as in any other Corel program.

You also should click on the maximize button in the upper-right corner of the window to expand the size of the CorelMove window so that it takes up the entire screen area.

Elements of animation

After you name your sequence and press the Enter key, CorelMove displays the interface shown in Figure 17-1. The interface features a blank stage, similar in function to the stage of a theater. This is where you assemble the objects that you want to animate. CorelMove divides these objects into three camps:

✔ Just like actors in a play, *actors* in CorelMove move and otherwise attract our attention. Each actor is actually a series of *cels*, as demonstrated in Figure 17-2. When played in sequence, these cels simulate movement or action.

The term *cel* comes from celluloid, which refers to the individual frames of film on which animated movies are produced.

✔ *Props* are still images, such as backdrops and inanimate foreground items — rocks and tables and stuff.

✔ *Sounds* are just that — sounds. Unfortunately, to use sounds, you have to have a multimedia PC equipped with a sound board.

You can introduce these objects in two ways. You can create new objects by clicking on the Actor, Prop, and Sound tools, or you can import prefab objects by using the Library roll-up. The second method requires much less work on your part than the first, which is why it's both the preferred method and the one I explain in this book.

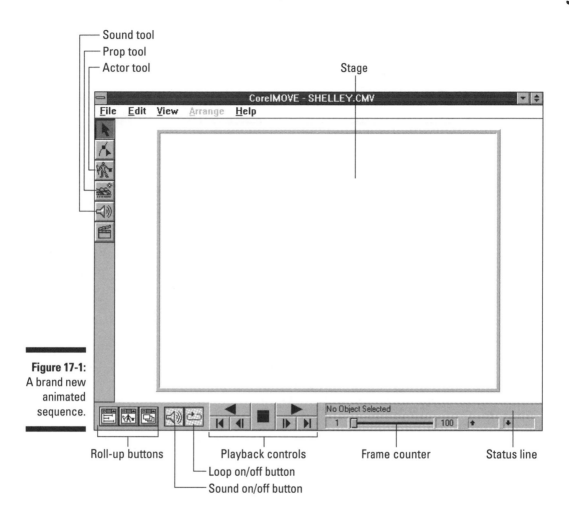

Figure 17-1: A brand new animated sequence.

Getting stuff from the library

The following steps explain how to use the Library roll-up to assemble an animated sequence:

1. **Choose View⇨Library roll-up.**

   Or click on the middle roll-up button (see Figure 17-1). An empty Library roll-up appears (like the one in Figure 17-3, except without the car).

2. **Click on the right-pointing arrowhead to display a pop-up menu. Then click on the Open Library option.**

   The Open Library dialog box appears on-screen.

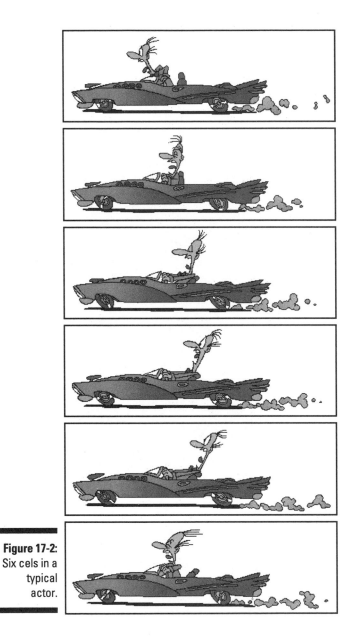

Figure 17-2:
Six cels in a
typical
actor.

3. Locate and select the library you want to open.

You'll find a library file called SAMPLIB.MLB in the \LIB subdirectory inside the \MOVE directory: \COREL50\MOVE\LIB\SAMPLELIB.MLB.

If you own a CD-ROM drive, insert the second of the two CD-ROM disks included with CorelDraw 5 and look inside the \CLIPART\MOVE\LIBRARIE subdirectory. This directory contains several libraries.

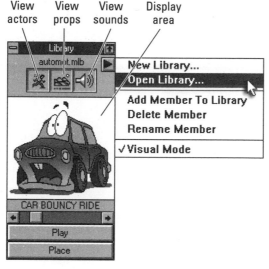

View actors   View props   View sounds   Display area

Figure 17-3:
The Library roll-up provides access to collections of actors, props, and sounds.

4. Click on the OK button.

Or press Enter to open the library. The first object in the library appears inside the central portion of the Library roll-up (the display area), as in Figure 17-3.

I wish I knew the name of the person or persons who created the actors and props included in CorelMove's prefab libraries because the artwork is uniformly wonderful. I mean, with these gems, who needs talent? You can construct entire animated sequences without drawing a single stroke. You are so-o-o lucky.

After you open a library, you can use the controls in the Library roll-up as follows:

✔ Click on the View buttons (labeled in Figure 17-3) to display different kinds of objects. When you first display the Library roll-up, all three buttons are selected and display three varieties of objects. If you click on the View Actors button, for example, the Library roll-up hides the actors and shows only the props and sounds.

✔ Note that most libraries on the CD contain only actors and sounds. To access props, open one of the three props libraries (PROPS1.MLB, PROPS2.MLB, and PROPS3.MLB).

✔ Use the scroll bar below the display area to access different objects in the library.

✔ To display library objects in a list, as in Figure 17-4, rather than one object at a time (see Figure 17-3), click on the right-pointing arrowhead and then deselect the Visual Mode option.

Figure 17-4:
Deselect the
Visual Mode
option to
display
objects in
a list.

✔ Click on the Play button to play an actor or sound. This command lets you preview how the actor moves. Sounds are silent unless your computer is equipped with a sound board. When you display a prop, the Play button is dimmed. To stop playing, click on the Play button again.

✔ When playing an actor inside the Library roll-up, CorelMove occasionally has to scale a cel to fit inside the display area. This means that an actor may grow and shrink as it moves. This *Alice in Wonderland* effect is purely a function of the Library roll-up; the actor does not grow and shrink when you place it in your animated sequence.

✔ Click on the Place button to add an object to the stage, which is the central portion of the interface (refer to Figure 17-1).

✔ When you place a prop, it automatically appears in back of any actors on the stage. Props are generally backdrops — the scenery in front of which the action takes place, as it were.

✔ Placed sounds don't display on the stage because, well, you don't see sounds — you hear them.

Playing Your Animation

After you introduce a few actors and props into your animated sequence, as in Figure 17-5, you should play your animated sequence to see how it looks. To do so, press the F9 key or click on the Play button in the playback controls, labeled in Figure 17-6. All the actors go through their motions. The props just sit there, of course. And if you have a sound board, you can listen to any sounds you placed from the Library roll-up.

CorelMove is set up to play your animated sequence over and over in an endless cycle. When you get sick of watching it and decide that it's time to do something constructive, press the Escape key or click on the Stop button.

Props

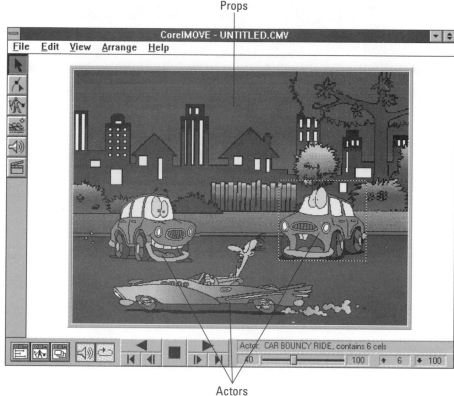

Figure 17-5:
A scene
composed
of three
actors (the
cars) and
one prop
(the
backdrop).

Actors

If you want your sequence to play once and then stop, click on the Loop on/off button (refer to Figure 17-1) to turn the looping function off. Then, after you finish playing your sequence, press the Home key to return to the first frame.

Other playback controls

As shown in Figure 17-6, each playback control (except the Reverse button) has a corresponding command in the View menu. The buttons and commands work like this:

✔ Click on the Reverse button to play the sequence backwards, which is great for amusing any little ones in the family. (Why is that kids will watch anything backwards? And then ask you to do it again?)

✔ Click on the First Frame button, choose View⇨Frame⇨First, or press the Home key to return to the first frame in the sequence.

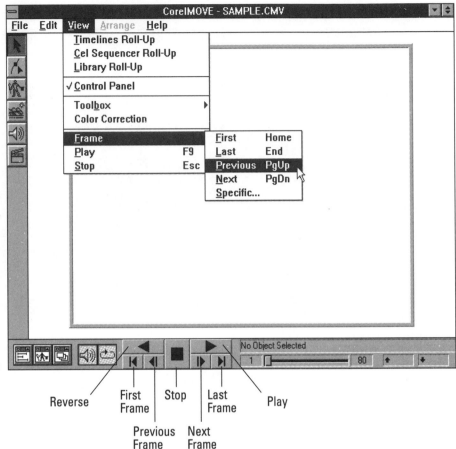

Figure 17-6:
The commands in the View menu and their equivalents among the playback controls.

Reverse   First Frame   Stop   Last Frame   Play

Previous Frame   Next Frame

✔ Click on the Last Frame button, choose View⇨Frame⇨Last, or press the End key to advance to the last frame in the sequence.

✔ Press the PgUp key to go to the previous frame in the sequence. Press PgDn to go to the next frame. You can also use the commands and buttons labeled in Figure 17-6, but why expend all that effort? Believe me, you burn off very few calories shuffling the mouse around, so I encourage laziness and lots of it.

✔ Choose View⇨Frame⇨Specific to display a dialog box asking which frame you want to go to. Just enter the frame number, press Enter, and off you go.

✔ You can also go to a frame by dragging the box in the frame counter (refer to good old Figure 17-1).

Frame of reference

Before you go any further, there are a few things you should know about frames in an animated sequence and how they affect objects like actors and props:

✔ An actor repeats over and over throughout the course of a sequence. If an actor contains two cels, for example, cel 1 appears in frame 1 of the sequence, cel 2 appears in frame 2, and then cel 1 repeats in frame 3, and so on. Fortunately, the actors included in CorelMove's prefab libraries are designed to repeat. In other words, the last cel in the actor goes seamlessly into the first to create a continuous loop.

✔ You can change the length of a sequence by choosing Edit⇨Animation Info or by pressing Ctrl+A. When the Animation Information dialog box appears, as shown in Figure 17-7, change the value in the Number of Frames option box. Then press the Enter key.

Figure 17-7: Change the number of frames in a sequence by entering a new value in the Number Of Frames option box.

✔ If you reduce the value in the Number of Frames option box, CorelMove just throws the extra frames away. And thanks to the fact that the program lacks an Undo command — that's right, no Undo — there's no way to retrieve them.

✔ The frame counter and status line keep you apprised of what's going on in your sequence (see Figure 17-8). The number on the left side of the frame counter tells you which frame you're looking at now, better known as the *current frame*. The value on the right side of the counter is the total number of frames in the sequence.

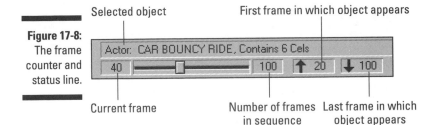

Selected object

First frame in which object appears

Figure 17-8:
The frame
counter and
status line.

Actor: CAR BOUNCY RIDE, Contains 6 Cels
40   100   ↑ 20   ↓ 100

Current frame

Number of frames
in sequence

Last frame in which
object appears

> ✔ When you select an object, the status line describes it (see Figure 17-8).
> The numbers on the far right side of the frame counter — the ones
> accompanied by up and down arrows — tell the first and last frames in
> which the object appears.

The reason I mention the last few items is that any object begins at the current
frame and continues to the last frame in the sequence. When you first introduce
objects in a new sequence, you're at the first frame, so the object starts at
frame 1 and ends at frame 100, thereby filling the entire sequence. But if you
introduce an object after playing a few frames, the object may make its debut in
the middle of the sequence. For example, if you click on the Place button in the
Library roll-up when you're at frame 40, the object appears in frames 40
through 100 but does not appear in frames 0 through 39.

To change the frames at which an object debuts and ends, choose Edit⇨Object
Info or double-click on the object to display the Actor Information dialog box
shown in Figure 17-9. Then change the values in the Enters At Frame and Exits
At Frame option boxes.

Figure 17-9:
Change the
values in the
Enters At
Frame and
Exits At
Frame
option
boxes to
specify the
frames in
which an
object
appears.

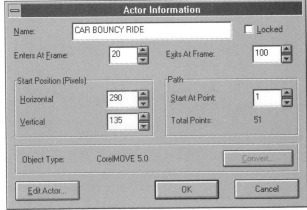

Actor Information

Name: CAR BOUNCY RIDE   ☐ Locked

Enters At Frame: 20   Exits At Frame: 100

Start Position (Pixels)   Path
Horizontal   290   Start At Point: 1
Vertical   135   Total Points: 51

Object Type: CorelMOVE 5.0   Convert...

Edit Actor...   OK   Cancel

Editing Actors and Props

You can edit the appearance of an actor or a prop by bringing up the Paint Editor, shown in Figure 17-10. To display the Paint Editor, select the object and choose Edit⇨Object. Or better yet, press the Ctrl key and double-click on the object.

The Paint Editor consists of the Tools palette and an image window that contains the object that you want to edit. You edit the object exactly as you would an image in Corel Photo-Paint. Select one of the tools in the palette and drag in the painting area of the image window (refer to Figure 17-10).

The tools include two selection tools (a Rectangular Marquee and a Lasso), a Pencil, a Paintbrush, a Fill tool, a Spraycan, a Text tool, an Eraser, an Eyedropper, and some geometric shape tools. Experiment with them and you'll quickly learn how to use them. If you have problems with a specific tool, look up my explanation of the tool that looks just like it in Corel Photo-Paint, as discussed in Chapter 15.

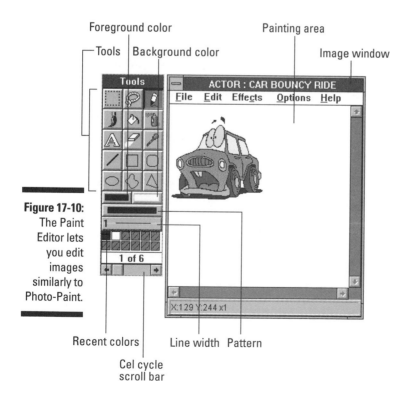

Foreground color

Painting area

Tools Background color

Image window

Figure 17-10:
The Paint
Editor lets
you edit
images
similarly to
Photo-Paint.

Recent colors   Line width   Pattern

Cel cycle
scroll bar

The other items in the Tools palette work as follows:

✔ Press and hold on the Foreground Color button to display a pop-up menu of color options. While continuing to hold down the mouse button, place the cursor on top of the color you want to use. Then release the mouse button to change the foreground color. The same goes for the background color.

✔ Use the Pencil, Spraycan, Text, and geometric shape tools to apply the foreground color. Only the Eraser paints with the background color.

✔ To select the foreground color from the image window, click in the painting area with the Eyedropper tool. To select a background color, right-click with the Eyedropper.

✔ Press and hold on the Pattern button to display a pop-up menu of pattern options. The Paintbrush or Fill tools paint with the selected pattern.

✔ Press and hold on the Line Width button to select from a pop-up menu of line width options. The options affect the thickness of lines drawn with the pencil and geometric shape tools.

✔ To change the size of the Paintbrush cursor, double-click on the Paint-brush icon in the Tools palette. Doing so displays a pop-up menu of brush shapes. Click on the one you want to use.

✔ Below the line width, the Tools palette keeps track of the most recent colors you've used. You can select any recent color by clicking on it. Change the background color by right-clicking on a recent color.

Unlike the main CorelMove interface, the Paint Editor actually allows you to undo operations. In fact, as if to make up for its past oversights, the Paint Editor provides three commands for remedying mistakes:

✔ To undo the last alteration, press Ctrl+Z or choose Edit⇨Undo.

✔ Choose Edit⇨Keep Paint whenever you get to the point that you like what you've done. It's sort of like a mini-save command.

✔ To revert the image to the way it looked the last time you chose the Keep Paint command, choose Edit⇨Revert Paint. If you've never chosen Keep Paint, choosing Revert Paint restores the painting to the state in which it appeared when you first displayed the Paint Editor.

Stuff under the Effects menu

The commands under the Effects menu enable you to transform the image in myriad ways. Although you can figure out most of these commands without my help, there are a few things you should know:

✔ Morph Cels allows you to automatically create more cels between two adjacent cels. You can create a smoother animation without having to manually re-create cels, especially if you change one of the cels. This function is a great time-saver if the changes between the cels aren't that significant. If you morph a car into an elephant, well . . . don't say I didn't warn you.

✔ Choose the Tint All Cels command to shade the actor or prop with a bit of the foreground or background color. Why you'd want to do this, I haven't the slightest idea. Maybe if a fish were swimming through the ocean, you'd want to tint it greenish blue as it swims away.

✔ The Anti-alias command make things fuzzier. Anti-aliasing is a techno term for enlarging an image to twice its normal size and then mathematically reducing it back to its previous size, slightly blurring the image in the process.

Want my advice? Don't use the Anti-alias command. It's supposed to remove the jagged edges from images, but it really just makes them blurry. What's the point of making your viewers feel more myopic than they already are?

✔ As you might expect, the Rotate, Scale, and Mirror commands affect the selected portion of an image. If you want to rotate, scale, or reflect all cels in an actor to the same extent, however, don't select anything. When no portion of an image is selected, the commands read Rotate All Cels, Scale All Cels, and Mirror All Cels.

Options for actors

When you're editing an actor, the Paint Editor provides a handful of commands that you don't find when editing a prop. They include the following:

✔ Use the cel cycle scroll bar (refer to Figure 17-10) to advance from one cel to the next inside an actor.

✔ Choose a command from the Options⇨Onion Skin submenu to view two cels at the same time. When you choose the Next Cel command, for example, you see the current cel superimposed over a faded version of the next cel in the actor. As shown in Figure 17-11, the effect resembles tracing an image on a sheet of onion-skin paper. This technique is extremely useful for gauging how neighboring cels look with respect to each other. In fact, it's based on a technique used by professional animators.

✔ To reverse the order of cels in an actor, choose Edit⇨Reverse Cels.

✔ To add one or more cels, press Ctrl+T or choose Edit⇨Insert Cels. A dialog box appears in which you can enter the number of cels you want to add and specify whether they should occur before or after the current cel. Select the Duplicate Contents checkbox to copy the contents of the current cel into all new ones.

Figure 17-11:
Tracing one cel on top of another by using the onion-skin feature.

- Choose Edit⇨Remove Cels to delete one or more cels. If you specify multiple cels, CorelMove deletes consecutive cels starting with the current one. For example, if you're working on cel 5 and you ask to delete three cels, the program deletes cels 5, 6, and 7.

- The Options⇨Transparent command makes all the white portions of a prop or actor transparent. The Opaque command makes them . . . well, this is your chance to try out the old deductive-reasoning skills.

The Undo command doesn't work after you add, remove, or reverse cels.

Applying your changes

To apply your changes to the actor or prop on the stage, choose File⇨Apply Changes. If you're finished editing the object, just press Alt+F4 or choose File⇨Exit. CorelMove asks whether you want to apply your changes. Respond as you see fit.

Adding Some Movement to the Proceedings

If you've experimented with any actors, you've probably noticed a disappointing effect when playing them back. Although they walk and wiggle and bob up and down just fine, they don't go anywhere. They just walk and wiggle and bob up and down in place like they're doing it for the exercise. Don't these things have any purpose in their imaginary lives?

To move actors, you have to use the Path tool, the second tool in the toolbox, just below the Arrow tool. It looks exactly like the Shape tool in CorelDraw. Here's how it works:

1. **Select the Path tool.**

   CorelMove displays the Path Edit roll-up.

2. **Click on an actor.**

   A small, black circle appears above the actor, as shown in Figure 17-12.

3. **Position the actor where you want the movement to begin.**

    To accomplish this, drag on the small, black circle.

   If you want the actor to appear from off-stage, you can place the dot outside the animation window.

4. **Click at the point where you want the movement to end.**

   You now have two points: a black circle at the place where you just clicked and a white square where the black circle used to be. The black circle is the "to" point, the location to which the actor moves. The white square is the "from" point, the location at which the movement starts. A line stretches the two points to show the path of the movement.

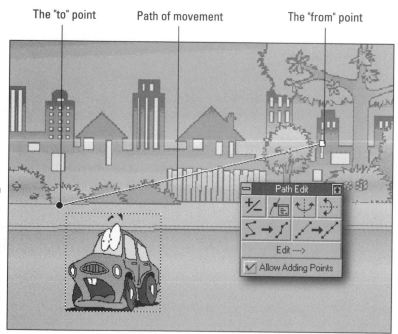

The "to" point   Path of movement   The "from" point

Figure 17-12: The to and from points indicate the distance that the actor will travel.

5. If necessary, drag the "to" point where you want it.

Very few folks get it right on the first click.

6. Click on the Scale Path button in the Path Edit roll-up.

The Scale Path button is the one that looks like +/-. A dialog box opens and lets you specify the number of points in the path. Actors move one point per frame. As things stand now, the actor should move to the "to" point by the second frame and then just sit there for the rest of the sequence. You need to give the path enough points to keep the actor moving.

7. Click on the Path Line to add more points.

If you want the actor to move around in circles, for example, you have to add more points to your path. Click to establish corners, just as if you were drawing a free-form polygon.

8. Enter 100 into the Desired option box, and then press the Enter key.

This action assumes that the actor appears throughout the entire sequence. If the actor doesn't appear in all 100 frames, or if your sequence is longer or shorter than 100 frames, enter the number of frames in which your actor appears in the Desired option box. My actor starts in frame 20 and continues through frame 100, so I enter the value 81 (80 plus 1 to account for the first frame).

9. Press F9.

Or click on the Play button to watch your actor move across the screen.

The following items describe the functions of the other buttons in the Path Edit roll-up, as shown in Figure 17-13:

✔ If you want to remove some points from the path, again click on the Scale Path button and enter a new value in the Desired option box. This is not the number of points you want to add or delete, but rather the number you want to retain.

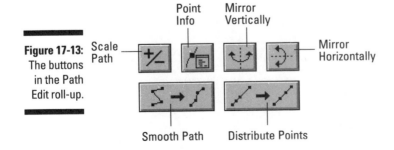

Point Info   Mirror Vertically

Figure 17-13: Scale Path
The buttons in the Path Edit roll-up.

Mirror Horizontally

Smooth Path   Distribute Points

✔ Click on the Point Info button or double-click on a point to display the Point Information dialog box, which lets you change the coordinate location of the point (don't bother) and designate a point as the loop point. If your path contains fewer points than there are frames in the sequence, the actor can loop from the loop point to the "to" point in the path for the remainder of the sequence. In other words, the actor follows the path, and when it reaches the "to" point, it hops to the loop point and continues on to the "to" point again. There can only be one loop point per path.

✔ Click on the Mirror Vertically button to flip the path vertically. Click on the Mirror Horizontally button to flip it the other way.

✔ If your path zigs and zags all over the place, click on the Smooth Path button to smooth it out and establish consistent transitions between frames.

✔ After you add points to a path, you may decide that you want to relocate the "from" or "to" point. Unfortunately, the other points remain where they are. But instead of dragging all these points into position manually, just click on the Distribute Points button to spread the points evenly throughout the path.

✔ If you really make a mess of a path, click on the Scale Path button, press 2, and press Enter. The path now has two points, the "from" point and the "to" point, allowing you to start over again.

Chapter 18

A Lightning-Fast Tour of CorelVentura

*W*ay back in Chapter 1 — gosh, it seems like ages ago, doesn't it? — I mentioned that CorelDraw now includes CorelVentura, formerly known as Ventura Publisher. I also explained that this desktop publishing program goes far beyond the page layout and creation capabilities offered by CorelDraw itself. Although CorelDraw is fine for putting together small documents, such as birthday party invitations, leaflets, and flyers, it's not so hot for generating anything larger. That's where CorelVentura comes in.

So What Exactly Does Ventura Do?

Before I tell you what CorelVentura *is,* let me tell you what it *isn't.*

It's *not* for creating letters to Mom, short, one-of-a-kind reports, or anything that you can bash out on a word processor (which, with the new generation of word processors, is an awful lot).

CorelVentura's reason for existence is to take information that you create elsewhere and assemble it into a professionally crafted document. The draw-ings you create in Draw, clip art you accumulate from wherever, and text you author in a word processor are brought together to live happily ever after as a CorelVentura publication.

CorelVentura is simply wonderful if you are self-publishing *The Great (fill in the politically correct term of your choice) Novel* or are responsible for laying it out for someone else. It accomplishes the things professors like to see in upper-level papers magnificently. It excels in doing scholarly works or putting together excruciatingly long documents. It is also boss when you have to do the same thing over and over, exactly (or almost exactly) the same every time, as you do in a newsletter or magazine.

Ventura takes a highly structured approach to the page-layout process. Once placed in CorelVentura, text and graphics are scientifically, positively guaranteed to appeal to your accountant side. Everything is neatly tagged, labeled, pigeonholed, lined up, dressed right, standing at attention, and ready for audit.

Even though the thought of this much organization may send people who call themselves *artists* immediately into a narcoleptic attack, a page-layout program like Ventura is an indispensable tool in constructing long, complex documents.

Creating a Publication

In Ventura-ese, a *publication* is the whole banana. When smooshed all together and properly ordered, all the chapters in a work, along with the table of contents, index, tables of authority, tables of figures, footnotes, and the crud that was left over at the bottom of the garbage disposal, become a *publication*.

You may think that creating a publication would be a complex task best accomplished by Merlin, but it's really rather easy. To kick things off, just do the following:

1. Choose File⇨New.

(Or, if this spell gets tiring, you can always press Ctrl+N.) This magical incantation opens the New Publication dialog box shown in Figure 18-1.

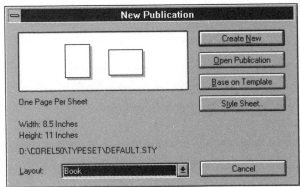

Figure 18-1: The New Publication dialog box starts the ball rolling.

2. **Select from the various layouts in the Layout drop-down menu.**

3. **Start a new publication by clicking on the Create New button.**

Don't even think about copying an existing CorelVentura file or publication to any location without reading the "Copying Can Be a Trying Experience" section later in this chapter.

I Was Framed!

CorelVentura bases the page-layout process on *frames*: to everything a frame, and a frame to everything. As a matter of fact, when you first open a file, what you see on-screen is a frame. (I know that you're just waiting for me to go off on some horrid diatribe about being framed, but I'm much too innocent to stoop so low.)

A good way to look at Ventura's frame obsession is to visualize your Great Aunt Tillie's photo wall. Think of the wall itself as a frame, defining and setting off all the other stuff on it. Think of all the pictures of kids, pets, and strange, unknown relative-type folks as little frames within the big wall frame.

A page in Ventura, at its simplest, is only one frame. However, each additional element, such as a header, footer, or picture, gets a frame of its own. A page can have anywhere from one to ten kabillion frames on it. This is a pretty neat thing, because when you put something in a frame, you can move it about on the page while everything else stays put.

Because frames are normally designed to stuff stuff in, it should come as no major surprise that they serve this purpose in CorelVentura.

I think that the picture of Uncle Fred's pet piranha would look best over there by the photo of Chris's ex-fiancee, don't you?

Adding a frame

To add a frame, you use the Frame tool, oddly enough. You'll find the Frame tool on the toolbar on the left side of the Ventura window; it's the third tool from the top. You drag the frame into place, as follows:

1. **Select the Frame tool.**

   The cursor takes on the shape of the corner of a frame.

2. **Click the left mouse button in the page on the point at which you want the top left corner of the frame to begin, and drag the frame to size.**

   As you drag, a bounding box represents the frame, as shown in Figure 18-2.

Frame tool
Arrow tool

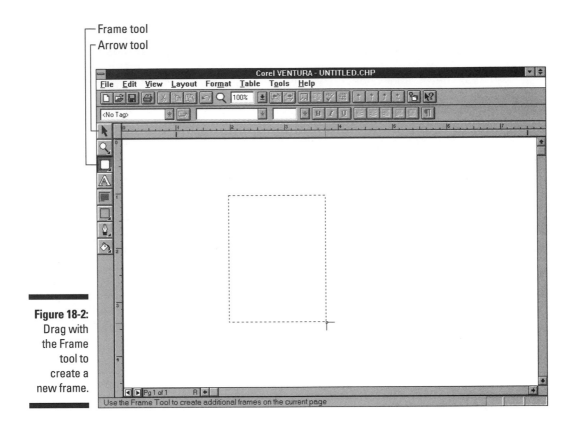

Figure 18-2:
Drag with
the Frame
tool to
create a
new frame.

3. Select the Arrow tool.

As shown in Figure 18-3, the frame is surrounded by handles that you can use to drag the frame into a more exact shape.

Resizing a frame

When you place a frame on the page, it seldom is exactly perfect. Follow these steps to make it larger or smaller:

1. Select the frame with the Arrow tool.

2. Position the Arrow tool on any of the eight handles in the selected frame and click the left mouse button.

The cursor changes into a double-headed arrow. If it changes into a four-headed arrow, you have just discovered how to move a frame about the page. You've placed your mouse pointer inside the frame, not on a handle. Keep moving your mouse pointer over a handle until you get the right cursor.

3. Drag the frame to its new size.

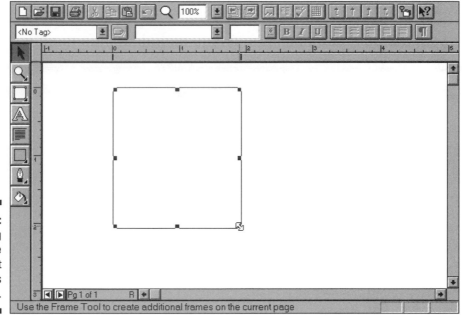

Figure 18-3:
Selecting
the frame
makes eight
handles
appear.

Repositioning a frame

You can move frames around on the page just like you move graphics in CorelDraw. The process is rather simple:

1. **Position the Arrow tool anywhere inside the frame and click the left mouse button.**

   The cursor changes into a four-headed arrow. If it changes into a double-headed arrow, you have just discovered how to resize a frame. See the preceding section for more info.

2. **Drag the frame to its new location.**

Formatting a frame

You can format a frame as well as the stuff you put inside the frame (your actual graphics and text) in a whole bunch of ways. Follow these steps:

1. **Select the frame with the Arrow tool.**

2. **Press F6 or select Format⇨Frame.**

   This step opens the Frame Settings dialog box shown in Figure 18-4.

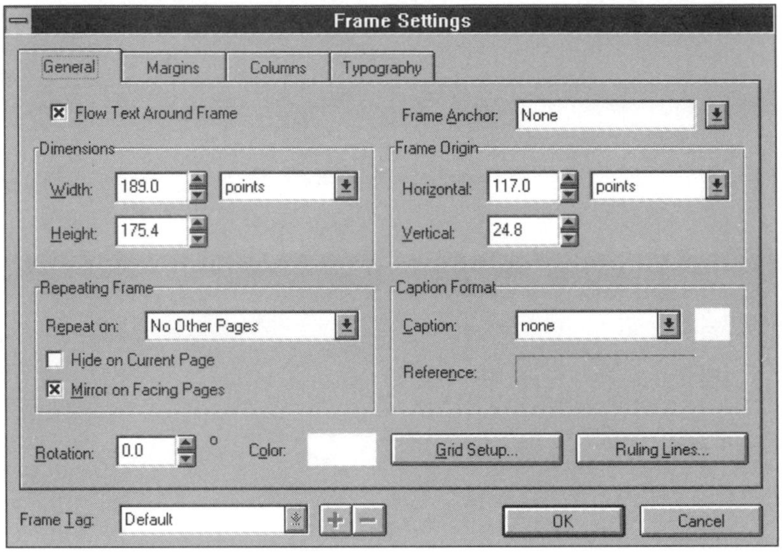

```
┌─────────────────────────────────────────────────────────────┐
│ ─                      Frame Settings                         │
├─────────────────────────────────────────────────────────────┤
│  ┌─General─┐ ┌─Margins─┐ ┌─Columns─┐ ┌─Typography─┐           │
│                                                               │
│  [X] Flow Text Around Frame      Frame Anchor: [None    ] [±] │
│  ┌─Dimensions──────────────┐ ┌─Frame Origin───────────────┐  │
│  │ Width:  [189.0] [÷] [points ▼] Horizontal: [117.0] [÷] [points ▼]│
│  │                                                        │  │
│  │ Height: [175.4] [÷]         Vertical:  [24.8] [÷]      │  │
│  └─────────────────────────┘ └────────────────────────────┘  │
│  ┌─Repeating Frame─────────┐ ┌─Caption Format─────────────┐  │
│  │ Repeat on: [No Other Pages ▼] Caption: [none      ▼] [ ] │
│  │ [ ] Hide on Current Page     Reference: [          ]   │  │
│  │ [X] Mirror on Facing Pages                             │  │
│  └─────────────────────────┘ └────────────────────────────┘  │
│  Rotation: [0.0] [÷] °  Color: [ ]  [Grid Setup...] [Ruling Lines...]│
│  Frame Tag: [Default    ▼] [+][-]        [ OK ]   [ Cancel ]  │
└─────────────────────────────────────────────────────────────┘
```

Figure 18-4:
You accomplish frame formatting in this dialog box.

3. **Select the stuff you want to change in each tab and the formats you want to apply.**

   I discuss the various options in the following sections.

4. **Click on OK.**

The General tab options

- ✔ **Flow Text Around Frame:** When this box is checked, text that is in a frame positioned below the currently selected one flows around the borders of this frame. In other words, the picture of Uncle Fred's pet piranha won't cover up the words under it; the picture will just move the words aside.

- ✔ **Frame Anchor:** The name of the anchor, if any, appears here. This subject is heavy, but anchors are designed to keep a frame in place, just like those on a boat.

- ✔ **Dimensions:** The size of the frame. If you want to see how big it is in millimeters or any measurement other than ciceros, select the measurement units you want from the drop-down list box.

- ✔ **Frame Origin:** The horizontal and vertical location of the frame's upper-left corner. You can put other measurements in the Horizontal and Vertical text boxes to reposition the frame on the page with a boring degree of exactness.

- ✔ **Repeat On:** This option is extremely useful when you use a frame as a repeating design element in your publication. You can define the frame and all of its attributes and have it repeat on every page in your document or on just the left or right pages. You can also hide the frame on any given page by selecting the Hide on Current Page check box. Use the Mirror on Facing Pages box when your publication has different margins on the left and right pages. This option places the repeating frame in the same relative position on the page.

- ✔ **Caption:** Nothing makes a figure happier than a snappy caption. Selecting this option allows you to place a caption above, below, to the left, or to the right of the frame. Cool.

- ✔ **Reference:** This option lets you include the figure number, chapter number, or table number in the caption.

- ✔ **Rotation:** You don't like straight up and down stuff? No problem — rotate that frame.

- ✔ **Grid Setup:** You can snap to a grid in CorelVentura just like you can in Draw. Select this option to set up your sticky grid.

- ✔ **Ruling Lines:** This option opens another dialog box that allows you to draw a box around all or part of the frame.

The Margins tab options

Listen up — I may test you on this stuff later. You select Margins tab when you want to establish the margins of a frame. Bet you can't guess which margins you can change! If you said, top, bottom, left and right, inside, and outside, you get the prize.

The Columns tab options

You use these settings to tell Ventura how many columns you want to include in a selected frame. You can also establish the gutter (space between columns) and indicate whether you want intercolumn rules (lines between the columns).

Another thing you can do here is tell Ventura whether you want to balance the text of the columns.

Which margin goes where?

Inside and outside margins refer to the position of the page with respect to a book's binding.

When you open a book, page one is always on the right side, so the inside margin on page one (and generally on all odd-numbered pages) is the left margin. The outside margin is the right margin.

This state of events is reversed for even-numbered pages.

The only time that this rule does not hold true is in single-sided publications. In these documents, *all* pages are odd pages, and settings for the right page are used for the entire publication (or chapter).

The Typography tab options

This tab gives you some sophisticated options that you can apply to text within a frame, which include the following:

- **Widows and Orphans:** These options attempt to keep single lines of text from starting or ending a page. You can select a different cutoff, like "I don't want a widow (top of page) of less than 3 lines or an orphan (bottom of page) of less than 2."

- **Vertical Justification and so on:** This stuff is for the really adventuresome. All of us self-respecting Dummies would be wise to select Default in these lists and leave the real nitty-gritty to those who get off on minutiae. These measurements determine how Ventura balances text. They are pretty tough to explain, let alone comprehend.

Bringing in Text

Finally, after all of that messing around, you're going to do something that you can see.

Because the whole purpose of CorelVentura is to get down and persnickety with the appearance of text and graphics, don't bother using the sophisticated features of your word processor. Some elements in that stupendous piece of textartstuff that you spent hours developing will be lost when you import the file into Ventura.

Write your text in a simple format and wait until you get it into Ventura to gussy it up. Save your text file in ASCII (.TXT) format if Ventura does not support your word processor directly.

If you want to create a fancy extrude or blend effect, use CorelDraw. I know you have it, and it works great. You can even cut your Draw creation to the Clipboard and paste it right into Ventura. More than way cool!

To insert text in a publication, follow these steps:

1. **Insert or select the frame in which you want to put the text.**

   To find out how to insert a frame, see "Adding a frame" earlier in this chapter.

2. **Select File⇨Load Text (or press F9 if you feel lazy).**

   Doing so opens up the Import dialog box shown in Figure 18-5.

3. **Navigate through the directories until you find the text file you want.**

   You may need to select All Files [*.*] from the List Files of Type drop-down list to see all the files in a given directory.

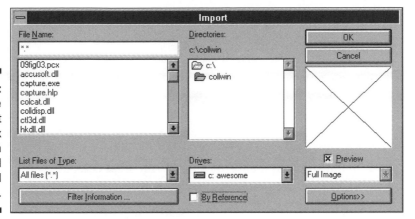

Figure 18-5:
You use the
Import
dialog box
to bring in
almost all
external
files.

If you want to limit your search to files of a particular type, you can select those files from the List Files of Type drop-down list. If you select a particular type (for example, .TXT), only files ending in that extension show up in the scrolling window under the File Name text box.

CorelVentura can bring in text from almost any word processor in some format or another. If your word processor's native file type (name and file extension) is not shown in the List Files of Type drop-down list in the Import dialog box, you can save your word processing work as an ASCII (.TXT) file or in one of the formats that Ventura supports.

4. Double-click on the file or select it and click on OK.

Your file is brought into Ventura and positioned in the selected frame.

If the frame is smaller than the amount of text you imported, CorelVentura fills the frame as fully as it can. The name of the file is also added to a special file list that you can see by pressing Alt+F6. To continue placing the text in another frame, draw a frame or select a predrawn frame and click on the imported file's name in the drop-down list of files. (Press Alt+F6 or Tools⊃File List Roll-Up to open the file list if it's not already on-screen.)

If nothing seems to happen when you import a file, you probably forgot to select a frame with the Arrow tool first.

Bringing in the Good Stuff: Art

To insert art into a publication, do the following:

1. Insert or select the frame in which you want to place the art.

To learn how to insert a frame, see the "Adding a frame" section earlier in this chapter.

2. Select File⇨Load Graphic (or press F10 if you feel lazy).

This step brings up the Import dialog box.

3. Navigate through the directories until you find the graphic you want.

You may need to select All Files [*.*] from the List Files of Type drop-down list to see all the files in a directory.

Selecting the Preview box can be a big help here. If you check this box in the Import dialog box, you can see a copy of the picture in the preview area of this dialog box before putting the graphic in your document.

4. Double-click on the file or select it and press OK.

The file is brought into Ventura, and its name is placed in the file drop-down list in the formatting toolbar.

Corel does not provide a means to import every possible kind of graphic into Ventura. However, if you can get a graphic into the Windows Clipboard, you can bring it into Ventura. To do so, perform these steps:

1. Create the graphic.

2. Choose Edit⇨Select All.

3. Choose Edit⇨Copy.

4. Open CorelVentura.

5. Select Edit⇨Paste to paste in the graphic.

Copying Can Be a Trying Experience

Copying a CorelVentura publication from one place to another is not as easy as you may think, but it's not impossible. (For information on why copying a publication isn't as simple as it sounds, read the upcoming sidebar.)

Don't use the DOS Copy command to move chapters or publications from one place to another.

To copy a publication, do the following:

1. Open the Publication Manager by selecting Publication Manager from the File menu (Ctrl+M for us lazy types).

2. In the Scan Directories tab, show Ventura where to find your publication.

3. Go to the File Operations tab (see Figure 18-6) and click on the File Operations radio button.

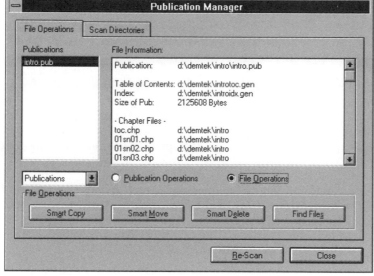

Figure 18-6:
The File
Operations
Tab, ready
to move or
copy a
publication.

4. **Select the publication in the Publications list window.**

5. **Select either Smart Move or Smart Copy to do the dastardly deed.**

    This step opens a new dialog box that asks where you want the stuff to go.

6. **In the Pub section of this dialog box, indicate the location to which you want the publication or chapters copied and then click on the Make All Directories the Same button.**

7. **Select OK to copy all of the files that are contained in the publication, including graphics, to the new place you stipulate.**

A filename is special to CorelVentura

One of the nicer features of CorelVentura can also be a royal pain. Ventura does not store all of a publication's files in a separate place. Instead, the filenames of all the different files that make up a publication include "pointers" to the directory to which they were first imported.

A simple DOS Copy command does not change these pointers, so if you transfer a publication to disk, for example, you must use the Smart Copy (or Smart Move) command in the Publication Manager to change the file pointers to their new location.

Understanding Tags

Tags are really neat things, and if you are going to mess with CorelVentura, you should know a little bit about them. A *tag* is a series of instructions that the program applies to a paragraph. You can format the tag just about any way you want.

For instance, you may always want your body text to be 12-point Times New Roman, flush left. You can define this format as a style and call it *Body Text*. After you do so, applying this previously defined formatting to a paragraph is a simple matter of selecting the paragraph with the Paragraph tool and applying the Body Text tag.

Tags can be very complex, containing boxed text and other weird stuff, or quite simple, as in the preceding example.

Defining a new tag

Defining a tag can be a simple process. To define a tag, follow these steps:

1. **Select Format⇨Paragraph Tags.**

2. **Meander through the many dialog boxes that show up, changing the Character, Alignment, Spacing, Defaults, and Typography of the paragraph in question.**

3. **Click on the plus sign button near the bottom of the dialog box.**

4. **Give the tag a meaningful name, such as "Indented Bullet," in the Add Paragraph Tag dialog box that opens after you click on the plus sign.**

5. **In the Tag Type drop-down list, select the general category of the tag.**

   Indented Bullet would be a body text thingamajig.

6. **Click on OK.**

Hey, I said that it *can* be simple; I didn't say that it *is!* These dialog boxes give you the opportunity to change everything but the paragraph's diapers. And once defined, the attributes stay that way forever.

Using a tag

If you thought that defining a tag was easy, just wait until you use one. Just kidding — really, your cat could do it if cats had opposing thumbs. Follow these steps:

1. **Using the Paragraph tool, select the paragraph(s) to which you want the tag to apply.**

The Paragraph tool looks like a page and lives over there on the left side of your screen. Yeah, right below the letter *A*.

2. **Select the tag that you want from the Tag List drop-down list box and press Enter.**

The Tag List is the first drop-down list box on the formatting toolbar. Bang, pop! The tag is applied.

Venturing Forth

Thousand-page books are written about programs like CorelVentura. If this little chapter fires up your imagination, you can find one of those weighty tomes at your local bookseller. Go forth and buy a couple. You can always use them in your workout program — maybe strap them to your calves when you go on a power walk.

"HEY, I NEVER SAW A SLOW RESPONSE TIME FIXED WITH A PAPERWEIGHT BEFORE."

Part V
The Part of Tens

The 5th Wave   By Rich Tennant

"YES, I THINK IT'S AN ERROR MESSAGE."

In this part...

Sure, sure, we're all addicted to statistics and sound bites, so no one knows the full story about anything. But I figure what's good enough for Moses is good enough for me. I mean, the guy kept it simple — two tablets, ten factoids — and everybody ate it up. "Thou shalt not kill" kind of sticks in your mind. It has a certain undeniable directness that's downright impossible to argue with. You can toss it out at a party or share it with a friend in a time of need.

Jill:	I swear, Jack's driving me nuts. I'm about ready to strangle the chump in his sleep.
Humpty Dumpty (a friend from a neighboring story line):	Now now, Jane. (Wagging finger.) "Thou shalt not kill."
Jill:	Oh, right, I forgot about that one. (Considers.) But I can wallop him with my pail, right? It doesn't say anything about walloping folks with a pail, does it?
Humpty Dumpty:	No, I believe that's acceptable.

Of course, the following lists don't quite measure up to the Ten Commandments (or Mother Goose, for that matter). In fact, they're more the Guinness Book of World Records variety. But they're still lots of fun and, wow, talk about memorable! You can even toss them out at a party — if you want to look like a computer geek.

Chapter 19

Ten Way-Cool Special Effects

● ●

In This Chapter

▶ Making a 3-D sphere

▶ Extruding a cube

▶ Flipping text to create a shadow

▶ Applying the envelope feature to text

▶ Creating fuzzy text

▶ Creating perspective text

▶ Blending the colors of two shapes

▶ Filling the background with a texture

▶ Applying special effects in Photo-Paint

▶ Sharpening the focus of an image

● ●

CorelDraw is a stalwart, functional program. You know that. I'm pretty sure that Ross Perot proved it in one of his NAFTA ads. You can do all kinds of things to make your life more efficient. But who cares? I mean, life isn't about efficiency. It's about liberty, justice, and the pursuit of happiness.

I want you to make me a promise. Any time you hear that America is losing its competitive edge and is five years behind the rest of the industrialized world and that you should be doing something you're not doing and have no intention of doing, refer to this chapter. Here's where you rock and roll, folks.

In this chapter, you can pull out the plugs and tell everyone what they can do with their statistics and their data and their organizational charts. Some of these techniques are based on ideas covered in previous chapters, but don't expect any warmed-over repeats. Here's your chance to indulge in some purely frivolous and amazing special effects.

Make a 3-D Sphere

I'll start things off with a new one, namely that of creating a three-dimensional sphere like the one shown in Figure 19-1. Isn't it a beauty? Can you imagine taking in that baby through the view port of your rocket ship? Or perhaps losing communications with an unmanned probe in the vicinity of this gorgeous orb?

Figure 19-1:
Your very
own radial
gradation.

Here's how to create one just like it:

 1. Inside CorelDraw, draw a circle.

You do so by Ctrl+dragging with the Oval tool.

 2. Press F11 or select the Fountain Fill tool from the Fill tool flyout menu.

This action displays the Fountain Fill dialog box.

3. Select Radial from the Type drop-down list box.

Doing so creates a radial gradation, which progresses outward in concentric circles, as in Figure 19-1.

The way things stand now, the white spot is dead in the center of the gradation. But that doesn't look right. It needs to be up and to the left a little, maybe. You can move the white spot by using the Horizontal and Vertical options in the Center Offset area.

4. **Enter –20 in the <u>H</u>orizontal option box and 20 in the <u>V</u>ertical option box.**

   The white spot scoots to the left and up.

5. **Press Enter.**

   That's it. You're done.

On-screen, the gradation probably looks like a bunch of stripes rather than the continuous tones shown in Figure 19-1. But it should print much more smoothly.

Create a Floating Cube

You'd think that you create spheres and cubes in similar ways, but they require completely different approaches. The following steps explain how to create a floating cube by using the Rectangle tool and the Extrude roll-up:

1. **Draw a square.**

   Ctrl+drag with the Rectangle tool.

2. **Select the Arrow tool and click on the square.**

   The rotate and skew handles appear.

3. **Drag on a corner handle to rotate the shape.**

   Rotated cubes look like they're floating. If you want to create a cube on solid ground, don't rotate it.

4. **Press Ctrl+E.**

   Or choose Effe<u>c</u>ts⇨<u>E</u>xtrude Roll-Up to display the Extrude roll-up.

5. **Drag the vanishing point to determine the direction of the extrusion.**

   Change the Depth value to your taste.

6. **Click on the Light Source icon in the roll-up (it's the fourth one from the left).**

7. **Click on the #1 Light Bulb icon.**

8. **Click on the Color icon in the Extrude roll-up (the icon on the far right).**

9. **Select the Solid Fill radio button.**

10. **Click on the color square to see a display of your palette colors. Then click on a color for the cube.**

11. **Click on the Apply button in the Extrude roll-up.**

    Your cube is finished.

If your cube doesn't look exactly the way you want it to look, you can adjust the settings in the Extrude roll-up as described in the "Extruding in the workplace" section of Chapter 9.

Set Shadowed Type

Folks invariably ooh and ah when they see the effect shown in Figure 19-2, but it's really easy to create. Here's how:

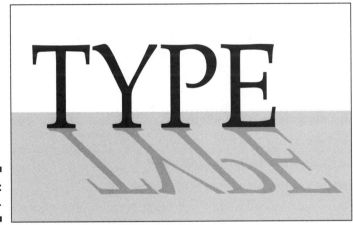

Figure 19-2:
Text at dusk.

1. **Press the Caps Lock key.**

   This effect works best when you use all capital letters. Lowercase letters sometimes descend below the baseline, which ruins the shadow effect.

 2. **Create some text with the Artistic Text tool.**

   Click with the Artistic Text tool and type a single, short line of text.

3. **Use the Text roll-up to enlarge the type size to 48-point.**

   You display the Text roll-up by pressing Ctrl+F2. Then type **48** in the Type Size option box and click on the Apply button.

4. **Open the Transform roll-up (Effects⇨Transform Roll-Up).**

   Alt+F9 also displays the roll-up.

5. **Click on the Scale and Mirror icon (the 3rd one from the left) and then click on the Vert Mirror button.**

   The Vert Mirror button is the lower button under the Mirror section of the roll-up.

6. **Click on the Apply to Duplicate button.**

   This option creates a duplicate of the text block as it flips it.

7. **Press the down-arrow key until the baselines of the two text blocks align.**

   In other words, the bottom of the letters in the different text blocks should touch.

8. **Click on a light gray color in the color palette.**

   The flipped text changes to gray.

9. **Click on the flipped text block.**

   The rotate and skew handles appear.

10. **Drag on the bottom handle to skew the text.**

    The shadow appears at an angle.

Make Type Bulge

CorelDraw is about the only program on the planet that lets you create type that bulges off the page, as shown in Figure 19-3. This interesting text effect is remarkably easy to create by using the envelope feature. Follow these steps:

1. **Repeat the first three steps from the preceding section.**

   Press the Caps lock key, click with the Artistic Text tool, enter a word or short line of text, and then increase the type size to 48-point or larger.

2. **Using the Arrow tool, drag up on the top handle of the text block until it's roughly as tall as it is wide.**

   The text stretches vertically.

3. **Press Ctrl+F7 to display the Envelope roll-up.**

4. **Click on the Add New button.**

 5. **Click on the Single-Arc mode icon.**

   This is the second tool in the roll-up. Eight handles now surround the text block.

6. **Drag the top handle upward, drag the bottom handle downward, drag the left handle further to the left, and drag the right handle to the right.**

   Ultimately, you're trying to turn the square confines of the text block into a circle.

7. **Click on the Apply button.**

   The text now puffs out as though you were viewing it through a fish-eye camera lens.

Figure 19-3:
This text
looks like it's
about ready
to pop.

Make Type Fuzzy

CorelDraw has built-in fuzzy logic. Take a look as you lift your coffee mug or mouse off your desk; the shadow beneath it gets fuzzier and fuzzier as you lift it up. This happens because the light source (whether a light bulb or the sun) is not a point but an area. The two different sides of the light source create a fuzzy zone. You'll see how realistically you can imitate this effect when you try the following:

1. **Select the Artistic Text tool and then type the word *Hello*.**

   Select a thick font such as Fujiyama or Bahamas to get the most out of this effect. Pick a size of about 300 points.

2. **Press Ctrl+D to Duplicate.**

3. **Press Ctrl+D again to Duplicate again.**

   You should have three Hellos on-screen. Move one out of the way for now.

4. **Select two of the text objects.**

5. **Press Ctrl+A to Align.**

   Align the two objects centered both horizontally and vertically. The two objects should now be on top of each other.

6. **Click on a white space to deselect the objects.**

7. **Click on one of the two text objects.**

8. **Make the text 50 percent black by clicking on the 50% Black color box with the left mouse button.**

   Watch the status bar as you move your cursor across the palette, and stop moving the mouse when the status bar says you're on the 50% Black color box.

9. **Make the outline white by clicking on the white color box with the right mouse button.**

10. **Make the outline thick by selecting the Outline tool and then selecting the largest thickness available on the flyout menu.**

11. **Move this object to the back by pressing Shift+PgDn.**

12. **Select the second text object by pressing Shift+Tab.**

    Confirm that you have the second hello by looking at the status line; it should have no outline.

13. **Make the text 50 percent black by clicking on the 50% Black color box with the left mouse button.**

14. **Make the outline 50 percent black by clicking on the 50% Black color box with the right mouse button.**

15. **Reselect both objects and press Ctrl+B to blend.**

    The Blend roll-up menu should appear. Make sure that the value in the Steps option box is 20.

16. **Click on Apply and then close the roll-up.**

    You just created the shadow portion of the fuzzy text.

17. **Reposition the third text and place it above and to the left of the blended group.**

    Just in case, press Shift+PgUp to ensure that this object is on top; it's the object that creates the shadow. You should have something that looks like Figure 19-4.

Figure 19-4:
Creating
fuzzy type.

Put Your Message in the Sky

You can use CorelDraw's perspective function to create text that appears stretched across the sky. Figure 19-5 shows an example in which a consumer-oriented message flies over the viewer's head.

1. **Use the Artistic Text tool to create some text.**

   This time around, you can use lowercase letters if you want to. Furthermore, the type size doesn't really matter because you end up stretching it all over the place anyway.

2. **Choose Effe_c_ts⇨_A_dd Perspective.**

   Four handles appear in the corners of the text block.

3. **Drag the handles until you get the desired effect.**

   Experiment to your heart's content.

4. **Click on a light gray in the color palette.**

   Doing so colors the text gray, the first step in creating the drop shadow that heightens the perspective effect.

5. **Press Ctrl+D.**

   Or choose _E_dit⇨_D_uplicate to create a duplicate of the text block slightly offset from the original.

6. **Select black from the color palette.**

   This black duplicate now appears to cast a gray shadow.

Figure 19-5: An important message hovers above the heads of an eager audience.

Design a Custom Color Gradation

Draw lets you create your own custom color gradations by using the Blend roll-up. In essence, you can blend one shape filled with one color into a different shape filled with a different color. Here's how it works:

1. **Draw two shapes.**

   For this example, draw a large rectangle and then draw a smaller oval that fits inside the rectangle (use the Rectangle and Ellipse tools).

2. **Select the rectangle with the Arrow tool and select black from the color palette.**

   This action fills the shape with black.

3. **Right-click on the X icon on the left side of the color palette (the Delete Color button).**

   Doing so deletes the outline from the shape, which is an important step in creating custom gradations. If you don't delete the outline, borders appear between the colors in the gradation.

4. **Select the oval, select white from the color palette, and right-click on the X icon.**

   The ellipse is now white with no outline.

5. **Press Ctrl+B.**

   Or choose Effects⇨Blend Roll-Up to display the Blend roll-up.

6. **Select the rectangle and the oval.**

   Assuming that the oval is still selected, just Shift+click on the rectangle.

7. **Click on the Apply button in the Blend roll-up.**

   Draw automatically creates a gradation between the two shapes.

CorelDraw makes this gradation by generating 20 transitional shapes between the rectangle and ellipse, each shaped and filled slightly differently. If you want to increase the number of shapes to create a smoother gradation, increase the value in the Steps option box near the top of the roll-up and then click on the Apply button again.

Add a Wild Background

To create zany background effects, do the following:

1. **Draw an enormous rectangle.**

   Make it as big as the page. You want it to cover the entire background.

2. **Press Shift+PgDn.**

   This command sends the rectangle to the very back of the drawing.

 3. **Select the Texture Fill tool from the Fill tool flyout menu.**

   The Texture Fill tool looks like a cloudy sky and sits to the left of the PS tool. Selecting this tool opens the Texture Fill dialog box.

4. **Select Samples from the Texture Library pop-up menu.**

   The pop-up menu is located in the upper-left corner of the dialog box.

5. **Select the desired texture from the Texture list.**

   Press Alt+T. Then use the down- and up-arrow keys to highlight different textures in the list. A preview of the texture appears in the upper-right portion of the dialog box.

6. **Click OK or press the Enter key.**

   Draw applies the texture to the selected rectangle, which results in a breathtaking textured background.

Try Some Image Enhancements

In Corel Photo-Paint, you can apply some serious special effects to images. Figure 19-6 shows just a few examples that I applied inside Photo-Paint by choosing commands from the Effects menu.

- ✔ The Invert command changes all the white to black and all the black to white, as in a photographic negative.

- ✔ The Jaggy Despeckle command randomizes the pixels in the image, which gives the image a rough, gritty quality.

- ✔ The Psychedelic command mixes up the colors all over the place, thus fooling the viewer into seeking medical attention.

These aren't the only special effects you can apply, of course — just a sampling of the ones that are easy to use and produce the most pronounced alterations. In Photo-Paint, you'll probably want to experiment with several other commands under the Effects menu.

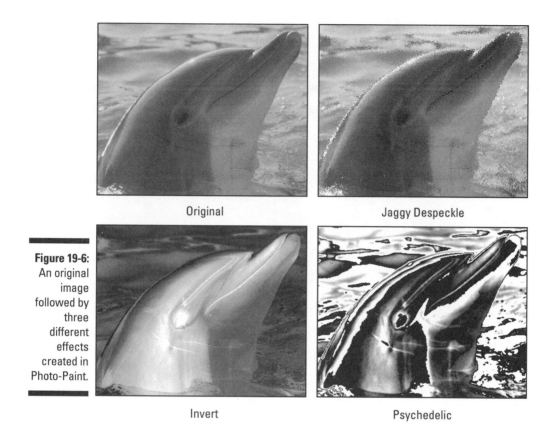

Original   Jaggy Despeckle

Figure 19-6:
An original
image
followed by
three
different
effects
created in
Photo-Paint.

Invert   Psychedelic

Play with the Focus

Have you ever taken what you thought was going to be a great photograph
when you were on vacation only to find that you didn't focus the camera
correctly when you got the picture developed?

Wouldn't it be great if you could focus the photo after the fact? Well, in Corel
Photo-Paint, you can.

Choose Effects⇨Sharpen⇨Sharpen to display a dialog box that allows you to
specify the degree to which you want to focus the image by entering a percentage value in the Sharpen Amount option box. Figure 19-7 shows the effects of
three sample percentage values on the dolphin image.

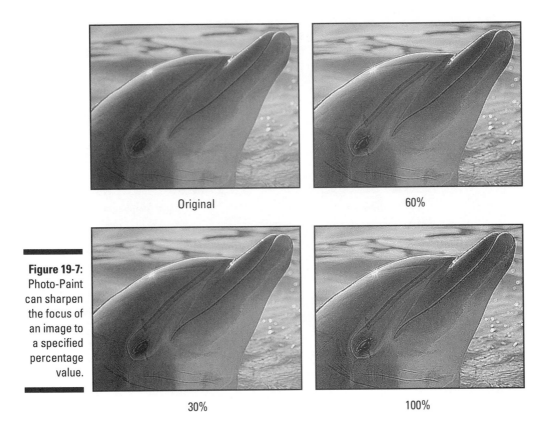

Original   60%

Figure 19-7:
Photo-Paint
can sharpen
the focus of
an image to
a specified
percentage
value.

30%   100%

Chapter 20
Ten Time-Saving Shortcuts

- -

In This Chapter

▶ Choosing commands in the File menu

▶ Working with dialog boxes

▶ Using Alt key shortcuts

▶ Accessing the zoom tools

▶ Selecting drawing and editing tools

▶ Undoing, redoing, and repeating

▶ Editing objects in the drawing area

▶ Choosing Clipboard commands

▶ Bringing to front and sending to back

▶ Using the Enter and Escape keys

- -

*A*nd now, from the ridiculous to the sublime. In between having fun with CorelDraw and creating every wacky special effect you can think of, you may as well work in a little productivity so that you don't go completely broke and have to put the kids up for adoption or rent them out for scientific research. Absolutely every Draw user should memorize the mouse and keyboard equivalents covered in this chapter — and get in the habit of using them on a regular basis.

Opening, Saving, and Quitting

Ctrl+O, Ctrl+N

To open a document in any Corel program, press Ctrl+O. In most Corel programs, you can press Ctrl+N to create a new document.

Ctrl+S

To save a document in any program, press Ctrl+S. Do so early and often.

Ctrl+F4

To close a document in programs that offer this capability, such as Photo-Paint and CorelChart, press Ctrl+F4 or double-click on the control menu in the upper-left corner of the document window. If you haven't saved your most recent changes, press Y or Enter to do so.

Alt+F4

To quit a program and return to the Program Manager, press Alt+F4. Again, press Y or Enter to save your most recent changes.

Alt+Esc, Ctrl+Esc, Alt+Tab

Alt+Escape switches you to a different running Windows program. Ctrl+Escape opens a list of running programs. Double-click on the one you want to use. Alt+Tab switches you back and forth between two running programs.

All of these shortcuts are applicable not only to CorelDraw programs but also to nearly every Windows program on the planet.

Navigating Inside Dialog Boxes

You can move around a dialog box without using the mouse. To activate the next option on a dialog box, press the Tab key. To return to the previous option, press Shift+Tab.

To display the pop-up menu for an active option, click on the down-arrow button. Then use the up- and down-arrow keys to highlight the desired option and press Enter to select it. You can also use the arrow keys in scrolling lists.

To select a specific option, press the Alt key in combination with the underlined letter in the option.

Displaying Menus

To display a menu, press the Alt key in combination with the underlined letter in the menu name. When the menu appears, you can simply press the underlined letter in a command name — no Alt key required — to select it.

The Control menu is a special case. Press Alt+spacebar to display this menu.

In some cases, you may be more comfortable navigating through the menus with the arrow keys. Press and release the Alt key to highlight the menu bar. Then press the left- and right-arrow keys to highlight different menu names. Press the up- or down-arrow keys to display a menu and highlight different commands. If a highlighted command brings up a submenu, press the right-arrow key to display it. Press the left-arrow key to hide the submenu.

Press and release the Alt key again to hide the menus and deactivate the menu bar.

Zooming from the Keyboard

F2, Shift+F2, F3, F4, Shift+F4

Press F2 and click the mouse to magnify the drawing area to twice its previous size. Press Shift+F2 to zoom to the maximum view size of the selected objects. To zoom to the maximum view size at which you can see all objects in the drawing area, press F4.

To reduce the view size to half the current level of magnification, press F3. To zoom out so you can see the entire page, press Shift+F4.

Selecting Tools in CorelDraw

F5, F6, F7, F8, Shift+F8, F10

Of all the programs Corel sells, only CorelDraw lets you access the main drawing and editing tools from the keyboard:

- ✔ Press F5 to select the Pencil tool.
- ✔ Press F6 to select the Rectangle tool.

> ✔ Press F7 to select the Ellipse tool.
>
> ✔ Press F8 to select the Artistic Text tool. Shift+F8 selects the Paragraph Text tool.
>
> ✔ Press F10 to select the Shape tool and edit a path.

Pressing the spacebar toggles you back and forth between the Arrow tool and the tool you were using last.

Although you can't select the Arrow tool from the keyboard, you can get to this tool by right-clicking on an empty portion of the drawing area. This assumes that you haven't assigned a specific operation to the right mouse button by using Special⇨Preferences (Ctrl+J). Ha, I managed to sneak in another one.

Undoing a Mistake

Ctrl+Z, Alt+Backspace

To undo an operation in any program bundled with CorelDraw, press Ctrl+Z or Alt+Backspace.

Alt+Enter

You can restore an operation that you undid by pressing Alt+Enter (Redo). Otherwise, again press Ctrl+Z or Alt+Backspace.

Ctrl+R

For extra credit, Draw lets you repeat an operation by pressing Ctrl+R.

Manipulating Objects with the Arrow and Shape Tools

To select an object with the Arrow tool (or the Pick tool in Photo-Paint), click on it. To select multiple objects, click on the first object you want to select and Shift+click on the others.

You can also drag on an empty portion of the document to surround multiple objects in a marquee. Press Shift while marqueeing to add objects to the selection.

To deselect specific objects that are currently selected, Shift+click on them.

Drag an object to move it. Ctrl+drag to move the object strictly horizontally or vertically. To nudge a selection a few fractions of an inch (as specified in the Preferences dialog box), press one of the arrow keys.

All these techniques also work when you edit nodes with the Shape tool in CorelDraw. Furthermore, you can double-click on a node to display the Node Edit roll-up. Double-clicking on objects in other Corel programs likewise tends to display specialized roll-ups or dialog boxes.

Making Copies of Objects

Ctrl+C, Ctrl+X, Ctrl+V

In all Corel programs, you can copy one or more selected objects to the Clipboard by pressing Ctrl+C. To cut an object from the document and transfer it to the Clipboard, press Ctrl+X. To paste the contents of the Clipboard into the document, press Ctrl+V.

Ctrl+Ins, Shift+Del, Shift+Ins

You can also use these old-style keyboard equivalents. Copy by pressing Ctrl+Insert. Cut by pressing Shift+Delete. To paste, press Shift+Insert.

Ctrl+D

In CorelDraw, you can bypass the Clipboard and make an immediate duplicate of a selected object by pressing Ctrl+D.

Changing the Stacking Order of Objects

Shift+PgUp, Shift+PgDn

 To bring a select object to the front of the stacking order, press Shift+PgUp. To send it to the back of the document, press Shift+PgDn. Or you can use those cute icon buttons along the ribbon bar. Click on the left button to send the object to the front of the stacking order; click on the right button to send it to the back.

Ctrl+PgUp, Ctrl+PgDn

You can scoot a selected object one object forward or backward by pressing Ctrl+PgUp and Ctrl+PgDn, respectively.

Activating Buttons

Remember that pressing the Enter key always activates the button surrounded by a heavy outline. This is usually the OK button, but sometimes pressing Enter activates a button other than OK — especially while you're using the Preferences dialog box.

To activate the Cancel button, press Escape. In fact, rely on the Escape key to get you out of just about any weird situation in which you don't know what to do. If you don't recognize a dialog box, press Escape to get out of it. If all the menus and other interface elements disappear, press Escape to bring them back. If you change a value in the data manager in CorelChart and think better of it, press the Escape key. This key almost always returns you to familiar territory.

If the Enter key doesn't activate the highlighted button in a dialog box, try pressing the Enter key in the numeric keypad instead.

Chapter 21

Ten Little-Known, Less-Used Features

*I*n case you haven't figured it out yet, CorelDraw is a veritable grab bag of graphics functions. For $500 (or whatever you paid), you get more programs and features than any other software package I can think of. But face it: Like any grab bag, Draw is split evenly between essential capabilities and extravagant, super-complicated excesses. This chapter concerns the latter. I discuss ten features that you'll probably never use. But, by gum, you paid for them, so you should know about them. I'll start with the borderline excess and move my way up to functions that you never, ever in a billion years expected to find in a drawing package.

Turning CorelDraw into a Parking Garage

You find layers in just about every drawing program with high-end pretensions, but only a handful of experienced artists use layers on a regular basis. Granted, those experienced artists swear by layers. They'll tell you how layers saved their artwork from certain, overwhelming confusion. But for my part, I can take or leave layers, and I would never recommend them to anyone who isn't drawing vast blowouts of manifold exhaust systems or tubercular cancer cell networks or something equally complicated and mind numbing. Still, I'm a simple guy with simple tastes. You may enjoy complexity.

Here's how layers work: Imagine that all the objects in a CorelDraw document are cars. Sure, the cars come in various shapes, sizes, and colors, and they're heaped all over each other, but they're still cars. Flat cars without engines. And no drive train warranties. Anyway, one day, there gets to be way too many cars and you think to yourself — because you're some kind of city official or something — "How can I sort out these cars to make things more efficient and less of a screwball mess?" The answer is to build a multilevel parking garage.

Well, that's layers. By choosing Layout⇨Layers Roll-Up (Ctrl+F3) , you display the Layers roll-up, which lets you divide your document into a transparent, multilevel parking garage viewed from a helicopter. Each layer contains a bunch of objects — as many as you want — that are fully segregated from objects on other layers.

Unless you specify otherwise, objects on different layers don't look different and they don't print differently. They're merely organized into separate banks to help eliminate confusion and provide greater control and flexibility. For example, you can hide different layers to get them out of your face; you can print only certain layers to isolate others; you can lock the objects on a layer to prevent accidental alterations; and you can make objects on layers appear in different colors. The icons in the Layers roll-up assist you in determining what's locked, visible, printable, and so on.

Blending Between Objects

I sort of spoiled the surprise with this one when I mentioned blending as a way to create custom color gradations in Chapter 19. Luckily, there's more to blending than just creating gradations. In fact, blending is one of CorelDraw's most complicated functions. You can do all kinds of things with this feature that you never wanted to do — and you never will do — so it fits right in with the tone of this chapter.

As described in Chapter 19, you display the Blend roll-up by choosing Effects⇨Blend Roll-Up or by pressing Ctrl+B. Then you select two objects, click on the Apply button, and watch CorelDraw create a bunch of intermediate objects (called *steps*) between the two. The steps gradually change in form and color as they progress from the first object to the last. You can specify how many steps Draw creates, rotate the steps, make the steps follow a path, and even control the amount of space between steps.

Blending is sort of like morphing — you know, that effect in that commercial in which some feline or other gradually turns into a car. Or when all those faces change into each other at the end of that Michael Jackson video. Unlike morphing, in which each step occurs in a different frame of videotape to create the effect of a gradual transition, in blending, all the steps appear in the drawing area at the same time. As a result, no one uses blending for any other purpose than creating custom gradations. If you're really adventurous, though, you can take a blend from CorelDraw and link it into CorelMove, where it acts as a morph and each object appears on each cel. The procedure is very complicated and explaining how it works could take an entire chapter, so I'm not going to get into it. But I will tell you this — don't try it alone . . . you could poke out a pixel or something.

Backing Your Objects with Data

Wow, is this feature ever obscure. When you right-click on an object, you display the Object pop-up menu. (If you have assigned some other function to the right mouse button, such as zooming or node editing, press and hold the right mouse button on an object.) Click on the Data Roll-Up option in the Object pop-up menu to display the Object Data roll-up. Here, you can enter any data you want about the selected object. For example, you can assign it a name, type its phone number, and enter the name of its closest relative in case of emergency. You can associate any data you want with the object.

Why on earth would you want to do this? Well, Corel's example is catalogs. If you have a drawing of a rotary combine engine, for example, you might want to write down the name and price of the product along with a few comments. Later, you could print this information or use it in a different program. Yeah, I'm always wishing that I could do that.

Trapping Colors

Sounds like I'm taking you on a little hunt, huh? Well, not really. You may remember the "Printing full-color artwork" section of Chapter 13, in which I discuss how to print color separations. Cyan, magenta, yellow, and black primaries are printed on separate pages and reproduced in separate passes. First, all the cyan pages are printed, then the magenta ink is added, then yellow, and finally black.

It turns out that this process is the same one used to print the Sunday comics in your local newspaper. Actually, nearly all color newspaper and magazine art is created this way, but the comics are the best example because they invariably have registration problems. Maybe the red in Hagar's beard is printed on Helga's face, or perhaps Robotman's outfit is leaking yellow onto a neighboring panel. These errors are caused by improper alignment of the cyan, magenta, yellow, and black inks.

CorelDraw allows you to compensate for bad registration by overlapping the colors a little. For example, imagine a circle with a cyan fill and a black outline. If the colors don't register exactly right, a gap occurs between the fill and outline colors. Draw can fill this gap by spreading the colors. The black outline becomes slightly thicker, and the cyan fill becomes slightly larger. This process is known as *color trapping*.

To activate CorelDraw's trapping function, do the following:

1. **Press Ctrl+P or choose File⇨Print.**
2. **Click on the Options button in the Print dialog box.**
3. **Select the Separations tab and select the Print Separations checkbox.**
4. **Select both the Always Overprint Black and Auto-Spreading checkboxes.**
5. **Click on OK and then click on OK again.**

Phew, what a lot of work. Might as well get out your crayons and draw the artwork from scratch. It would be equally as convenient.

Separating Color Channels in Photo-Paint

CorelDraw offers some rarefied features, but it's not until you leave Draw and explore the other Corel programs that the features become truly obscure. In Photo-Paint 5, you can take a color image and split it into several separate images called *channels,* each of which represents a primary color. For example, you can split an image into four channels, one each for cyan, magenta, yellow, and black, just as when printing color separations. Or you can separate the image into three channels, one each for red, green, and blue (the primary colors for light). To do so, just choose the desired command from the Image⇨Split Channels To submenu.

What's the point of channel splitting? Well, you can apply a special effect to a single color channel to get a doubly weird effect. If a color image looks a little fuzzy, it may turn out that only one color channel needs sharpening. Or you may want to create a psychedelic effect by splitting the channels and then reassembling them differently by using the Combine Channels command. For example, you can swap the red and green channels to change a red apple with a green leaf into a green apple with a red leaf.

In other words, you'll never use this function.

Scanning Directly into Photo-Paint

All right, here's something you might actually do someday. If you've sunk a few thousand bucks into a scanner, you can scan images directly into Photo-Paint. Scanners convert photographs — the kind you shoot with a camera — into on-screen images.

To take a bit of real life and make it appear magically on your computer screen, choose File⇨Acquire Image⇨Acquire. Then click on the Scan button inside the Corel Image Source dialog box. When the scanner is done working, your photograph appears on-screen.

If you don't have a scanner, however, nothing happens. You can try smushing the photograph against the screen, but I don't think Corel has figured out how to make Photo-Paint read images that way. Maybe you can try smushing the photo and shouting at the same time. It's worth a try.

Crunching Numbers in CorelChart

In CorelChart, the Data Manager can perform calculations. To access this function, click on an empty cell — the cell *must* be empty — and choose Data⇨Enter Formula or press F12. A dialog box with a calculator inside it appears. Can you believe that? This program actually has a calculator. Anyway, click on the buttons on the calculator as if you were using the real thing. You can even select a few expert calculations from the Functions list on the right (provided that you can make heads or tails of them). When you're finished, click on the Enter button. Chart makes the required calculations and displays the solution in the selected cell.

Although I've sort of been poking fun at some of the features in this chapter — it's been very subtle, of course, so you probably didn't notice — I like the Enter Formula command. I don't think I've seen a program handle calculations better than CorelChart.

Compressing Files in CorelMosaic

If your files are taking up too much space on disk, you can make them smaller by using CorelMosaic. When placing graphics in libraries, Mosaic automatically compresses the files to make them take up less disk space. It accomplishes this task by examining the computer code used to explain the graphic. It then removes all the excess stuff that doesn't need to be there and creates a smaller file.

Press Ctrl+N or choose File⇨New Catalog/Library to create a new library file. This command creates a new, empty window. Then choose File⇨Open Collection (Ctrl+O) to open a window that displays all graphics in a directory on disk. To compress a graphic, just drag it from the directory window into the empty library window. Mosaic automatically copies the graphic and compresses it.

To free up space on your hard drive, you must delete the original graphic from disk. You can do so in the Windows File Manager or use the DEL command at the dreaded DOS prompt. Because a compressed version of the graphic is stored safely in the library file, you can delete the original with a clear conscience.

Editing Sounds by Using CorelMove

Not only can you import sounds in CorelMove, you also can edit them. You can actually open the sound and change the way it, er, sounds. To do so, locate a sound in the Library roll-up (View⇨Library Roll-Up) and click on the Place button. Then choose View⇨Timelines Roll-Up. Locate the sound inside the Timelines roll-up — it should have a speaker icon in front of it — and double-click on the sound to display the Sound Information dialog box. Click on the Edit Sound button to display the Wave Editor window, which displays the sound as a waveform graph. You can select portions of the sound and apply commands to amplify the sound, play the sound backwards, add echoes, and so on.

Of course, you can't hear your changes unless your computer is equipped with a sound board. Too bad, because you'd be awfully impressed.

Optical Character Recognition with CorelTrace

After scanning a typewritten page, CorelTrace can recognize the characters in the scanned image and generate a text document that you can open in a word processor, such as WordPerfect or Microsoft Word. This function is absolutely the last I expected to see worked into what is ostensibly a drawing package. Face facts, it'll be a cold day in Port-au-Prince before you decide to use it.

Chapter 22

Ten (or so) File Formats and Their Functions

. . . .

In This Chapter

▶ .CDR

▶ .EPS and .AI

▶ .CGM and .WMF

▶ .DXF

▶ .PCX

▶ .TIF

▶ .BMP

▶ .GIF

▶ .JPG

▶ Photo CD

▶ Word processor text, spreadsheets, and Micrografx files

. . . .

CorelDraw supports more file formats than any other graphics program on the PC. You can create a graphic in just about any program on an IBM-compatible or Macintosh computer and open it or import it into CorelDraw. Likewise, you can export an image from Draw so that it can be opened in just about any program. If CorelDraw were a person, it would be able to speak every language except . . . well, any language I mention would be politically incorrect, so I'd better keep my mouth shut.

Native CorelDraw, .CDR

.CDR is the native file format, which means that when you choose File⇨Save As, enter a name, and press Enter, CorelDraw uses the .CDR format. This format retains every shred of information about your drawing, including nodes, segments, fills, outlines, and layers. Unless you plan on sharing your drawing with another user or opening it in another program, stick with this format.

Also be sure to select the Save Presentation Exchange Data checkbox in the Save Drawing dialog box. If you deselect it, you strip out blends, contours, powerlines, dimensions, and text fitted to path if it happens to be edited while being embedded or linked in another OLE-based application. Got that? Me neither. If you want to check out what it's all about, read Chapter 17 in Corel's manual. In my opinion, it's not worth the headache.

Encapsulated PostScript, .EPS and .AI

PostScript is the printer language explained in Chapter 13. The Encapsulated PostScript (.EPS) file format contains a complete PostScript definition of the graphic right in the file. It's as if the artwork contains a little PostScript capsule. When you print an imported .EPS file from CorelDraw or some other program, the program sends the PostScript capsule to the printer and lets the printer figure it out.

However, the printer has to support PostScript in order to print .EPS graphics. If you don't own a PostScript printer, don't use .EPS.

The Adobe Illustrator (.AI) format is an editable variation of the .EPS format. In other words, when you import an .EPS graphic into a program, you can't edit it. You can display the graphic inside your document, but you can't manipulate the paths, reformat the text, or do anything else. You can only place it on the page and print it.

When you import an .AI file into CorelDraw, you can edit every little bit of it. This format is ideal if you want to share your artwork with someone who works with a Macintosh computer. It is also widely supported by other Windows programs.

Metafile Formats, .CGM and .WMF

Computer Graphics Metafile (.CGM) is a dinosaur-like file format that's certified by the American National Standards Committee. Predating the .EPS format, .CGM is preferable to .EPS when you're printing to non-PostScript printers. It's also very popular within large institutions where the wheels grind very slowly, such as the U. S. Government.

The Windows Metafile Format (.WMF) is the rough equivalent to .CGM in the Windows environment, although no institutions have come out to certify it. The Windows Clipboard uses .WMF format. If you plan to transfer a drawing to another Windows program and print to a non-PostScript printer, you may want to give .WMF a try.

AutoCAD, .DXF

AutoCAD may be the most venerable graphics program for the PC. Technically a computer-aided design (CAD) program created with engineers, architects, and other precision-oriented professionals in mind, the program's been around so long that even amateurs and novices sometimes get into the act.

The AutoCAD format, known as .DXF, is widely supported by CAD programs. Desktop publishing and drawing programs also support it to a lesser extent. Much to its credit, CorelDraw can import and edit .DXF graphics. However, unless someone specifically tells you to send a graphic in .DXF format, you shouldn't export to it.

Paintbrush, .PCX

Formats with the extensions .PCX, .TIF, .BMP, .GIF, .JPG, and .PCD are image file formats. They save artwork as pixels, not as objects. Although CorelDraw is perfectly capable of importing these formats, you should not export to them unless you want to convert your graphic to pixels. However, it is perfectly acceptable to both open and save in these formats in Corel Photo-Paint because Photo-Paint works with pixels exclusively.

The .PCX format was originally designed for PC Paintbrush and is now the most widely supported graphics format on the PC. When in doubt, save your image in .PCX format.

One of the most common uses for the .PCX format is trading images between Photo-Paint and CorelDraw. In other words, you can save a Photo-Paint image in .PCX format and then import it into Draw.

Tag Image File Format, .TIF

The Tag Image File (.TIF) format was developed to be the standard image file format — even more of a standard than .PCX. Although it still plays second fiddle to .PCX in terms of raw support on the PC, .TIF is more likely to be supported by programs running on other kinds of computers, namely the Mac. Furthermore, if you're exporting an image for use in a mainstream desktop publishing program such as PageMaker, QuarkXPress, or Microsoft Publisher, .TIF is the way to go because it is generally a more reliable format and offers compression options to reduce the size of the image on disk.

Corel also supports .TIF 6.0 file formats, which Mac-amundos know as a CMYK TIF. On top of that, Corel supports .SEP files for Scitex fans, as well as the new Photo-Paint .CPT format that uses layering.

Windows Bitmap, .BMP

.BMP is the native format of that squalid little Paintbrush program included in your Accessories directory in the Program Manager. The only reason Photo-Paint and CorelDraw support .BMP is for importing purposes. Don't export to the .BMP format unless . . . gee, I can't think of any reasons.

CompuServe Bitmap, .GIF

The .GIF format was created especially for trading images over the CompuServe Information System, which is a mammoth bulletin board that you can call by using a modem. Anyway, .GIF offers compression capabilities, but it only supports 256 colors. Like .BMP, .GIF is generally for importing purposes only.

Joint Photographic Experts Group, .JPG

The new format among ultra-high-end users is JPEG (or .JPG), which stands for the Joint Photographic Experts Group (the group of folks who came up with the format). The .JPG format is designed to compress huge images so that they take up less space on disk. Compression-wise, .JPG wipes the floor with .TIF and .GIF. However, you actually lose data when you save to .JPG format. In most cases, the loss is nominal and most users can't even see the difference, but it's something to keep in the back of your mind.

Generally speaking, you don't need to worry about .JPG format unless you start creating very large images — larger than 400K on disk — with Corel Photo-Paint.

Kodak's Photo CD, .PCD

CorelDraw and Photo-Paint can import Kodak Photo CD files. Neither program can save to the format because Kodak won't let them. The .PCD format is what's known as a *proprietary format*.

In case you haven't heard of it, Photo CD is the latest thing from Kodak for storing photographs on compact discs. You take a roll of undeveloped film to a service bureau, hand over $25 or so, and get your photos scanned onto a CD. As long as you have a Photo CD-compatible CD-ROM drive hooked up to your computer, you can then open and edit the images in Photo-Paint. What will they think of next?

Word Processor Text

CorelDraw 5 can import text from your favorite word processor. That includes Microsoft Word for Windows 1, 2, and 6 (what happened to 3, 4, and 5?), Microsoft Word for the Mac 4 and 5, the Rich Text Format (.RTF), Lotus AmiPro 2 and 3, WordPerfect 5, 5.1, and 6, and the faithful old .TXT files as well.

Spreadsheets

Yup, you can import spreadsheets from Microsoft Excel Versions 3 and 4 and Lotus 1-2-3 Versions 1, 2, and 3. Don't ask me why someone would want to import a spreadsheet in CorelDraw.

The Competition

Heck, CorelDraw can even import images created in a competing draw program, Micrografx Designer. Draw wumps Micrografx Designer in its volume of clip art alone, let alone everything else it can do. Being a classy, polite program, however, Draw ignores the fact that you're importing from a rival and accepts the file graciously.

Chapter 23

Ten Commandments of CorelDraw

· ·

In This Chapter

▶ Thou shalt not unlock the original disks

▶ Thou shalt not neglect to save on a regular basis

▶ Thou shalt not forget where thou savest thy files

▶ Thou shalt not hesitate to press Ctrl+Z or Alt+Backspace

▶ Thou shalt not choose a command when thou mayest press a few keys instead

▶ Thou shalt not close thy roll-ups

▶ Thou shalt not choose Copy when Duplicate will do

▶ Thou shalt not create text in Photo-Paint

▶ Thou shalt not neglect the temporal needs of thy local computer expert

▶ Thou shalt not freak out and beat thy computer mercilessly

· ·

I was quite persuaded we were there when we were ten miles off; and when we really were there that we should never get there.

— *Bleak House*, Charles Dickens

That's a real quote, for once, by the great Chaz Dickens from his upbeat *Bleak House,* describing the pleasures of riding in a hansom cab. But he may just as well have been describing his impression of reading this book. You keep thinking that it'll end soon: the relentless sarcasm, the ground swell of unendurable technicalities, the gaping chasm of information opened up before you. Well, it has finally come to an end. You now know everything about CorelDraw that anyone has a right to know.

As for you folks who skipped here because you liked the title of this chapter, or worse yet, are reading this in a store without having even purchased the book . . . well, you haven't earned the following pearls of wisdom, that's all I can say. For further thoughts on this subject, skip to page 253. Then read all of page 128, part of page 219, and the three words in the upper-right corner of page 12 held up to a mirror.

(Psst, you folks who read the book. There's nothing of importance on any of those pages. I just used that clever ruse to keep the folks who haven't read the book busy for a while. See, you have to suffer to appreciate the Ten Commandments of CorelDraw, and you haven't suffered until you've read this book. So without further ado, here are some rules to work by. Keep them under your hat.)

Don't forget to cut page 73 into horizontal strips with a pair of pruning shears and plant the strips four inches deep in fertilized soil.

Thou Shalt Not Unlock Thy Original Disks

The 3 ½-inch disks that come with CorelDraw have a little tab in the upper-right corner that should be open, which is the locked position. If your disks have two holes, make sure that both are open. When a disk is locked, your computer can't copy to it or otherwise alter the contents. This way, you can't do something dumb like accidentally copy the contents of your hard drive to disks for which you paid hundreds of dollars.

Of course, if you have a CD-ROM drive and bought Corel's CD version of the software, copying to the CD disk isn't possible, so you're protected from yourself.

Thou Shalt Not Neglect to Save on a Regular Basis

Press Ctrl+S every time you think of it, if not more frequently. Honestly, you shouldn't let 10 minutes go by without saving your document. Go ahead, practice right now. See how it feels. Experiment with using different fingers. Try it out until it feels habitual. This way, any time you have a breather, your hand naturally rests on Ctrl+S.

Thou Shalt Not Forget Where Thou Savest Thy Files

It doesn't do any good to save a file if you're going to call it FILE.CDR and forget what you did with it. Use meaningful and distinct names and make sure to pay attention to the directory in which you save the file.

Every three or four days — every Tuesday and Friday morning, for example — copy the new files you've created from your hard drive to disks. That way, if something goes wrong with your computer, which undoubtedly will happen one day, you won't lose your work.

Thou Shalt Not Hesitate to Press Ctrl+Z or Alt+Backspace

If you make a mistake, press Ctrl+Z. If that doesn't seem to work, choose Edit⇨Undo. The Undo command can restore deleted objects, change transformed objects back to the way they looked before the transformation, and generally discombobulate erroneous operations. In CorelDraw, you can undo several operations in a row. Only in CorelMove do you ever find yourself without a chance to undo.

Thou Shalt Not Choose a Command When Thou Mayest Press a Few Keys Instead

Moving the mouse requires more concentration, more coordination, and more time than pressing keys on the keyboard. If you can access a command, tool, or any other function by using a keyboard equivalent, use the keyboard. Memorize the stuff in Chapter 21 if you haven't already.

Thou Shalt Not Close Thy Roll-Ups

When you finish using a roll-up, your natural reaction may be to close it so that it no longer clutters up your screen. If you ever want to use the roll-up again, you have to choose a command or press a keyboard equivalent again. You're better off double-clicking on the title bar (or clicking on the up-arrow button) to collapse the roll-up and leave only the title bar visible. This way, you can quickly redisplay the options in the roll-up just by double-clicking on the title bar (or clicking on the down-arrow icon).

Thou Shalt Not Choose Copy When Duplicate Will Do

If you just want to make a quick copy of one or more selected objects in CorelDraw, press Ctrl+D or choose Edit⇨Duplicate. Better yet, just press + on the keypad, which creates a duplicate directly in front of the original. There's no sense in bothering with the Cut, Copy, and Paste commands unless you want to copy an object from one drawing and paste it into another.

Thou Shalt Not Create Text in Photo-Paint

As if it's not bad enough that all text in Photo-Paint is jagged, the Text tool works about as reliably as a pig on roller skates. If you want to add text to an image, select the entire image, copy it, switch to CorelDraw, paste it into a new or existing drawing, and use Draw's text tools to create the text. This way, you get smooth text plus the advantage of Draw's better editing and formatting capabilities.

Thou Shalt Not Neglect the Temporal Needs of Thy Local Computer Guru

Can't live with 'em, can't live without 'em. That's what folks say about their resident computer gurus. Granted, they can be arrogant, obnoxious, and irritable, but they have something you need: information and knowledge. Therefore, appease them. The time to get a computer expert on your side is when there is no crisis. Gifts and random acts of kindness work best. Then when a crisis does occur, your computer expert is already predisposed to help you.

If you're really ambitious, pay careful attention to how the computer expert solves your problems and learn how to solve the problems yourself. With some careful study, *you* can attain the rank of computer expert. Then I'll be instructing people how to appease you with gifts and random acts of kindness.

Thou Shalt Not Freak Out and Beat Thy Computer Mercilessly

Computers don't respond to violence; they just respond to your commands. This isn't to say that they always respond correctly — computers can be very problematic — but yelling at them, slapping monitors, and pummeling on keyboards don't have any effect. Computers aren't yet smart enough to understand threats.

If things are really going awfully, save your work, exit CorelDraw, exit Windows, and press Ctrl+Alt+Delete to restart your computer. Then start up Windows again, start up CorelDraw, open your document, and see whether things go a little more smoothly. If that doesn't work, call your computer expert and beg for help, all the while hinting at more gifts and random acts of kindness.

"WE'VE EXPANDED THE MEMORY ON THIS ONE SO MANY TIMES IT'S STARTING TO GET STRETCH MARKS."

Installing CorelDraw 5

When CorelDraw 5 Arrives — Don't Let This Happen to You!

While sitting at my desk, I scan today's mail. What's this? A letter from the IRS reminding me of a tax audit in two weeks. Forget that. The other large envelope looks more intriguing.

Great — it's only car insurance stuff. An invoice falls into my lap. This can't be right! The premium has skyrocketed 322 percent! I use the invoice as a three-pointer into the trash. Missed!

I save the best for last — a box from Canada. Packed inside is an old Canadian newspaper. I can't help but notice the crumpled headlines announcing "Retro-active Taxation." I'm glad I don't live in Canada!

Digging to the bottom of the box, I finally get to it — my escape for the week — a brand-new version of CorelDraw. I rip apart the plastic shrink-wrap and search for the installation instructions. What? I need 50MB of free hard drive space to load Corel? They must be kidding! I only have 30MB left on my whole internal hard drive!

I take out my worn but still legible charge card and reluctantly order a new hard drive for my computer. What's $500 anyway? At least this five has only two zeros after it.

After hanging up the phone with the mail-order company, I read further in the setup and installation guide. Here's a great feature. I don't have to use all of Corel's applications; I can just add the programs and features I want to use to minimize the space used on the hard drive. I call back the mail-order company and cancel my new hard drive order. Too late. They've gone bankrupt.

If you are upgrading from Version 4 to 5, grab your manual or find the closes computer guru for help. That upgrade installation is too advanced for this bc especially if you want to retain all the customized features and actions of the previous version.

Getting Started

These are the basic steps for installing CorelDraw 5:

1. **Turn on your computer.**

2. **Start Windows.**

   You cannot install the full-featured CorelDraw without Microsoft's Windows Version 3.1.

3. **In the carton of disks that comes with CorelDraw, look for the disk labeled *Disk #1*.**

   If you're installing from the CD version, you have only one disk to load.

4. **Insert Disk #1 into the appropriate disk drive.**

   The computer recognizes this disk slot as Drive A or B. If the front of your computer only has one slot available, it's probably Drive A. If you notice two slots on the front, the top one is usually Drive A and the bottom is Drive B.

5. **Choose File⇨Run from the Windows Program Manager menu bar.**

   The Run dialog box appears.

6. **Type the following in the Command Line box:**

   If Disk #1 is in Drive A, type

   ```
   A:\SETUP
   ```

   If Disk #1 is in Drive B, type

   ```
   B:\SETUP
   ```

A dialog box similar to Figure A-1 appears in the middle of your screen. Click on Continue with your left mouse button. A second setup dialog box prompts you to enter your name and the serial number of your software (see Figure A-2).

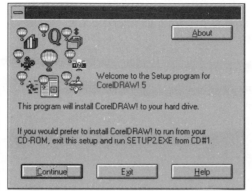

Figure A-1:
The first
"welcome
aboard"
message.

Figure A-2:
CorelDraw
5's
registration
dialog box.

You can find the serial number labels in Volume 1 of the User Manual. Look inside the cover to locate the technical support card — it's in the right-hand corner.

If you can't find the serial number, you can't install the program — worse yet, you may have to buy another copy. If you're missing a serial number, call Corel Corporation first.

Full Installation for Byte-Biters

If you have plenty of hard drive space available, don't care what you're filling your computer with, and want everything that the software has to offer, pick the Full Install button in the CorelDraw 5 Installation Options dialog box (see Figure A-3). Just follow the program's instructions during the remaining portion of the installation and insert the appropriate disks. Whenever you're asked a question during the installation process, click on the Yes, OK, or Continue button in the questioning dialog box.

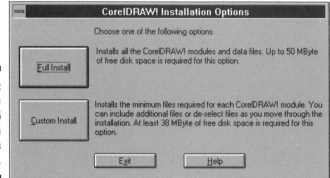

Figure A-3:
The
CorelDraw 5
Installation
Options
dialog box.

If you see a message similar to the one shown in Figure A-4, click on OK with the mouse and read "Custom Installation for Byte-Budgeters" later in this Appendix.

Figure A-4:
The
Insufficient
Disk Space
dialog box.

When CorelDraw finishes the installation process, it notifies you with a dialog box. You can now run any of Corel's applications from the newly created Corel program group in the Program Manager. Just double-click on the balloon icon labeled CorelDRAW! to start the state-of-the-art drawing program.

Custom Installation for Byte-Budgeters

As shown in Figure A-3, Version 5 has an option button named Custom Install. Clicking on this button allows you to select only the programs and features you need or think you need. At the same time, Corel's installation program keeps a running tally of the amount of hard drive space your choices use. It also keeps an accurate list of the free space available on your hard drive.

Occasionally, when the installation program needs to recalculate the hard drive memory required to install your custom selections, you see a small dialog box like the one shown in Figure A-5.

Figure A-5:
The
installation
program
checks the
disk space.

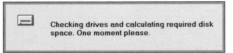

Checking drives and calculating required disk space. One moment please.

Minimum Installation — CorelDraw Only

This section explains the minimum installation of CorelDraw 5 only. If you want only the Draw program — and don't need Chart, Show, or anything else — this section is for you.

Don't get confused here. All of Draw (the drawing program) will be installed, but the extra programs bundled with Version 5 (Publisher, Chart, Photo-Paint, Show, and Move) will not. You save a lot of precious hard drive space by keeping programs you don't need off your computer.

When you first click on the Custom Install button in CorelDraw 5's Installation Options dialog box (see Figure A-3), the Choose which applications to install dialog box appears, as shown in Figure A-6. Notice that every box in the left column is marked with an X, which means that all programs in the CorelDraw 5 package are selected for installation.

To make the installation a minimum one, you need to click on every checked box except the one for CorelDraw. The Setup Program recalculates the amount of hard drive space that your new configuration will steal and displays it at the bottom of the dialog box.

In this custom minimum installation, the value labeled Space Required at the bottom of the dialog box continues to shrink in K size every time you click on a checked box to deselect it.

When you have appropriately deselected all the Xs with a click of the mouse, your screen should look like that in Figure A-7. The Space Required value (space required by CorelDraw) should be smaller than the Space Available value (space available on your hard disk). If not, then you need to visit your favorite computer store to discuss buying a bigger hard drive or adding a second one to your computer.

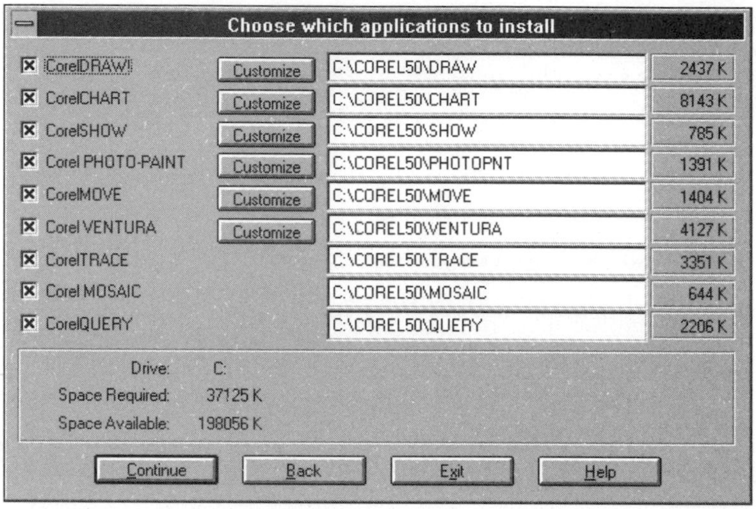

```
┌─────────────────────────────────────────────────────────────┐
│ ─            Choose which applications to install             │
├─────────────────────────────────────────────────────────────┤
│ ⊠ CorelDRAW!    [Customize]   C:\COREL50\DRAW        2437 K   │
│ ⊠ CorelCHART    [Customize]   C:\COREL50\CHART       8143 K   │
│ ⊠ CorelSHOW     [Customize]   C:\COREL50\SHOW         785 K   │
│ ⊠ Corel PHOTO-PAINT [Customize] C:\COREL50\PHOTOPNT  1391 K   │
│ ⊠ CorelMOVE     [Customize]   C:\COREL50\MOVE        1404 K   │
│ ⊠ Corel VENTURA [Customize]   C:\COREL50\VENTURA     4127 K   │
│ ⊠ CorelTRACE                  C:\COREL50\TRACE       3351 K   │
│ ⊠ Corel MOSAIC                C:\COREL50\MOSAIC       644 K   │
│ ⊠ CorelQUERY                  C:\COREL50\QUERY       2206 K   │
├─────────────────────────────────────────────────────────────┤
│          Drive:      C:                                       │
│     Space Required:  37125 K                                  │
│     Space Available: 198056 K                                 │
├─────────────────────────────────────────────────────────────┤
│    [ Continue ]    [ Back ]    [ Exit ]    [ Help ]           │
└─────────────────────────────────────────────────────────────┘
```

Figure A-6: CorelDraw 5's default selection options.

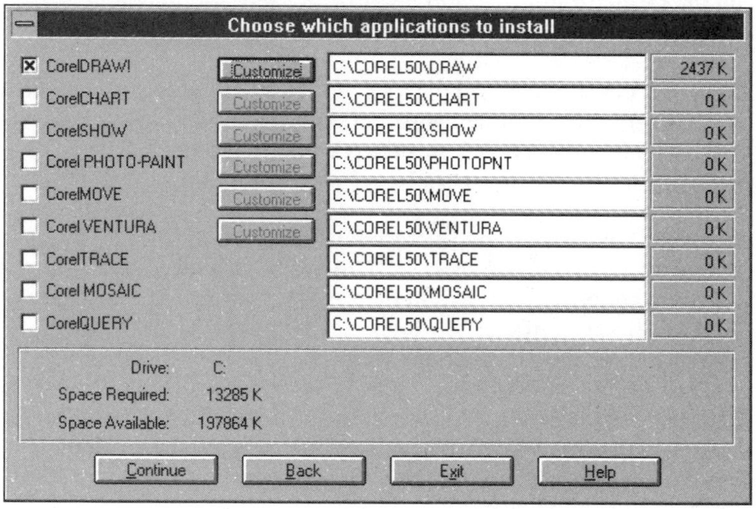

```
┌─────────────────────────────────────────────────────────────┐
│ ─            Choose which applications to install             │
├─────────────────────────────────────────────────────────────┤
│ ⊠ CorelDRAW!    [Customize]   C:\COREL50\DRAW        2437 K   │
│ ☐ CorelCHART    [Customize]   C:\COREL50\CHART          0 K   │
│ ☐ CorelSHOW     [Customize]   C:\COREL50\SHOW           0 K   │
│ ☐ Corel PHOTO-PAINT [Customize] C:\COREL50\PHOTOPNT     0 K   │
│ ☐ CorelMOVE     [Customize]   C:\COREL50\MOVE           0 K   │
│ ☐ Corel VENTURA [Customize]   C:\COREL50\VENTURA        0 K   │
│ ☐ CorelTRACE                  C:\COREL50\TRACE          0 K   │
│ ☐ Corel MOSAIC                C:\COREL50\MOSAIC         0 K   │
│ ☐ CorelQUERY                  C:\COREL50\QUERY          0 K   │
├─────────────────────────────────────────────────────────────┤
│          Drive:      C:                                       │
│     Space Required:  13285 K                                  │
│     Space Available: 197864 K                                 │
├─────────────────────────────────────────────────────────────┤
│    [ Continue ]    [ Back ]    [ Exit ]    [ Help ]           │
└─────────────────────────────────────────────────────────────┘
```

Figure A-7: Selections for installation of CorelDraw 5 only.

If the Space Required value is smaller than the Space Available value, click on the Continue button.

When the installation program asks you questions during the installation process, always click on the Yes, OK, or Continue button in the questioning dialog box and insert the appropriate disks. After you reach the end of the installation, double-click on the CorelDraw balloon icon from the Corel group in the Program Manager. CorelDraw magically appears before you, and you're ready to start using this book — don't forget your pocket protector.

If you need any of Corel's other programs or options later, read "Getting Started" in this Appendix again and then go to the last section of this Appendix, "A sample custom installation of Corel Photo-Paint."

On your own again

If you're not sure which programs to load in your first installation, I suggest that you read about Corel's individual applications in the first chapter of this book. You can use the minimum install options discussed in this Appendix first to install Draw only and then install other Version 5 features and applications later if you need to.

Table A-1 lists each application and a description and use for each. You may want to review this table to help you make your Custom Install choices.

Table A-1	Corel's Many Programs	
Program	*Description*	*Use*
CorelCapture	A screen-capture program	Use to print (or save to disk) a picture of whatever's on-screen.
CorelChart	A data chart maker	Use if you want Merrill-Lynch to hire you.
Corel DataBase Editor	A database editor	Use to build and modify database files.
CorelDraw	Vector drawing with text manipulation	What this book is all about.
CorelKern	Utility for modifying kerning pairs of PostScript fonts	A tool for your typographer friends.
CorelMosaic	A graphics file viewer and organizer	Helps organize all your Corel files.
CorelMove	An animation program	Use if you want Disney to hire you.
Corel Photo-Paint	Bitmap painting and photo retouching	A must if you have a scanner.
CorelQuery	A tool for use with database files	Use to turn up specific information in a database.
CorelShow	A slide show developer	Egomaniacs use this to show off their work.
CorelTrace	Converts bitmap paintings into vector drawings	A must if you're a graphic artist.
CorelVentura	A document maker	Use if you want *National Geographic* to hire you.

Adding a new part of CorelDraw 5 to your hard drive

When you refer to Figure A-6, you see that most Version 5 applications have a Customize button.

When you select the Customize button, an Options dialog box shows all subfiles, filters, help files, and samples already checked and ready to be loaded to your hard drive. If you click the Continue button at this point, the application still loads with all of its components.

The benefit of the Customize button is that you can reach every component of an application to check or uncheck it. With the check marks, you access just what you need before the installation process begins.

Note that CorelCapture, CorelKern, and CorelDatabase Editor don't have their own installation checkboxes in the Choose which applications to install dialog box. CorelCapture is an option within the Photo-Paint custom options; click on Photo-Paint's Customize button and check the CorelCapture checkbox if you want to install it. Similarly, CorelDatabase Editor is an option within the CorelVentura custom options. CorelKern is automatically installed when you install CorelDraw.

A sample custom installation of Corel Photo-Paint

You can also use these steps as a general guide if you decide to install other programs later.

Suppose that today you want to install the sample images that come with Corel Photo-Paint because last week you didn't have your new hard drive and had only enough room to install the Corel Photo-Paint program without the samples. Do the following:

1. **Start from the Choose which applications to install dialog box (see Figure A-6).**

   Refer to previous sections to get to this point.

2. **Uncheck all the boxes except for Corel Photo-Paint.**

3. **Select the Custom option in the Corel Photo-Paint line.**

   The Corel Photo-Paint Options dialog box appears.

4. **Uncheck all the boxes except for the one next to Samples (see Figure A-8).**

Figure A-8:
The Corel
Photo-Paint
Options
dialog box.

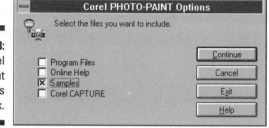

5. **Click on the Continue button in the Corel Photo-Paint Options dialog box.**

   You see the Checking drives information box that looks like Figure A-5.

6. **Click on the Continue button in the Choose which applications to install dialog box (see Figure A-6 again).**

Remember that you're only installing the Corel Photo-Paint samples and nothing more. If you are asked questions during this small custom installation, always click on the Yes, OK, or Continue button in the questioning dialog box. You are prompted to insert some disks, but the installation of the sample files does not take very long.

Index

Title	Author	ISBN	Price

12/20/94

INTERNET / COMMUNICATIONS / NETWORKING

Title	Author	ISBN	Price
CompuServe For Dummies™	by Wallace Wang	1-56884-181-7	$19.95 USA/$26.95 Canada
Modems For Dummies™, 2nd Edition	by Tina Rathbone	1-56884-223-6	$19.99 USA/$26.99 Canada
Modems For Dummies™	by Tina Rathbone	1-56884-001-2	$19.95 USA/$26.95 Canada
MORE Internet For Dummies™	by John R. Levine & Margaret Levine Young	1-56884-164-7	$19.95 USA/$26.95 Canada
NetWare For Dummies™	by Ed Tittel & Deni Connor	1-56884-003-9	$19.95 USA/$26.95 Canada
Networking For Dummies™	by Doug Lowe	1-56884-079-9	$19.95 USA/$26.95 Canada
ProComm Plus 2 For Windows For Dummies™	by Wallace Wang	1-56884-219-8	$19.99 USA/$26.99 Canada
The Internet For Dummies™, 2nd Edition	by John R. Levine & Carol Baroudi	1-56884-222-8	$19.99 USA/$26.99 Canada
The Internet For Macs For Dummies™	by Charles Seiter	1-56884-184-1	$19.95 USA/$26.95 Canada

MACINTOSH

Title	Author	ISBN	Price
Macs For Dummies®	by David Pogue	1-56884-173-6	$19.95 USA/$26.95 Canada
Macintosh System 7.5 For Dummies™	by Bob LeVitus	1-56884-197-3	$19.95 USA/$26.95 Canada
MORE Macs For Dummies™	by David Pogue	1-56884-087-X	$19.95 USA/$26.95 Canada
PageMaker 5 For Macs For Dummies™	by Galen Gruman	1-56884-178-7	$19.95 USA/$26.95 Canada
QuarkXPress 3.3 For Dummies™	by Galen Gruman & Barbara Assadi	1-56884-217-1	$19.99 USA/$26.99 Canada
Upgrading and Fixing Macs For Dummies™	by Kearney Rietmann & Frank Higgins	1-56884-189-2	$19.95 USA/$26.95 Canada

MULTIMEDIA

Title	Author	ISBN	Price
Multimedia & CD-ROMs For Dummies™, Interactive Multimedia Value Pack	by Andy Rathbone	1-56884-225-2	$29.95 USA/$39.95 Canada
Multimedia & CD-ROMs For Dummies™	by Andy Rathbone	1-56884-089-6	$19.95 USA/$26.95 Canada

OPERATING SYSTEMS / DOS

Title	Author	ISBN	Price
MORE DOS For Dummies™	by Dan Gookin	1-56884-046-2	$19.95 USA/$26.95 Canada
S.O.S. For DOS™	by Katherine Murray	1-56884-043-8	$12.95 USA/$16.95 Canada
OS/2 For Dummies™	by Andy Rathbone	1-878058-76-2	$19.95 USA/$26.95 Canada

UNIX

Title	Author	ISBN	Price
UNIX For Dummies™	by John R. Levine & Margaret Levine Young	1-878058-58-4	$19.95 USA/$26.95 Canada

WINDOWS

Title	Author	ISBN	Price
S.O.S. For Windows™	by Katherine Murray	1-56884-045-4	$12.95 USA/$16.95 Canada
MORE Windows 3.1 For Dummies™, 3rd Edition	by Andy Rathbone	1-56884-240-6	$19.99 USA/$26.99 Canada

PCs / HARDWARE

Title	Author	ISBN	Price
Illustrated Computer Dictionary For Dummies™	by Dan Gookin, Wally Wang, & Chris Van Buren	1-56884-004-7	$12.95 USA/$16.95 Canada
Upgrading and Fixing PCs For Dummies™	by Andy Rathbone	1-56884-002-0	$19.95 USA/$26.95 Canada

PRESENTATION / AUTOCAD

Title	Author	ISBN	Price
AutoCAD For Dummies™	by Bud Smith	1-56884-191-4	$19.95 USA/$26.95 Canada
PowerPoint 4 For Windows For Dummies™	by Doug Lowe	1-56884-161-2	$16.95 USA/$22.95 Canada

PROGRAMMING

Title	Author	ISBN	Price
Borland C++ For Dummies™	by Michael Hyman	1-56884-162-0	$19.95 USA/$26.95 Canada
"Borland's New Language Product" For Dummies™	by Neil Rubenking	1-56884-200-7	$19.95 USA/$26.95 Canada
C For Dummies™	by Dan Gookin	1-878058-78-9	$19.95 USA/$26.95 Canada
C++ For Dummies™	by Stephen R. Davis	1-56884-163-9	$19.95 USA/$26.95 Canada
Mac Programming For Dummies™	by Dan Parks Sydow	1-56884-173-6	$19.95 USA/$26.95 Canada
QBasic Programming For Dummies™	by Douglas Hergert	1-56884-093-4	$19.95 USA/$26.95 Canada
Visual Basic "X" For Dummies™, 2nd Edition	by Wallace Wang	1-56884-230-9	$19.99 USA/$26.99 Canada
Visual Basic 3 For Dummies™	by Wallace Wang	1-56884-076-4	$19.95 USA/$26.95 Canada

SPREADSHEET

Title	Author	ISBN	Price
1-2-3 For Dummies™	by Greg Harvey	1-878058-60-6	$16.95 USA/$21.95 Canada
1-2-3 For Windows 5 For Dummies™, 2nd Edition	by John Walkenbach	1-56884-216-3	$16.95 USA/$21.95 Canada
1-2-3 For Windows For Dummies™	by John Walkenbach	1-56884-052-7	$16.95 USA/$21.95 Canada
Excel 5 For Macs For Dummies™	by Greg Harvey	1-56884-186-8	$19.95 USA/$26.95 Canada
Excel For Dummies™, 2nd Edition	by Greg Harvey	1-56884-050-0	$16.95 USA/$21.95 Canada
MORE Excel 5 For Windows For Dummies™	by Greg Harvey	1-56884-207-4	$19.95 USA/$26.95 Canada
Quattro Pro 6 For Windows For Dummies™	by John Walkenbach	1-56884-174-4	$19.95 USA/$26.95 Canada
Quattro Pro For DOS For Dummies™	by John Walkenbach	1-56884-023-3	$16.95 USA/$21.95 Canada

UTILITIES / VCRs & CAMCORDERS

Title	Author	ISBN	Price
Norton Utilities 8 For Dummies™	by Beth Slick	1-56884-166-3	$19.95 USA/$26.95 Canada
VCRs & Camcorders For Dummies™	by Andy Rathbone & Gordon McComb	1-56884-229-5	$14.99 USA/$20.99 Canada

WORD PROCESSING

Title	Author	ISBN	Price
Ami Pro For Dummies™	by Jim Meade	1-56884-049-7	$19.95 USA/$26.95 Canada
MORE Word For Windows 6 For Dummies™	by Doug Lowe	1-56884-165-5	$19.95 USA/$26.95 Canada
MORE WordPerfect 6 For Windows For Dummies™	by Margaret Levine Young & David C. Kay	1-56884-206-6	$19.95 USA/$26.95 Canada
MORE WordPerfect 6 For DOS For Dummies™	by Wallace Wang, edited by Dan Gookin	1-56884-047-0	$19.95 USA/$26.95 Canada
S.O.S. For WordPerfect™	by Katherine Murray	1-56884-053-5	$12.95 USA/$16.95 Canada
Word 6 For Macs For Dummies™	by Dan Gookin	1-56884-190-6	$19.95 USA/$26.95 Canada
Word For Windows 6 For Dummies™	by Dan Gookin	1-56884-075-6	$16.95 USA/$21.95 Canada
Word For Windows For Dummies™	by Dan Gookin	1-878058-86-X	$16.95 USA/$21.95 Canada
WordPerfect 6 For Dummies™	by Dan Gookin	1-878058-77-0	$16.95 USA/$21.95 Canada
WordPerfect For Dummies™	by Dan Gookin	1-878058-52-5	$16.95 USA/$21.95 Canada
WordPerfect For Windows For Dummies™	by Margaret Levine Young & David C. Kay	1-56884-032-2	$16.95 USA/$21.95 Canada

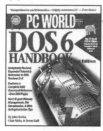

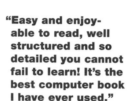

IDG BOOKS

Order Center: **(800) 762-2974** *(8 a.m.–6 p.m., EST, weekdays)*

12/20/94

Quantity	ISBN	Title	Price	Total

Shipping & Handling Charges

	Description	First book	Each additional book	Total
Domestic	Normal	$4.50	$1.50	$
	Two Day Air	$8.50	$2.50	$
	Overnight	$18.00	$3.00	$
International	Surface	$8.00	$8.00	$
	Airmail	$16.00	$16.00	$
	DHL Air	$17.00	$17.00	$

*For large quantities call for shipping & handling charges.
**Prices are subject to change without notice.

Ship to:

Name _____

Company _____

Address _____

City/State/Zip _____

Daytime Phone _____

Payment: ☐ Check to IDG Books (US Funds Only)
         ☐ VISA   ☐ MasterCard   ☐ American Express

Card # _____ Expires _____

Signature _____

Subtotal _____

CA residents add
applicable sales tax _____

IN, MA, and MD
residents add
5% sales tax _____

IL residents add
6.25% sales tax _____

RI residents add
7% sales tax _____

TX residents add
8.25% sales tax _____

Shipping _____

Total _____

Please send this order form to:

**IDG Books Worldwide
7260 Shadeland Station, Suite 100
Indianapolis, IN 46256**

*Allow up to 3 weeks for delivery.
Thank you!*